Bankruptcy 1995

BANKRUPTCY
1995

The Coming Collapse of America and How to Stop It

Harry E. Figgie, Jr.,

with

Gerald J. Swanson, Ph.D.

Foreword by former U.S. Senator Warren B. Rudman

Little, Brown and Company

Boston   New York   Toronto   London

First Paperback Edition

ISBN 0-316-28206-5 (pbk)

10 9 8 7 6 5 4 3

MV-NY

Published simultaneously in Canada by Little, Brown & Company
(Canada) Limited

Printed in the United States of America

We are in a real sense living
on borrowed money and borrowed time.

— Chairman of the Federal Reserve System
Board of Governors,
Paul A. Volcker,
February 20, 1985

This recession will be a picnic compared to where this
country will be in the year 1997.

— United States Senator Warren B. Rudman,
March 24, 1992

For my wife, Nancy; our sons, Dr. Harry E. Figgie III,
Dr. Mark P. Figgie, and Matthew P. Figgie;
and in memory of my parents,
Harry E. and Violet Phillips Figgie

Contents

Part 2
Averting Disaster

About the Numbers

THE figures used throughout this book come from a variety of governmental and nongovernmental sources. Most of the current and historical data come from documents issued by the Executive Office of the President, Office of Management and Budget (OMB). These include the budgetary statement *Budget Baselines, Historical Data and Alternatives for the Future,* issued in January 1993, and the *Budget of the United States Government* for Fiscal Years 1993 and 1994. Prior to 1985, the deficit figures cited reflect the net deficit. From 1985 on, the deficit figures cited reflect the gross deficit, or the total amount of government borrowing *before* monies were "borrowed" from federal trust funds to "reduce" the deficit artificially. Beginning in 1985, the government began to borrow significant trust fund surpluses to lower the reported deficit, and replaced these cash borrowings with IOUs. Many of the figures for future years were based on projections made by Data Resources Inc. (now DRI/McGraw-Hill), for the President's Private Sector Survey on Cost Control, also known as the Grace Commission. Explanations of specific information can be found in the chapter notes at the end of the book.

Foreword

by
Former U.S. Senator Warren B. Rudman

AMERICA is at war. Perhaps not your standard definition of war, but a very real war nonetheless. We are at war economically.

Our nation's wealth is being drained drop by drop, because our government continues to mount record deficits and, in order to finance its obligations, puts us at the mercy of foreign lenders. The security of our country depends on the fiscal integrity of our government, and we're throwing it away. We're doing nothing to protect it. Instead, it's politics as usual.

The blame for the economic collapse of our country ultimately will fall at all of our feet. But, to a large extent, it has its roots in a conspiracy of silence among most of our political leaders. That silence is due to basic fear . . . fear that if they directly confront the problem and honestly point out its severity to the American people, they may lose votes and elections.

The book you are holding is a godsend. Because it does what the government should have been doing all along. It deals with the issue in a brutally honest, straightforward manner.

It explains to the American people how serious the federal fiscal situation is, despite the government's best efforts to hide it. It defines how this crisis happened, what will happen to us in the near future if present trends continue, and, most important, what we — both government and individuals — must do to stop it. And it hits the heart of the issue not with fancy math or complicated models, but through well-researched facts and real-life lessons, and a good dose of common sense.

Harry Figgie and Gerry Swanson have studied this issue on a worldwide level for the better part of a decade. Neither is a politician. Neither needs to be concerned with being reelected or has reason to lie to the American people or to cover up the problem. They act out of a deep concern for the future of this country, which they — and I — believe will consist of economic disaster unless we take immediate remedial action.

For twelve years in the Senate, I fought the fight for debt reduction. I coauthored the Gramm-Rudman-Hollings balanced-budget law in 1985, which worked where it was allowed to, but was stonewalled where it could have done the most good (entitlements). I have been, and remain today, terribly frustrated with the unwillingness of our government to address the issue. That's why I chose not to seek reelection.

Through this book and its approach, perhaps Harry Figgie and Gerry Swanson can help get the message through to the American people. What it does best is bring the mammoth, almost incomprehensible problem of Washington's debt into the living rooms of everyday American citizens, and forces us to think about the likely consequences. You'll get a glimpse of what, realistically, could happen in a few short years to your life, your family, and your community when America's economic foundation is ripped out from under you.

It can and will happen if present trends continue. We are about to enter an era of $400 billion to $500 billion annual deficits, and reach the point where it's almost impossible to borrow the money we need. We are simply mortgaging the future for the present. And we — and our children and our grandchildren — will all pay dearly. The money we have worked so hard to save all our lives will be worthless.

Time is running out. With each day the situation becomes harder and harder to reverse. Officials know what needs to be done to cut the growing mountain of debt and have the talent to do it. But, as politicians, they lack the will.

So it falls to you to protect yourselves, to face the situation, and to force your elected officials to accept fiscal responsibility for our country's future. In this important respect, this book serves as a practical, hands-on guide for ways to effect change.

The 1992 elections may have been our last chance to head off fiscal disaster. To save this country, politicians must be willing to risk political careers, and citizens must be willing to make some personal sacrifices — which I tell you will be nominal now compared to what's to come.

Nothing is more important to the future of our country than getting this problem under control. We must treat it for the war it is, and come together — the president, Congress, and everyday citizens — to beat it, before it totally undermines our country's fabric, substance, and values.

Introduction
How I Came to Write This Book

In 1995, the United States of America, as we know it today,
will cease to exist. That year, the country will have spent itself into a bankruptcy from which there will be no return.
What we once called the American Century will end, literally,
with the end of the American way of life — unless you and I
act *now* to pull ourselves and the country back from near-
certain oblivion.

IN the fall of 1941, I entered Dartmouth College in Hanover, New
Hampshire. My father had urged me to go there for two reasons.
First, I wanted to become an engineer, but my father wanted me
to acquire some business education, too. Dartmouth, he told me,
had a program called Tuck-Thayer that would give me both. The
second reason was to pitch for Jeff Tesreau, the former Giant
great who was Dartmouth's baseball coach. My father considered
Jeff to be the best college pitching coach in the United States.
Some people at the time thought I might have a future in baseball.
So I went to Dartmouth, but only for a year, because World

1

War II broke out in the middle of my freshman year. In that year, however, I did something I would not have been able to do in my freshman year had I attended a traditional engineering school — I took an economics course from Professor Albert S. Carlson. One of the topics Professor Carlson covered was inflation, and he taught us about the terrible post–World War I hyperinflation in Germany's Weimar Republic. The currency there lost its value so quickly, he said, that people had to carry baskets of large-denomination bills to the store just to buy bread and potatoes.

Little did I realize that three years later, I'd be in the army and part of an infantry division that was fighting in Germany. Pinned down by gunfire in some town whose name I did not know in a house selected entirely by chance and necessity, I saw some large bills scattered on the floor. I recognized them because of Professor Carlson's class and my high-school German. They were 1923 Weimar Republic notes in denominations up to 50 million marks. The Nazis had declared them invalid, so I knew they were worthless as tender, but I put them in my haversack and carried them with me for the rest of the war.

When I finally got home, I put these six large-denomination bills into a scrapbook, and later I had them framed — the six bills ranged from 50,000 marks to 50 million marks and totaled 112 million marks. They've hung in my office for many years, a reminder to me of how utterly worthless paper money can become in a period of hyperinflation and how stable governments can give way to anarchy when hyperinflation occurs.

I am the founder and chairman of Figgie International, a diversified corporation based in Cleveland, Ohio, with $1.2 billion in annual sales. You may have heard of at least one of our twenty-eight divisions, Rawlings Sporting Goods, which manufactures, among other products, baseballs for the major leagues and official NCAA basketballs and footballs. I am also chairman and CEO of a much smaller, family-owned company, the Clark-Reliance Corporation, which has grown from a few hundred thousand dollars in annual sales to $35 million. It manufactures fluid control devices, such as valves for boilers, liquid level gauges, and sight-flow indicators. Clark-Reliance now also serves as a technical center for the development of world-class manufacturing techniques that we later introduce to divisions of the larger company.

Roughly eleven years ago, Dan McGillicuddy, who was then in charge of Figgie International's Washington, D.C., office, volunteered my services for something officially called the President's Private Sector Survey on Cost Control. The Grace Commission, as it became known, after the name of the man who chaired it, J. Peter Grace, chairman and chief executive officer of W. R. Grace & Company, was made up of 160 of the country's top business leaders from both sides of the political aisle plus two thousand corporate employees. It was charged by President Ronald Reagan to look for ways to eliminate government waste. (We eventually spent more than $76 million in private funds to identify such projects.) I didn't want to serve on the commission. I was busy with my own businesses, and I'm not fond of committees, meetings, and the Washington scene. Reluctantly, however, I agreed.

While a member, I received some numbers that Mr. Grace had commissioned from Data Resources Inc. (DRI; now DRI/McGraw-Hill), a respected Lexington, Massachusetts–based consulting firm. He wanted to know what the national debt and the federal deficit had been in the past and what they were projected to be in the year 2000. The economists gave him numbers for 1985, 1995, and 2000, as well as the debt and deficit figures back to the founding of our republic. (The deficit is the amount of government expenditures that exceed government revenues for a given time period, such as a year; the debt is the total amount that the government has borrowed over the years.) Being an engineer, naturally I wanted to see what the numbers looked like in graph form. First I plotted the points on semilog paper, which would show me the rate of change from year to year. Then I plotted them on regular graph paper. I was unprepared for the results that I got.

In the year 1995, I found, the American national debt would have grown beyond our ability to control it through taxation. In other words, even if the government that year dedicated every

Federal Deficit, Debt, and Interest
1980–2000
(In Billions of Dollars)

Year	Deficit	Debt	Interest on Debt
1980	$ (59.6)	$ 914.3	$ 52.5
1983	(195.4)	1,381.9	87.8
1985	(202.8)	1,823.1	179.0
1990	(386.7)	3,211.0	252.3
1995	(850.0)	6,560.0	619.1
2000	(1,966.0)	13,020.9	1,520.7
2000 as a multiple of 1980	33 times	14 times	29 times

SOURCE: President's Private Sector Survey on Cost Control.

penny it collected in personal income taxes to paying just *interest* on the debt, it wouldn't be enough. I first published my projections for the debt and deficit through the year 2000 in Figgie International's 1985 annual report, which included several graphs reproduced in this book. The deficit in the year 2000, I noted in that report, would be thirty-three times what it had been in 1980. The debt would climb to fourteen times its 1980 level, and interest on the debt, twenty-nine times.

Why did I chart those numbers? If the country was in danger of experiencing a financial and economic breakdown that could give us Weimar-like hyperinflation, I wanted to know how to protect and run companies in such an environment. Next, I called Gerry Swanson in Tucson, an economist I respect and with whom at that point I had worked for almost ten years in the area of our company-funded teacher education programs. I asked him to assemble a research team to look into the public-sector and private-sector problems that develop when governments lose control of their budget deficits and national debts. We selected South America for the initial studies. The knowledge Gerry would acquire, I felt, could be used to develop a handbook on operating a company in hyperinflation, because I hadn't been able to find anything on the subject. That handbook was later published and called *The Hyperinflation Survival Guide.*

Over the next seven years, the team traveled to eleven countries on three continents, visiting Argentina, Brazil, Bolivia, Czechoslovakia, Hungary, Mexico, Poland, Italy, Switzerland, Germany, and Great Britain. The team spoke with finance ministers, central bank directors, and the heads of major multinational companies, as well as with leading businesspeople, bankers, economists, and consultants in those countries. The team's findings confirmed my suspicions that the United States was headed for mortal trouble. In South American countries, the people the team members talked to maintained that we were on the same track that they had followed and just thirty years behind them. A letter I received from Felix de Barrio, an Argentinean business executive, was typical of their response: "So many times in the last few years," he said, "I have argued with U.S. citizens about the incredible mistakes being made in [the] U.S. economy, and so few times [have] I had anybody agreeing."

America has started on a downhill slope, he warned, because "individuals and politicians care first for themselves, second for their party, and only in [the] third instance for their country. Unfortunately," he added, "this is exactly what has happened in Argentina for the last 40 to 50 years. And look where we are now."

In 1988 and 1989, I made three speeches based on Gerry's team's initial research. I gave those speeches to groups of informed citizens — the League of Women Voters, the Town Hall of Los Angeles, and the City Club of Cleveland. The speech I gave to the League of Women Voters has generated more than 185,000 requests for reprints, all unsolicited. These requests still come in at the rate of 500 to 1,000 per week. A later speech I gave to the City Club of Cleveland in January 1993 elicited 50,000 requests for reprints within a month and a half.

From these requests, from the letters that accompany some of them, and from the telephone inquiries we receive, I know very well that the general population senses and is worried about the disaster our politicians are about to drop us into. In late 1991, a week before Christmas, Nancy, my wife of forty-three years, finally grabbed me by the arm and said, "Do something. You and Gerry have the data and the knowledge. You've been studying the subject for almost seven years, and know more about it than anyone in the country. You'd better act, because time is running out." But I didn't, using as my excuse the fact that I had two companies to guide through a tough recession, and I needed another project like I needed a hole in the head.

Then on January 28, 1992, I watched President Bush on television give his State of the Union message, something I seldom do. I waited anxiously for him to cite the deficit and our burgeoning debt as the highest priority problem we faced. Surely, I thought, it would be among the first challenges he would mention. Was I wrong. When he finally got to the deficit — this beast that's about to eat us alive — it was as a casual afterthought, the second-to-last point of his nine-point speech. He never did mention the debt as a problem.

That was it.

"You're right," I said to my wife. "We've got to wake this country up before the fall election. It's our last chance before 1995." That year has marked for me the date of America's fiscal Armageddon since I graphed the initial data in 1985, because the debt and deficit lines go absolutely vertical from that point on.

The day after the president's speech, I started the ball rolling for the book that you're now holding in your hand. First I walked down the hall from my office to that of Mike Prendergast, Figgie International's vice-president of public affairs (until his untimely death in 1992). Together, we called Henry Eaton, our outside public relations counsel at Dix & Eaton, and said, "We've got to get a book out by August." Among the three of us, we had zero expertise on how to write and publish a popular book, even though I'd written a book on cost reduction a few years before for general industry readership. A call to Gerry Swanson in Arizona got him on board as well.

The first thing our team found was that getting a book published normally takes a year from the completion of the manuscript, and ours wasn't written yet. Then we discovered we needed not only a writer or writers but someone called a literary agent. Talk about naïve. What we didn't know about getting a book published would have filled a book.

Ninety names and a lot of research later, Mike, Henry, and Scott Chaikin, who works for Henry, had found the people we needed — Helen Rees, book agent extraordinaire, and Donna Carpenter and the other writers and editors at Wordworks Inc., including Tom Richman and Abby Solomon, all magicians with the written word. Helen told us that in rare cases with a really timely book, she could get it "fast-tracked," and she thought she could have ours published by a top firm in the fall of 1992—that is, in just five months. (Normally, publishing a book takes a full year.) We were in business.

During our first meeting, Helen left the room for two hours because our data and story made her ill. Two weeks into the effort, Donna called to say she was so depressed that she had to take the weekend off. This is not a lighthearted project.

Thanks to my wife's urging and Bush's almost total disregard for what has to be the dominant issue before this country, plus the monumental efforts of a group of key people, including the firm of Little, Brown, its top executive, Bill Sarnoff, and editor-in-chief, Bill Phillips, the message in this book did get out to the American people before the 1992 election.

In fact, this book plus the dialogue sparked by such prominent individuals as Ross Perot, helped the debt and deficit become a major issue during the campaign. Now that the American people have elected a new president, they must continue to force his hand toward substantive action on the debt.

We must act now. We're out of time. Unless *you're* convinced that we're not crying wolf by the time you finish this book, then we've failed in our mission.

Paul Revere rode through the countryside warning the people, who, in turn, acted on his warning. Then Revere went back to silversmithing. When this crisis is over, I want to go back to doing what I love — being an entrepreneur and turning ailing little businesses into industry leaders.

A chain of random events taking place over more than fifty years has led to the publication of this book. The odds against all of these events happening in sequence and leading me to get this message out are incalculable. Had I not gone to Dartmouth, elected Professor Carlson's class, and been assigned to a particular army unit that would be in a particular town on a particular day, this book would not have been written. But I also had to have taken cover in a particular house where Weimar Republic money lay on the floor, used my high-school German to read it, and had the presence of mind to save it. (I never saw another piece of Weimar money for the rest of the war.) The Weimar Republic bills and I both survived the fighting, I framed them, and years later I joined the Grace Commission totally against my will. The data came to me, I knew how to graph it, and I had a friend, Gerry Swanson, who was capable of taking on a study of hyperinflation.

Still, the book would not have been written or seen publication if my wife hadn't insisted that we do something and if I hadn't uncharacteristically listened to Bush's speech. Finally, there was a group of writers and an agent and a publisher who could work together in a superhuman efort to get the book published before September 1992, so that the American public could have it in time to read, absorb, and act on it in time for the national elections. The earlier actions are random; the later ones are all outside of my normal operating realms. But if any one of these events spread over fifty years had not occurred, then this book would neither have been written nor published. I find this chain of events remarkable. My only explanation is that I am completing the mission I was assigned more than fifty years ago.

— Harry E. Figgie, Jr.

PART
1

The End of America As We Know It

The United States has a problem that is easy to understand, but whose effects are difficult to comprehend. Its solution is simple to prescribe, but hard to implement. This problem is more insidious than drug addiction, more pressing than recession; it is crueler than poverty and illness and more hazardous than a hole in the ozone.

Solving this problem is more important than anything else American politicians, business leaders, and ordinary citizens have to do. If it isn't solved soon, no other concerns will matter — not health care, not education, not the competitiveness of our industries.

This problem, which is of our own making, will precipitate an economic nightmare that will dwarf the Great Depression and turn the story of America into one of history's closed chapters. This problem has a name. It is *government debt.*

1

The Week from Hell

YOUR parents or grandparents thought the Great Depression of the 1930s was bad. Doomsday 1995 will be worse. Herewith, the week from hell.

Sunday

Betsy and Tom Roth woke up earlier than usual for a Sunday. Today was moving day. Not for them, but for Betsy's parents, Rose and Henry Adams, now in their seventies.

Rose and Henry had lived in their house for — "Let's see," Betsy thought as she lay in bed for an extra minute after hearing the alarm, "this summer, it would be fifty years." It was the house they'd moved into on their wedding day and the house in which Betsy and her brothers had grown up, but there wouldn't be any more anniversaries or birthdays for the Adamses in that house.

Betsy's parents couldn't afford the city taxes on the place, since Henry's pension from the union had been cut by two-thirds. The form letter they had received had said that the value of the pension fund's real estate and stock investments had dropped and left the fund unable to meet its full obligations. Everyone had to take a

11

cut. The sale had brought her parents only half of what the place had been worth a year earlier, but Betsy and Tom had felt the Adamses were lucky to find a buyer at all.

Toyota bought the house, because it wanted the land as part of a tract it was assembling for a huge new computerized auto spare-parts warehouse and distribution center. Temporarily, Betsy's parents would move in with her, staying in their granddaughter Sarah's room. Sarah was attending State U. and would be at school until June. Betsy knew that it wouldn't be easy for her parents to adjust to living with her — or for her and Tom and their son, Paul, to adjust, either — but what could she do? Lots of other families were doubling up these days.

Monday

Despite having to cope with two extra people for breakfast, Betsy arrived at work a couple of minutes before nine. She ran the accounts receivable department — right now consisting of her and an assistant they had hired last month — at a young, fast-growing software development company with thirty-five employees. When she got to her cubicle, she saw on her computer screen a message from the company's founder. "Company-wide meeting in the library at 9:15" was all it said.

Betsy quickly sorted through her work for the day. With sales more than double last year's and half again as many customers, there was always plenty to do. She filled her coffee cup and rolled her chair down the hall to the meeting room.

The company's young and personable founder came right to the point: "I'm sorry to have to tell you this," he said once everyone was settled down, "but after Friday this company will no longer exist."

Betsy couldn't believe what she was hearing. The company had always carried a line of credit with its bank and it had a hefty mortgage on its new building, but it had made all its payments on time. Now the bank was pulling the line of credit and calling the mortgage. The president, tears glistening in his eyes, said the bank would state only that it needed to rebuild its own capital and reduce its outstanding risk. There would be no appeal.

The venture capitalists who had invested early in the company, he added, had declined to put up any more money, and they could find no one interested in buying the company whole. Instead, the founder said, he was trying to sell some of the existing product lines to other companies. "There is, for instance, a French company that's interested in our factory-control software," he said, "and while they aren't willing to pay much, they're the only ones offering anything at all at this point." Maybe, he added, the buyer would keep some of the staff on for a short time, but he wasn't hopeful. In any case, everyone would be paid, he promised, through the end of the week.

Betsy was stunned. She knew how much the company's orders and sales had increased, but still it was shutting down. It didn't make sense to her. And paid only through the end of the week? She had returned to work because she and Tom needed the income from this job.

Tuesday

At 8:30 as Betsy was washing the breakfast dishes, her eyes still red from crying the night before, Sarah telephoned. "Did you hear the news, Mom?" she asked. Betsy said she had not. The morning paper lay unopened on the counter. "They're closing the university a month early. I'll be home in two weeks." Sarah paused, but Betsy said nothing. "And they said they don't know if they'll open it again in the fall because of the state's borrowing problem. Mom, I don't understand."

At 1:00 P.M., just after Tom Roth had finished eating the sandwich, apple, and candy bar that Betsy had packed in his lunch box, his supervisor approached him. "Tom," he said, "can you come into the foreman's office?" Tom was in the middle of reprogramming the computer-controlled lathe he operated, and he asked if it could wait until he was finished and the machine was back in operation. "No, you should come now," the supervisor said.

"Tom, Betsy just called. I'm sorry to have to tell you this, but there's been an accident involving your son," the foreman began as soon as Tom had shut the door. "Paul is in the hospital. Betsy said he's probably going to be all right. The other boy in the car, though — he's dead. Drowned. The Webster Avenue bridge collapsed. You know, the one they tried to pass the bond issue for, so they could replace it. Three cars went into the river. It was no one's fault. You'd better go." Tom got his jacket and left.

The radio was on in Tom's car, but he was barely listening as he drove rapidly toward the hospital. ". . . and despite heavy lobbying by groups representing the elderly," the announcer was saying, "House and Senate conferees agreed today to cut Social Security benefits and to move the age for collecting retirement benefits to seventy-five. A White House spokesman said the administration felt that Congress had overreacted to the current budget crunch. The president, according to the spokesman, said that the cuts would be only temporary.

" 'We will move to restore benefits to the level that retired American workers deserve,' the spokesman said, 'just as soon as our current fiscal problem, which was largely created by Congress, is resolved.' Reacting to news of the cuts, Wall Street investors accelerated their selling. At 1:00 P.M., the Dow-Jones Industrial Average stood at 2,127, down 87 points for the day, 125 points for the week so far, and more than 1,500 points off its high for the year. Some analysts say that the market's bottom isn't yet in sight, but a spokesman for Treasury Secretary . . ." Tom parked in the emergency room visitors' lot and hurried inside.

Wednesday

Betsy had stayed at the hospital overnight with Paul, who, except for a slight concussion, seemed to be all in one piece. A battery of tests showed no serious damage. The doctors said they might release him today. Without Betsy to prepare his usual breakfast, though, Tom left the house early so he could stop by the diner for hash browns and eggs.

Tom opened the paper as the waitress poured his coffee and glanced at the front page. "ENOUGH! SAY TRADE PART-NERS," read the headline. Tom skimmed the story that followed. "Japanese and European central bankers," the story began, "yesterday jointly declared that they would no longer act to support the U.S. dollar in international currency markets. Following the announcement, a widespread sell-off of the dollar drove its value lower on every major market. 'If the U.S. government can't or won't act responsibly on the issue of its pyramiding debt,' the joint communiqué read, 'other nations of the world can no longer be expected to carry the burden of . . . .' "

"Screw 'em," thought Tom, as he turned to the sports pages to look for yesterday's ball scores. As far as he was concerned, if the Japanese and Europeans didn't like the way the United States did its business, they could stop doing business here. Besides, he remembered when Americans were better off, before they began importing cars and VCRs. His first car — "Best wheels I ever owned," Tom often said when talking about it — had been a '57 Chevy.

When he arrived at work, Tom and the other machine operators were told that there'd been a change in the production plan. "The customer canceled the order," the foreman said. They were told to finish up the pieces on their machines, then to start performing the next maintenance service due for each machine. Tom knew that this meant there would be no work for the rest of the day, but union rules required a week's notice before any layoff. "Must have been a big order canceled," thought Tom, because the company had never shut off production so quickly before. He'd have an easy day and maybe, he figured, even an easy week before having to start real work again.

When he got home, Tom found Paul, released from the hospital, lying on the living room couch, his head bandaged and his cheek and eye bruised, a little quieter than usual. "Hey, Dad," he said when Tom walked in. Tom smiled. "Hey," he replied. Betsy came in, looking as if she'd missed a night's sleep. "Mom and Dad are upstairs, taking a nap, so we have the place to ourselves for a while," she said, as she sank into a chair.

"Recapping tonight's early news headlines," said the local news anchor, from the corner of the living room where the television sat, its volume low, "Meridian First Bank president Herbert Slocum this afternoon denied reports that the state's second largest bank was having trouble meeting depositors' demands for funds, but some bank customers, unconvinced, began withdrawing their money just before the bank closed at 4:00 P.M. The city council this afternoon . . ."

Tom caught a few words of the announcement. "Isn't that where we have our savings account?" he asked Betsy, who handled the family finances. She nodded, looking worried. She hadn't heard the news earlier, because she had been busy getting Paul settled. "Honey, maybe you should go down there tomorrow," Tom said, "and make a withdrawal. You know, with your having to look for another job and all, we probably ought to be careful." Betsy agreed that she would.

Thursday

Betsy went to her office this morning, since she had been out the day before and a great many details needed to be cleaned up before the end of the week. Maybe the company was closing down, but it was in Betsy's nature, a gift from her mother, not to leave any job half-done. She'd run over to the bank at noon, she told herself.

At 12:15, she turned her car into the Meridian First parking lot but was stopped by a police officer standing in front of a wooden barricade. The lot was full, he said. Betsy drove down the street, parked at a meter, and walked back. There was a large crowd — not a line, but a milling crowd — on the sidewalk in front of the granite and glass building. "Were you headed for the bank?" asked a man, a neighbor of the Roths. "Well, forget it," he said, "because they've shut down." He filled Betsy in. "About ten o'clock," he told her, "a bunch of guys in suits showed up and told the customers and most of the staff to leave. There must have been five hundred people waiting in line to get in. You know, they said that all that money's insured, but with all those other failures, I don't see how there will be any insurance left."

Betsy didn't know what else to do, so she returned to work, shutting her own office down. When she was through, she got into her car for the twenty-minute drive home. Finally, she had some time alone to think. She had the feeling that something important was going on, something she ought to pay attention to. She was beginning to think that there had to be some connection between the bank's closing, her company's shutting down, Tom's slack time, her parents' move, and Paul's accident. "But that's silly," she told herself. Surely, it was just a string of bad luck. Still, she couldn't shake the feeling. *Something* had to be going on. But what could it be?

While Betsy fixed dinner that night she talked to her mother, who sat at the kitchen table. "I don't know, Mom," she said as she snapped the green beans, "it seems like it's too much to be just, you know, a coincidence, all this stuff that's happening."

From the easy-listening station on the kitchen radio Betsy heard a news announcer say something about Treasury debt, and for some reason she pricked up her ears. ". . . The department's failure to find a buyer for its bonds today has thrown world financial markets into turmoil. Although the Treasury secretary has assured Congress that the government's financial status is as sound as ever, one senior senator, who preferred to speak off the record, said, quoting him now, 'The United States is as broke today as any South American banana republic has ever been.' Turning to the forecast, another springlike day tomorrow as temperatures . . ."

What the announcer had said didn't make Betsy feel any better.

In fact, it worried her more. But even the news report hadn't helped her make connections among the bank's failure, her son's accident, and her mother's sitting here in her kitchen.

Friday

Not all the workers at Tom's company could fit into the lunchroom at the same time, so they were going in two shifts — but not for lunch. This was a meeting called by management and the union muckety-mucks, and even before he crowded in with his co-workers, Tom knew the news wasn't going to be good. Rumors were flying. Already, Tom had heard that the German conglomerate that had bought the company the previous year was shutting this plant down and moving production to Mexico. The only thing that would remain here, rumor said, would be a sales office and a maintenance and service organization. Fifty people out of two thousand would keep their jobs.

But the real news turned out to be even worse than the rumors. In addition to the plant shutdown, the union chief told the assembled workers that the union was flat-out broke and could offer them no help, financial or other. Worse yet, a woman from the state unemployment office informed them that unprecedented numbers of claims and a failure by the federal government to pay its share into the insurance fund had left the state's unemployment account nearly drained. Benefits would be cut to only 25 percent of the normal level until, as the woman put it, "the folks in Washington come up with a way to bail us out."

They weren't even to return to their machines, the company vice-president said, but should move from the lunchroom to the locker room, where they could pick up any gear they had. Arrangements had been made, he said, to mail them their final checks. "But the new owners can't do that," said Jim, who ran the lathe next to Tom. "They have to give us sixty days' notice before they shut down. It's the law." Tom felt a stirring of hope.

"The foreign owners will do it, all right. They're leaving the country," said the vice-president. "Besides, who's going to prosecute them? With the chaos the country is in, no one is going to worry about one plant."

At that moment, a squad of security guards entered the room. Some of them took up positions along the back wall where the doors to the plant were. Others saw to it that the now *former* employees passed into the locker room and out of the factory's gate.

Tom didn't know what to think. He was numb with shock as he filed quietly out with his buddies. It had all happened so fast.

Friday evening after work was Betsy's time to do the weekly grocery shopping. With two more mouths to feed, her list was longer this week than usual, but she wheeled her cart to the checkout line after picking up only part of what she wanted. Betsy couldn't believe the prices. Swiss cheese that had been expensive at $4.99 a pound was now $7.29. The leg of lamb she had planned for Sunday dinner wasn't $4.00 a pound; it was closer to $10.00. The Italian-brand tomato sauce she usually bought had three price tags on it: $1.29, $1.49, and $2.09. Some things — the fresh produce from South America, for instance — weren't marked at all. Instead, there was a sign: "Due to rapidly escalating costs, these items will be priced at the register. We're sorry for the inconvenience."

Betsy wheeled her lightly loaded cart to the checkout and watched in astonishment as the bill mounted. It was almost twice what she usually spent. Instead of cash, she handed the clerk her Visa card, which the young man slid through the magnetic-strip-reading slot next to the register. The machine processed the data, then beeped. The young man turned back to Betsy, his face wearing a look of genuine sympathy. "I'm sorry," he said, "but your card is no longer valid, and I'm not supposed to return it to you."

"But," Betsy said, ". . . but . . ."

"This has happened to a lot of people today, ma'am," the clerk said. "It's not your fault. It's something about the banks shutting down. I really don't understand it myself. I'm sure it will be okay. I'm really sorry."

And suddenly Betsy felt deflated, weighted down. Hardly able to stand, she left her groceries at the end of the moving belt and walked through the automatic door to the parking lot.

Saturday

Betsy and Tom stayed in bed later than usual for a Saturday. "Maybe," Tom said in a weak joke, "this is the safest place to be." He wasn't really in a joking mood, and a small hangover from a few too many beers bothered him. They'd been talking in low voices about the week just past, trying to sort through the calamities that had hit them, one following on the heels of another.

"Thank God, Paul is going to be okay," said Betsy, but even as she said it she was wondering how they were going to pay the hospital and doctor bill that the cashier had handed to them when they checked their son out of the hospital. Tom's company insurance would pick up some of it, but after deductibles and uncovered charges they still owed more than two thousand dollars. Tom had hit the ceiling. "For one day in their lousy hospital," he'd yelled at no one in particular, "they want two thousand dollars."

That was the problem. Tom was angry, but he didn't know at whom to direct his anger. The union and his company seemed to have been in cahoots, both of them selling out Tom and the other workers to foreigners with lots of money, who didn't care that he'd put in more than twenty years with the company. And where did Congress get off shortchanging people on Social Security, when they'd been paying that tax all their lives? His immediate concern, though, was his unemployment benefits. With the little he was going to get, they'd have to dip into savings, Tom feared, before he lined up another job. (He didn't know about the bank yet.)

Betsy hadn't told Tom yet about the bank, the groceries, or

the credit card. He had been angry enough last night. How was she supposed to cash her last paycheck, she wondered, since the bank was closed? "For that matter," she thought, "the check will probably turn out to be no good."

Eventually, Tom and Betsy got up. She started coffee. The sun was bright in a blue spring sky. Tom walked outside and stood for a minute in the greening yard, letting the rays warm his face. The next week would almost *have* to be better than the last one, he thought. A nice day always made Tom feel better.

He stepped along the flagstones to the sidewalk where the newspaper lay and picked it up to check the baseball scores. The black banner headline distracted him. "DOLLAR IN FREE-FALL; NATION IS BANKRUPT," it said.

2

How We Got into This Mess

AS Tom and Betsy Roth so painfully found out, they're killing our country.

Who are *they?*

You know their names, and you know — or at least know of — one or more of the guilty. There are, to be precise, 536 of them, and they have hired about twenty thousand bright and energetic people to act as their accomplices and assistants. They pay themselves and their helpers very well, by the way, and why not? It's your money they are living on — that and the checks they bounce at the House bank and the loans they don't repay at the White House Credit Union. What could they possibly know of fiscal responsibility?

At the head of the list of the people who have been killing our country is the former president of the United States, George Bush, as well as the five presidents who preceded him. Also on the list are those who've occupied the positions of Senate Majority Leader and Speaker of the House. These are the ringleaders.

We elect them and the 434 other members of the U.S. House of Representatives and 99 other members of the U.S. Senate.

With them come the thousands of people we don't elect — their paid congressional and White House staffs.

Is it harsh to accuse our leaders and our honorable lawmakers of killing our country?

You won't think so when I tell you what they have done to our government and to our industries. You won't think so when you learn how they're destroying your chance of getting a better job or even keeping the one that you have.

You won't think I'm being harsh when you hear how you and your children — let alone your grandchildren — are going to fare in a second- or third-rate country that will be largely owned and controlled by politicians and corporations from cities such as Berlin, Riyadh, and Tokyo. *Their* first interest will not be *your* well-being.

And that company pension that you were planning on collecting to augment your Social Security benefits? Forget it, and forget them. When the country goes, they — and your insurance, bank accounts, and any other money you've managed to save — go with it. By 1997, the dollar will be worthless, according to former U.S. Senator Warren Rudman, the New Hampshire Republican who did not seek reelection to the U.S. Senate in 1992 because of his frustration over its unwillingness to address our fiscal crisis. The fact is, you're going to be on your own in twenty-first-century America — and probably even before that.

Why? Because our other so-called leaders in Washington — including *your* representative and *your* senators — have been bleeding this country to death, and not slowly. In the eighteen years since 1975, they have sucked the lifeblood out of the nation and put the country in hock for cash to cover up their unwillingness to tell us the truth. In the process, they are doing to us what George III, Adolf Hitler, Emperor Hirohito, and Nikita Khrushchev tried to do but failed: They are destroying this country and the dream that has sustained the American spirit for more than two hundred years.

Why are they killing our country? Because we let them, you and I. We've not only let them, we've encouraged them, because we wanted to keep hearing the lies they told us. Every interest group wanted to know — and still does — that *its* needs were going to be met. "No problem," the politicians have said, and that's what we wanted to hear. "Trust us," they said. We did, and we kept sending them back to Washington.

How are they killing our country?

That's what I'm going to explain in the rest of this book, but in a sentence or two, they're doing it by running up our tab — yours, mine, and ours — beyond any amount that we will ever be able to repay or control. If present trends continue, the federal government's accumulated debt will have reached approximately $6.56 trillion by 1995 and $13 trillion by the year 2000. That 1995 figure is roughly nine times the amount the government will collect in personal and corporate income taxes in that year. It's the equivalent of your piling up debts equal to nine times your annual income. It's being in hock for $450,000 on a salary of $50,000 a year. Are you broke at that point? Technically, no, but you sure have a serious problem, and so do your creditors, since you won't be able to make your payments.

By 1995, the United States won't be able to afford even the annual *interest* payment on this debt. If interest rates start to head up (as they undoubtedly will), the interest expense alone on the national debt could climb to a sickening $619 billion by 1995. Six hundred nineteen billion dollars will absorb almost all of the total personal and corporate income tax receipts that the government is projected to collect that year. To be exact, it will absorb 85 percent of these revenues.

Imagine that between your mortgage and your credit cards, you'd run up so much debt that the monthly interest payments alone were 85 percent of what you brought home in your paycheck. You'd have practically nothing left to buy groceries, gas for the car, new shoes for the kids, or anything else. Forget about paying off the debt itself. There's no chance of that. All you can worry about is the interest payment, and even that's almost more than you can handle. That's the situation the United States will be in — unable to satisfy its lenders.

In the movies, when borrowers disappoint the loan sharks, the mob sends goons to break their legs. As an insolvent borrower, this country's metaphorical legs will get broken . . . unless.

Unless what?

We don't have much time — two years at the most — to save ourselves. Save *ourselves,* I said, not ask someone to save us. No one will. Certainly not the lobbyists for foreign governments and foreign corporations who range free in the power corridors of Washington. They're there to help us take ourselves down. If we in the United States want to keep our country intact, hold on to our financial futures and political liberties, and pass something worth having on to our children, we're going to have to clean up this mess ourselves. We, the silent majority, who have let ourselves be shoved around by private-interest groups for years and years, will have to do what's needed.

I think that together, we — all of us — can. The hardest part of the job ahead is facing up to and accepting the truth about the cancerous mess that we're in. That's why Gerry Swanson and I have written this book. What's in it is the truth, plain and straightforward, because neither Gerry Swanson nor I have any reason to cover up or paste smiley faces on the threat confronting us. Any profits from this book have long since been assigned to charity. We make no profit whatsoever from it.

Gerry Swanson is a professor of economics at the University of Arizona and executive director of economic affairs for the Academy for Economic Education, a nonprofit organization that trains K-through-12 educators at selected universities across the United States how to teach economics and free enterprise. He is not a politician.

I am not a politician. I am a businessman who loves this country. Not only do I love this country, but until 1982, when I signed on as a cochair of the Grace Commission, I looked up to those people running it. If someone had told me back then that one day

I'd write a book that criticizes our country's president and political leaders, I would have shown him the door. But I've become convinced that our so-called leaders have in fact sold us out.

You don't have to be a rocket scientist to figure out how they are managing to kill our country — and not gradually, incidentally, but by taking increasingly larger bites out of our collective hide. All it takes is a little patience and the ability to hold your temper, because what you're about to read — in this chapter and in the rest of this book — should make your blood boil.

Lyndon Johnson

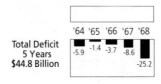

'64 '65 '66 '67 '68

Total Deficit
5 Years
$44.8 Billion

-5.9 -1.4 -3.7 -8.6

-25.2

The present debacle had its beginnings during Lyndon Johnson's presidency. From the time this country was founded, the U.S. government had typically operated on a pay-as-you-go basis. It spent what it took in and no more. If it needed to spend more, it raised taxes or tariffs to generate the income. In other words, it operated sanely and sensibly.

In general, the only time that the government borrowed to cover any substantial portion of its expenses was in time of war. And, if it financed a war, the debt was paid back. Fiscal responsibility was the name of the game. By 1963, when John F. Kennedy's assassination vaulted Vice-President Johnson into the White House, the U.S. government in 183 years had accumulated a total debt of just $310 billion.

Then Johnson, a street-smart politician, tried to do what no president should ever attempt. He tried to run two wars simultaneously, one against the Communists in Vietnam and the other against poverty in America. He tried, in other words, to provide both guns to the military and butter to the hungry. It couldn't and didn't work. Moreover, this policy led directly to our current crisis and was its genesis.

In his administration's early days, Johnson concealed his military buildup for the Vietnam war from even his top economic advisers, thereby initiating the modern trend of presidents concealing the true magnitude of their deficit spending. His advisers, who were no fools, suspected the buildup was under way and tried in vain to prove it. Despite their lack of success, they nonetheless argued for a surtax to pay for it. The president spurned their advice. He had no intention of damaging his popularity by raising taxes.

Johnson made sure that the Pentagon regularly sent consistently low spending estimates, stamped "For internal use only," to his Council of Economic Advisers. Arthur Okun, the youngest of these advisers and the most irreverent, scribbled beneath the stamp on one of the memos: "But not to be swallowed." From the beginning of the Vietnam buildup in 1965 to its height in 1968, military expenditures climbed an average of 18 percent each year, and taxes didn't go up at all.

Using deficit spending — and raising taxes — to finance wars was nothing new. That's what we'd done during both world wars, but Johnson wanted more. He wanted to make things better for those Americans who lived in hopelessness, so he initiated the Great Society programs. A noble cause, to be sure, but the timing was disastrous. The government had never financed a war *and* launched expensive social spending programs simultaneously. The resulting deficits were huge by historic standards. In 1968, the deficit came to $25 billion, which was twice as large as any other deficit since World War II. That deficit and the ones that followed led in the 1970s to a decade of inflation, as we'll see shortly.

The war against poverty involved the creation and expansion of so-called entitlement programs. An entitlement program is any system of government aid to individuals that says, in effect, that anyone who meets certain criteria is *entitled* to assistance — usually money or something that costs the government money, such as food stamps. Always, the costs of these programs have been terribly underestimated, probably purposely in order to sell them.

The country already had one large entitlement program, called Social Security. Anyone who reached the designated age or met other requirements was entitled to receive certain benefits. Johnson's Great Society legislation added more: Medicare and Medicaid, Aid to Families with Dependent Children (AFDC), the Food Stamp Program, and so on. To ensure congressional approval, he purposefully understated their cost — not always, but often enough.

The continued and unrestrained growth of these programs is a key cause of both our short- and long-term fiscal crises. Hard as it is to believe, the programs don't come up for an annual review by Congress or the president. Since they're not discretionary, they don't require an annual appropriation of funds, and they are subject to neither vote nor veto. Like Topsy, they just keep on growing, which is why they are often referred to as uncontrollable.

Entitlement programs may make good social policy, but they play havoc with fiscal policy. They lock the government into spending money that it may not have. Once you say that anyone who falls into a particular category can claim this or that kind of assistance, the government has no way of knowing how much it's going to spend on that aid until everyone who is going to has shown up to claim it. That's one problem with entitlement programs: They're hard to budget and they increase every year — in short, they have become uncontrollable.

If that were the only problem, it would be bad enough. But there's another difficulty with the kind of entitlement programs enacted during the Johnson years and afterward: They are too easy to expand and too hard to contract. Once people have been *entitled* to something for a period of time, they usually don't want to give it up. Why would they? Would you? So, any time anyone in Washington suggested that an entitlement program be cut back, the suggestion met with a maelstrom of opposition. For instance, try suggesting to some older people that Social Security benefits should be reduced or eliminated for those whose incomes fall above some limit that is well above the poverty line. You'll grow old yourself waiting for Social Security recipients to support any recommendation that cuts their benefits from the government.

The other side of that coin is that politicians can always buy votes for themselves by generously adding new groups to existing entitlement programs. It's easy. The program already exists. Incorporating the next deserving group costs only a little more, so why not? It makes the people in that group happy, and no one else is really paying attention anyway.

As a result, entitlement programs have grown far larger than anyone ever expected them to be. They're so large, in fact, that they now consume 65 percent of all government spending on everything except interest on the national debt. That means that for all practical purposes, 65 percent of the government's noninterest expenses are untouchable — in the absence, that is, of greater political courage than any president or Congress has so far been able to muster.

So, in budget terms, the lasting legacies of Johnson's five years in the White House are these: He adopted and promoted the dangerous idea that deficit spending by the federal government is okay even when the survival of the nation isn't at stake. And he created a plethora of social entitlement programs that have now, a quarter-century later, left the government politically unable, or at least unwilling, to control its pandering and thus nearly 65 percent of its annual budget after interest payments. These programs, by the way, amounted to only 30 percent of the budget during President Kennedy's term.

Richard Nixon

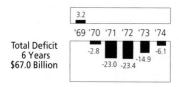

Total Deficit
6 Years
$67.0 Billion

Fiscally, Richard Nixon wasn't a bad character, as you can see from the graph above. He was no hero, to be sure, but he could have made a difficult federal debt situation far worse than he did.

Richard Nixon inherited the Vietnam war from Lyndon Johnson, but immediately began to wind down spending for the war as a percentage of federal revenues. And while the government under Nixon didn't cut back on entitlement program spending, it did reduce the programs' rate of growth.

True, in all but one year that Nixon was in office, the federal government ran a budget deficit, but these deficits were smaller at the end of his presidency than at the beginning. The government overspent its revenues by $23.4 billion in fiscal 1972, and by the time he helicoptered off the White House lawn for the last time in 1974, Nixon had cut the deficit amount to $6.1 billion — a help if not a solution to the borrowing problem that now, more than two decades later, is going to paralyze us.

Gerald Ford

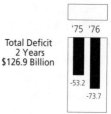

Total Deficit
2 Years
$126.9 Billion

'75 '76
-53.2
-73.7

Maybe Richard Nixon still had some respect for at least the *idea* of a balanced budget, but his unelected successor, Gerald Ford, certainly didn't. Take a look at the graph above. It shows that Ford stumbled into the trap that had been set during the Johnson administration. Perhaps it was his years in Congress that insulated him from a sound fiscal approach.

In 1973, the year before Ford stepped into the Oval Office, the country was slam-dunked by a recession. That, naturally, had the effect of throwing more people automatically onto the federal government's growing entitlement rolls and increasing the costs of those programs. Ford decided he wanted to use government spending to move the economy out of recession, an idea that had gained currency during the Kennedy administration and originated with the teachings of John Maynard Keynes. JFK had embraced the notion that governments could boost their economies out of recession by deliberately overspending. If the government spent more than it collected in taxes, it would, in effect, create money. The extra cash would get in the hands of consumers and businesses and jump-start the economy.

The idea sounded good to Ford, so in 1974 he asked for and got a partial tax rebate from Congress; the following year he got a tax cut. Cutting taxes while spending increased led, of course, to higher deficits. It also watered the inflation seed that Lyndon Johnson had planted. The sorry result of Ford's fiscal policies was that he saddled the country with $126.9 billion in budget deficits after fewer than three years in office. Unfortunately, both Ford and Johnson forgot that Keynes also taught that deficits were to be run only during deep recession and paid off as the economy improved.

Jimmy Carter

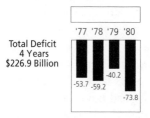

Total Deficit
4 Years
$226.9 Billion

'77 '78 '79 '80

-53.7 -59.2 -40.2 -73.8

No question, we were a lot worse off four years *after* Jimmy Carter took office than we were when he was elected. On that score, Ronald Reagan was right. Poor one-term Carter; he had both inflation *and* unemployment to contend with — it was a legacy of the Democrat Lyndon Johnson, but Republicans Nixon and Ford also contributed to Carter's woes.

When Johnson accelerated federal deficit spending for the Vietnam war and for Great Society programs, the economy was already in high gear. The additional government spending had a result that should have been predictable: It kicked off higher inflation. When you run a deficit while the economy is booming and unemployment is low, that's what you usually get, and it doesn't take a Ph.D. in economics to figure out why. Government spending injects money into an economy without adding any additional goods to spend the money on. So what do consumers do? They tend to bid up the price of existing goods. It follows a logical rule of human behavior: The more money you have, the more you're willing to pay for what you want.

Nixon and Ford had both tried some pretty foolish measures to wring inflation out of the economy. Nixon imposed wage and price controls, which no one except he and some of his economic advisers thought would work. They didn't. Ford had his WIN program — Whip Inflation Now. Remember that? But asking Americans to wear buttons with cute slogans didn't work, either. Neither Nixon nor Ford had the political courage to swallow the bitter pill that *would* have worked: reducing government spending and creating a balanced budget. To do that, they would have had to cut entitlement programs, make big reductions in defense, or make cuts in other areas of spending. They wouldn't do any of these things, so inflation kept galloping along.

At the same time, Carter inherited a growing unemployment problem that was no one's fault. The nature of the work force was changing. Women who had never worked before were competing with men for jobs. Plus the largest wave of Baby Boomers was now in the job market as well. The economy was expanding to accommodate these new workers, but not fast enough. Carter didn't know which problem — unemployment or inflation — to tackle first. Finally, he made a decision. He chose unemployment and attacked it with still more deficits. In effect, he opened the furnace door to increase the draft, and the flames of inflation leapt higher. Interest rates soared to 21 percent.

Carter used an economic tool on what was really a demographic problem. He got the result that we can say now he should have expected but not the one that he wanted. Unemployment stayed pretty much the same until his last year in office, but the inflation rate just got higher.

In the process, Carter, as you can see from the graph on page 31, set new records during his term for total annual budget deficits and for growth in the national debt, just like the two men who would follow him in the office. During the Carter presidency, the government overspent its revenues by a total of $227 billion. That was more than all the deficits piled up during World War II.

And what happened to those entitlement programs? With inflation running in the double digits, the people who were collecting the benefits saw their real value go down year by year. It was a matter of simple math. If the annual inflation rate stood at, say, 10 percent, a $500-a-month benefit would have only $450 in purchasing power a year later. Congress, always eager to spend money that will make constituents happy, decided to index some of these benefits, including Social Security, to the inflation rate. That move not only made our problems worse, but now threatens our future.

Indexing means that the benefit levels go up automatically to compensate recipients for the effects of inflation. That was nice for the people who collected Social Security and other government checks, but it just exacerbated the deficit problems that are associated with entitlements. Now, not only were entitlement programs considered untouchable by a president or a Congress that couldn't take the political heat that would come from telling some people "No," they were actually growing even more than before. Each time inflation ticked up a point, so did the entitlement benefits. By the end of the Carter reign, 54.6 percent of the government's annual budget for everything except interest on the debt was consumed by these uncontrollable programs. Even if the government had wanted to reduce spending — which, of course, it didn't — less and less of the budget was available for cutting.

The real tragedy of the Carter years? If at the start of his administration Carter had just capped the federal government's expenditures, a rising revenue stream would have enabled him to balance the budget in two years. As we know, he didn't, and in his single term in office, Carter's deficit spending brought the federal debt up to $909 billion.

Then came Ronald Reagan.

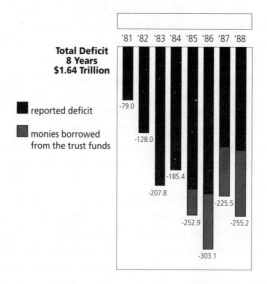

Ronald Reagan

ronald Reagan was explicit and emphatic, both as a candidate and then as president, that he would deliver a balanced federal budget. That was a central objective of his economic policy. And a lot of us believed him. Why not? He certainly sounded convincing.

In the first minute of his first televised address to the nation after taking office in January 1981, he pointed to that year's "deficit of nearly $80 billion" as evidence that "the federal budget is out of control." Two weeks later, in his first address to Congress, he echoed the same warning in a different way. "Can we, who man the ship of state, deny that it is somewhat out of control?" he asked. "Our national debt is approaching $1 trillion." At last, I thought, here's someone who will apply the brakes to our runaway debt.

But by the time Reagan's successor took office in January 1989, it was difficult to remember that these numbers had aroused a sense of alarm eight years previously. The $79 billion budget deficit that Reagan had inherited from Jimmy Carter in 1981 was the last expressed in double digits. From then on it jumped to triple digits. Further, over the next seven years, on Reagan's watch, the national debt nearly *tripled,* rising from $909 billion to an astonishing $2.6 trillion by the time he left office.

Why did it happen? The Reagan administration, which included George Bush, apparently wanted to achieve two goals: It wanted to balance the budget and start an arms race that would bankrupt the Soviet Union before the turn of the century. How could Reagan manage both? As it turned out, he couldn't, and the attempt will end up bankrupting us as well. Does this remind you of the Johnson era? Reagan, like Johnson, tried to supply both guns and butter. To do so, he, or his advisers, tried to hoodwink us by relying on an old chestnut and some new magic.

The old chestnut was government waste, fraud, and abuse. If his administration could identify all the many places where money was being misspent and fix them, Reagan would have part of what he needed to fund his military buildup while simultaneously reducing the debt. The other part, the new magic, would come from his so-called supply-side tax cut; lower tax rates would spur people into working harder and investing more, thereby stimulating the economy and ultimately yielding not less tax revenue but more.

The Reagan tax cuts, which were enacted when he took office in 1981 and again in 1986, were a success in the sense that they did what he said they would. They actually generated higher government revenues — not straight off, but eventually, though not anywhere near the levels they had to if they were to offset the deficit that was created. Something else positive happened for the economy during Reagan's administration. The chairman of the Federal Reserve, Paul Volcker, who had also served under Carter, finally broke the back of inflation by contracting the money supply. The other part of the Reagan strategy, though — finding and eliminating waste, fraud, and abuse — was by any measure a dismal and absolute failure, as you'll see in the next chapter.

As a result of the Reagan tax cuts and the economic growth that followed, the government's revenues grew by 76 percent between 1980 and 1988, but government spending grew by 80 percent. During this time, for every additional tax dollar the government took in, it spent $1.21. Most of the revenue growth, incidentally, came from an increase in the Social Security tax mandated in 1983. From 1980 to 1988, Social Security tax revenues climbed by 112 percent.

In short, Reagan's overall strategy failed to generate the additional revenue that he wanted to spend on the arms race. So what did he do? He spent it anyway. Defense spending jumped from $134 billion in 1980 to $290 billion in 1988, an increase of 116 percent.

Ronald Reagan's annual deficits were larger than those of any other president before him, and the $2.6 trillion debt he left the country when he yielded the Oval Office to his protégé, George Bush, eclipsed any debt figures this nation or any other had ever seen.

Ronald Reagan, whatever his other accomplishments in office, utterly failed to prod the Congress or the country to come to grips with what, by the end of his presidency, should have been the first item on the list of national priorities: eliminating the annual federal deficit. He and the Congress had done little to reverse the unbridled growth of federal entitlement programs, which in 1988 all by themselves ate up 54 percent of every dollar the government collected in revenue. He made a travesty of his campaign promises — as do all presidential and most congressional candidates.

Former senator Warren Rudman, who generally supported the president, says that in 1986 Reagan could have mustered the votes in Congress that would have been necessary to end the indexing of Social Security. He failed to use them, and the cost-of-living adjustment for Social Security benefits in 1991 amounted to a whopping $13.4 billion. The late Florida congressman Claude Pepper, who championed the political cause of elderly Americans, and the Washington group that claims the largest constituency of any lobby, the American Association of Retired Persons (AARP), brought so much pressure to bear that Reagan knuckled under. It's ironic that the group of people Claude Pepper fought the hardest for eventually will suffer the most when their fixed incomes and savings become worthless and $50 million will have no more value than one of my German 50-million-mark bills.

Increased defense spending, whatever its global strategic merits, made the problem of the deficit, which should have been our first concern, worse. By how much? In the last year of the Reagan administration, defense spending chewed up 32 percent of total revenue dollars. The government spent 54 percent of revenues on entitlement programs and 24 percent on interest. That's right. The total comes to 110 percent, more than all available revenues. And we still haven't mentioned all other government departments.

And how does the government get the rest of the money it needs? Right again. The government borrows it. Partially as a result of these failed fiscal policies and the large amount of borrowing from foreigners, we went in only ten years from being the largest creditor nation in the world to the largest debtor nation. What a tragedy.

So that's the legacy we inherited from the Gipper: an inability to operate almost all the basic functions of government without borrowing from creditors around the world. It's a sorry state for any country to find itself in, but especially one that thinks of itself — inaccurately now, to be sure — as the richest and most powerful on earth.

As any family or individual who overspends learns, sooner or later the bills come due. Ronald Reagan ran the country's credit cards *almost* up to their limits. George Bush followed suit.

George Bush

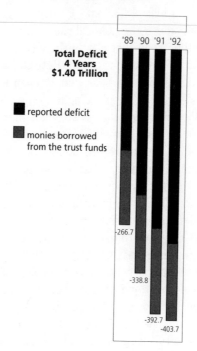

Total Deficit
4 Years
$1.40 Trillion

'89 '90 '91 '92

■ reported deficit

■ monies borrowed
from the trust funds

-266.7

-338.8

-392.7
-403.7

In four years in office, George Bush set new records for outspending government revenues, as the accompanying graph shows. In these four years, Bush's deficits came to nearly 85 percent of the deficits Reagan took a full eight years to rack up. For now, at least, Bush holds the title of all-time champion overspender.

Let's try to be charitable toward Bush for a moment. In one sense, he can point the finger of blame for his overspending at presidents and Congresses going all the way back to Lyndon Johnson. It's certainly true that he came into office facing a prodigious challenge. By the end of the Reagan years, the portion of the federal budget that could be easily controlled — that is, reduced — by the president or the Congress had become pitiably small. If entitlement programs and other mandatory spending, such as federal deposit insurance and debt interest payments, are taken as givens, only 33 percent of the budget was left for elected officials to fool with in 1989.

Matters then grew only worse. By the end of Bush's presidency, interest and entitlement spending had grown, leaving only 27 percent of the budget that is now considered controllable. Interest alone totaled 61 percent of all personal income taxes in 1992 — that means that just paying our creditors took the equivalent of 61 cents of every dollar the federal government withheld from your paycheck that year.

Nonetheless, Bush's greatest failure as president wasn't that he didn't solve or eliminate the problem that's leading us all to the Week from Hell. We can forgive that, because of the magnitude of the problem he inherited, but it's a lot harder to forgive the fact that he hardly tried. Instead, he went in the opposite direction, and so did Congress.

The Congress

Congress is no less and probably more guilty in the coming death of the United States than the string of presidents we've had for the last thirty years. You've recently seen that most of our representatives can't manage their own finances and checkbooks, their own post office, and their congressional restaurant tabs. How do we expect them and their staffs to manage the nation's finances? Most of them are lawyers or professional politicians who have never had to make a payroll or run any organization that had to make a profit. In fact, many of them regard business as an antagonist they must police.

When you look back over the past thirty years, you see that elected representatives and their staffs have also become captive to the most well-financed and effective lobbying groups that ever brought influence to bear on any legislative body anywhere at any time. In that period, which began with the onset of the Vietnam war, splinter groups and special-interest groups learned how to use their power to divide and conquer in Washington. Members of Congress learned that to get reelected, they had to provide something for each group, as well as jobs and aid for their constituencies.

It wasn't only domestic-interest groups that were hiring professional interest peddlers. Foreign countries and foreign corporations — from Japan, Korea, Mexico, and a myriad of others — have spent millions of dollars to hire ex-government officials at huge salaries to represent their own selfish interests. They've done so very effectively, and these lobbyists and their bosses didn't and don't give a damn about the United States. Their goal is to make up for compensation lost during government service.

I have a very highly placed friend in the government in Washington who, at the start of the Bush administration, explained to the Treasury secretary and the budget director the fiscal crises toward which the country was rapidly moving. They ignored him. He then went to the Republican leaders of Congress, and they ignored him. He tried the Democratic leaders and got the same result. He told me of his attempts and failures to get someone — anyone — in Washington to listen to a few facts and acknowledge the conclusion to which these facts clearly pointed.

I advised him to go directly to the president, because I knew my friend had the stature to be admitted to the Oval Office. He had tried, he said, but couldn't get past then-Chief-of-Staff John Sununu. "Even if I could," my by-now-despondent friend said, "it would be a waste of time. Bush is only interested in things international. He has no interest in domestic issues."

I was — and remain — stunned.

Bill Clinton

President Clinton has two choices. Like his predecessors, he can do nothing to head off the coming calamity over America's nearly-out-of-control debt. Or he can wrestle our problem to the ground, as he promised during his presidential campaign. (For more information on Clinton's presidency, see Chapter 10.)

If he ends up doing nothing, we can be pretty certain of what will happen. The growth rate of the federal budget deficit will accelerate. From more than $400 billion in 1993, it will, if present trends continue, balloon in 1994 to $730 billion, according to Grace Commission projections. It will climb still further in 1995, reaching $850 billion. If this rapid deficit growth continues, interest payments are projected to exceed the amount of money the government collects in personal income taxes by 1995. Interest will account for 92 percent of personal income taxes in 1994. By 1995, interest on the debt alone will reach 105 percent of all personal income taxes collected.

Don't be fooled, incidentally, when our leaders play around with the numbers. They may claim, for example, that interest on our debt will come to only 47 percent of "total revenues" in 1995 — as if that weren't bad enough. But included in their definition of total revenues are Social Security receipts, as well as corporate and personal income taxes.

As you will see in Chapter 5, our 1985 projections were right on target for seven straight years, and there is little on the horizon to indicate that they won't prove accurate in the future, regardless of what our politicians try to tell us.

By 1995, even if American politicians haven't acknowledged it yet, the rest of the world will have figured out that the United States is going to default on its debt. That's when and why our country and lives will come apart.

Now, look at the next graph. It shows unmistakably that we in the United States will suffer — soon — for the almost unbelievable debt that our so-called leaders are accumulating in our name.

Take careful note of this constantly increasing and accelerating deficit, which in turn creates a roaring debt. We are tight up against a fiscal Armageddon. They *are* killing our country, and whatever it takes, we can't let them go on.

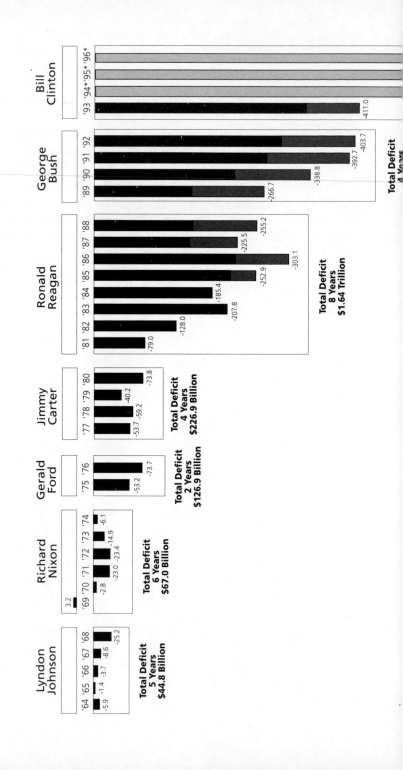

Federal Budget Deficits
Since 1964

(In Billions of Dollars by Fiscal Years)

■ **reported deficit**

■ **monies borrowed from the trust funds**

□ **projected deficit**

The shaded areas on the deficit bars from 1985—1993 represent the amount that is borrowed from trust funds and other government accounts to offset the reported deficit. The black portion shows the reported deficit. The black and gray areas together show the true, or gross, deficit.

-730.0

-850.0

-950.0

**Total Deficit
4 Years
$2.94 Trillion**

***Based on Grace
Commission
Projections**

3

So Proudly We Failed

PRESIDENT Clinton's first "deficit-reduction" proposal, issued in April 1993, marked the sixth time in the past eleven years that Washington politicians have announced a new plan, passed a new law, or reached a new agreement that they promised would bring spending under control in order to reduce and eventually eliminate budget deficits. As we have seen in each of the past five instances our politicians have been wrong. Well, either wrong or lying — or both.

If there were elected officials in Washington who both knew how to attack the government's propensity to overspend and *wanted* to attack it, they were a pitiful few, and they had their hands tied. Most elected officials realize, in fact, that their reelection to office depends on their perpetuating a system that encourages waste and deficit spending. We, the American people, are to blame for this sorry situation. The sad truth is most of us don't even realize what has been done to our country in so short a time. Consequently, we have sat back as a silent majority and let the special- and foreign-interest lobby groups destroy our country.

If Washington officials really wanted to cut billions of dollars in unnecessary spending from the federal budget, they could have followed the recommendations of the Grace Commission, created by President Ronald Reagan in 1982. They didn't.

If Washington officials really wanted to control the budget process in order to phase out deficit spending, they could have stuck to the terms of the Gramm-Rudman-Hollings Act as it was passed in 1985. They didn't.

If Washington officials really wanted to put an end to deficit spending, they could have lived up to the two revisions of Gramm-Rudman-Hollings in 1987 and 1990. They didn't.

Or Washington officials genuinely interested in staving off the calamity that budget deficits and a huge national debt are about to bring down on the country could have abided, at least, by the terms of the so-called budget agreement of 1990. But they didn't. In fact, the first budget proposal of the Clinton administration would have exceeded the 1990 budget caps by $123 billion over the next four years.

In every past attempt to control their own irresponsibility in spending the public's money, Washington officials in the White House and Congress have failed and will continue to do so without a major change in both their attitude and direction.

Amazing Grace

In February 1982, President Reagan commissioned the President's Private Sector Survey on Cost Control to look for ways to eliminate waste in federal spending. Known more familiarly as the Grace Commission, it consisted of such business leaders as James E. Burke, chairman and CEO of Johnson & Johnson; Robert W. Galvin, chairman and CEO of Motorola Inc.; John J. Horan, chairman of Merck & Company, Inc.; and Donald R. Keough, president of the Coca-Cola Company. I, too, was part of the Grace Commission.

The report that we submitted to President Reagan in January 1984 advanced a total of 2,478 cost-saving recommendations. They ranged from adopting a single accounting system for the federal government (there were then some 332 incompatible systems in place) to privatizing building-maintenance services to tightening federal cash-management practices (cash-management procedures remain so poor that money sits idle in noninterest-bearing accounts, costing taxpayers billions of dollars each year).

If the president and Congress had adopted everything in the Grace Commission report, the federal government could have cut its spending by $424 billion from 1984 to 1987. By the year 2000, the annual savings from these recommendations would have reached $1.9 trillion per year.

You can guess what happened. Reagan (even though it was his idea) and legislative leaders politely thanked the Grace Commission for the report, then dismissed or ignored most of what was in it. Instead of receiving support and leadership, the report was shelved.

The recommendations we made for reducing government waste weren't radical. Most were painfully obvious. For example, one proposal called for closing a western army base that had been built in the 1800s for use as an outpost in the Indian wars, which have long since ended. Another base in Virginia that we targeted for closing was so antiquated it had a moat around it, but that state's junior senator insisted that it "would not be closed on his watch." It wasn't. In fact, of the 4,000 Defense Department installations in the country, only 312 could be called significant and necessary. The remainder were support facilities — storage depots, for example — with fewer than 150 employees each. Most of these could have been closed without one iota of harm to our military capabilities. The problem? Congress, which seems to look on the Pentagon as its own personal pork barrel, had laws in place that made shutting down unneeded military bases a time-consuming, almost impossible task.

In general, waste in government spending isn't difficult to uncover. The Grace Commission found that one-third of all U.S. tax dollars were consumed by waste and inefficiency in the federal government alone. Examples both large and small are plentiful.

For instance:

- Waste and mismanagement — the $436 hammer. Bought by the U.S. Navy, this ordinary hardware-store hammer cost $7 *plus:* $41 to order; $93 to determine that it worked; $102 for something called manufacturing overhead; $37 to ensure the availability of spare parts; $3 to pack the hammer for shipping; $90 to pay a contractor's general administrative costs; $56 to pay a finder's fee; and $7 for the capital cost of money. The total: $436.
- Waste and mismanagement — a study funded by the federal government to measure the average size of airline stewardesses' noses.
- Waste and mismanagement — the Rural Electrification Administration (REA), which loaned, for example, $2 billion in 1992 for a loss of $350 million that year alone. Formed in 1935 to bring electricity to rural America, the agency continues to get funding even though 99 percent of rural Americans by now have electricity. (The REA uses its money to provide electric service to farms at reduced rates.) This, like many other agencies of its era, is a protected congressional pet.
- Waste and mismanagement — the U.S. Forest Service, the world's largest road builder, which spent $487 million in 1991 to lay and maintain roads on federal lands for private timber companies. It makes so little from timber sales, however, that it lost more than $1.8 billion in 1991.

For more ways Congress should cut spending, see Chapter 12, "A Debt-Buster's Tool Kit for Congress."

The men and women who served on the Grace Commission did their job. The president got what he asked for: specific, well-identified, and documented cases of waste that could be eliminated through either administrative or legislative action. But the president and the Congress didn't do *their* jobs by taking that action.

While the Grace Commission found $1.9 trillion in potential *annual* savings to be realized in the year 2000, the government had realized a total of just $197 billion by the early 1990s. And much of these savings came about because Peter Grace and syndicated columnist Jack Anderson founded Citizens Against Government Waste, so they could continue the fight that Reagan and Congress had either abandoned or evaded. Such failure to act in areas where reform would have proved so easy is a crime. Unfortunately for America, however, it's just not illegal.

The Gramm-Rudman-Hollings Waltz

After the Grace Commission, the next major bit of what also turned out to be public posturing by political leaders was the Balanced Budget and Emergency Deficit Control Act of 1985, otherwise known as the Gramm-Rudman-Hollings Act, after the names of its three sponsors. This cost-cutting piece of legislation was passed by Congress in December 1985. In its essence, it is not complicated.

The true federal budget deficit that year came to $252.9 billion. Gramm-Rudman-Hollings required that it be lowered by about $36 billion per year for each of the following five fiscal years, which would have brought the "net" deficit to zero by 1991. (The gross deficit would have been brought down to about $40.6 billion.)

These reductions weren't optional, something Congress and the president *could* do if it were convenient and they so desired. It was a law — like having to pay your income tax or being prohibited from robbing people of their money or goods. This law said that if the actual deficit exceeded the target deficit specified for any year, half of the excess automatically had to be cut from defense spending and the other half had to be cut from nondefense programs.

The law's sponsors say they never expected that Congress would have to make the mandatory cuts, because they expected to balance the budget largely from rising revenues. Moreover, they thought that the mere prospect of automatic cuts in their favorite spending programs would be threat enough to force lawmakers and the president to agree to a budget that honored the Gramm-Rudman-Hollings limits.

How did the legislators do in meeting their goals? Take a look at the chart below and the graph on page 50:

| Year | (in billions of dollars) | | | Actual Deficits |
| | Target Deficits | | | |
	(1985)	(1987)	(1990)	
1987	$144			$226
1988	108	$144		255
1989	72	136		267
1990	36	100		339
1991	0	64	$327	393
1992		28	317	404

In 1987 and again in 1990, Congress revised its targets. Under the 1987 revision, the new goal for fiscal year 1992 was a $28 billion deficit; in 1990, the goal for 1992 was a $317 billion deficit. And what was the real deficit for 1992? A whopping $403.7 billion, and that was after the nation's second largest single tax increase. Also, Congress always exempted entitlement programs from this law, an act that in and of itself assured the law's rapid destruction.

As it turned out, all the Gramm-Rudman-Hollings legislation did was force Congress and the administration to find new ways of relabeling, reclassifying, and rescheduling, but not reducing, their spending. This approach to solving economic woes reminds me of what was said of Brazil's plight in a 1992 issue of *The Economist:* "Brazil has managed to get out of trouble through the engaging Latin trick of *empurrar com a barrige:* pushing the problem ahead of you with your belly instead of stopping to grapple with it."

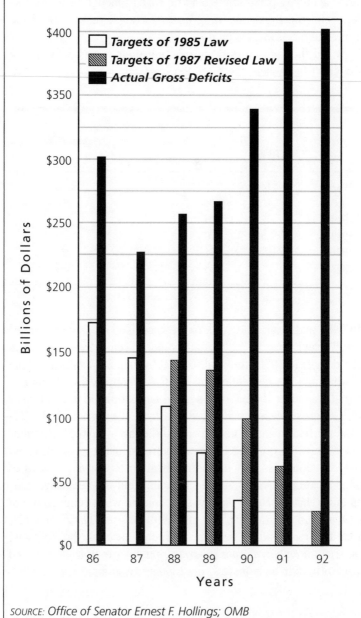

Gramm-Rudman-Hollings
Targets versus Actual Deficits

Billions of Dollars

☐ Targets of 1985 Law
▨ Targets of 1987 Revised Law
■ Actual Gross Deficits

$400
$350
$300
$250
$200
$150
$100
$50
$0

86 87 88 89 90 91 92

Years

SOURCE: *Office of Senator Ernest F. Hollings; OMB*

Debtspeak, or Budget Chicanery

It's hard not to be cynical about legislators and officials in the executive branch who are either fooled by their own words or assume that the public will be. Most of the decisions and actions taken in Washington in the name of deficit reduction in the last eight years have reduced nothing but the deficit's visibility. Maybe elected officials believe that if no one sees something, it isn't there, or that if the public sees less of something, it has grown smaller. These latest machinations remind one of the old shell game. Now you see it, now you don't.

If attempted deception were a federal offense, almost everyone involved in the federal budget process would be guilty of the crime. But, like the movie gang that couldn't shoot straight, the Washington gang hasn't even disguised its deception well.

In Newspeak, the language spoken in George Orwell's *1984,* "yes" meant "no." In the deficit reduction language spoken in Washington, D.C., "reduction" has come to mean "increase." You could pick any year, but the debate over the 1991 budget is as good as any. Congress reported that the budget package it passed would create savings of 2.4 percent in 1991 and 4.8 percent in 1992. In fact, the amount Congress budgeted for those years was actually higher than in 1990 — by 11.1 percent for 1991 and 16.2 percent for 1992. How could more be less?

Congressional budget writers defend their terminology by explaining that the spending levels budgeted for 1991 and 1992 were lower than earlier *projections* of spending for those two years. You probably don't have to ask who makes the projections.

Whether the deception worked is less important than that the budgeted deficits for 1991 and 1992 were larger, not smaller, than the deficit in 1990. Just calling something a reduction doesn't make it so, of course; it doesn't even hide the truth well. What it does do, however, is keep legislators and voters alike from dealing honestly with reality, because to do so is to acknowledge that an attempt was made to deceive and that it failed. The child who fibs about raiding the jelly jar can't acknowledge the jam on his or her face even when it's plainly there for the world to see.

Other deceptions practiced by congressional committees and the executive Office of Management and Budget (OMB), the arm of the administration charged with budgetary matters, are more pernicious, because they actually do conceal the size of the real annual deficit from anyone who is not schooled in the techniques of fiscal flimflam.

Some of the budgetary chicanery involves shifting items from one place to another on the government's books. In 1989, for example, the accounts of the U.S. Postal Service were deleted from the federal budget, thereby "saving" $1.8 billion. Nineteen ninety, incidentally, was the first year in which the Postal Service ran a deficit ($1.6 billion), a feat it repeated in 1991 ($1.3 billion). The cost of the 1991 Persian Gulf war was also omitted from the budget, as if the money spent there somehow didn't count. The war's funding, the lawmakers said, was a one-time emergency expense rather than a longtime commitment, so it didn't have to go on the budget.

Off-budget items are those excluded by law from the budget totals. Some off-budget entities, such as the Postal Service, were removed from the budget; others, such as the Federal Deposit Insurance Corporation (FDIC), were created outside the budget. The items are treated off-budget, either because they're so-called extraordinary "one-time" expenses, such as the S&L bailout, or they have their own revenues and operate as quasi-government agencies, such as the Post Office.

Other off-budget programs include:

- Direct loans. These are made by a variety of government agencies, including the Small Business Administration (SBA) and the Export-Import Bank.
- Loan guarantees. Student loans fall into this category, as do loans guaranteed by the Federal Housing Administration (FHA), Veterans Administration (VA), Rural Electrification

Administration (REA), and the Small Business Disaster
Loan program. When borrowers don't repay these loans,
the taxpayer has to foot the bill. The present outstanding
student loan default bill is a fiasco bordering on fiscal
larceny. It amounted to about $13.5 billion in 1992.

- Federal insurance. These off-budget programs include the
  Federal Deposit Insurance Corporation and the Resolution
  Trust Corporation (RTC), which was created in 1989 to
  handle the assets of the failed savings and loan institutions.
  (Solvent S&Ls are covered by the FDIC.) Even though the
  money comes right out of the Treasury — which means it
  comes right out of your pocket — Washington politicians
  don't count the $500 billion they'll spend to bail out banks
  and savings and loans as budgeted expenditures.
  Remember, the first S&L estimate was a mere $50 billion,
  and now look at it. The politicians' approach is to lie about
  the magnitude of the amount we owe until the public gets
  used to it.

- So-called government-sponsored enterprise loans.
  Examples include the Federal Home Loan Mortgage
  Corporation (Freddie Mac), Federal National Mortgage
  Association (Fannie Mae), Student Loan Mortgage
  Association (Sallie Mae), and Federal Agricultural Mortgage
  Corporation (Farmer Mac). These loans are put in a
  separate category, because the institutions that offer them
  lend the money directly. (Banks issue the other type of
  loans we mentioned, which the government then
  guarantees.) This category is the fastest growing of all
  government lending programs. How fast is it growing?
  From 1965 to 1990, the amount of these loans outstanding
  jumped some 5,000 percent. Keep in mind that even
  though these are considered private loans for budgetary
  purposes, the government must cough up the money when
  there's a default.

- Pension Benefit Guarantee Corporation (PBGC). This one's

a real time bomb. The PBGC provides insurance to guarantee the payment of pension benefits if a company becomes unable to meet its obligations. The amount of retirement funds that the PBGC insured in 1990 came to $43 billion.

Another trick used by deficit-reducing budget writers: Shift military and civil service paydays and other scheduled government payments forward into the next fiscal year — thereby creating the illusion of reduced spending without incurring the pain of actually making cuts. It hardly matters to taxpayers whether the government pays people on September 30, the end of one fiscal year, or October 1, the beginning of the next. In either case, the money is spent.

The numbers that appear in budgets are based on *estimated* revenues and expenses, so another way the president and Congress make a budget look better than it is is to play with these estimates. One would want to inflate revenue estimates and reduce estimated expenses, and Congress and the administration routinely do that. For instance, they will paint the rosiest picture possible of anticipated tax collections by overestimating national economic growth for the upcoming budget year. Then they will take a bite out of estimated expenses by predicting lower interest rates and therefore lower carrying charges on the national debt. Naturally, reality always gives the lie to these projections, but by then that fiscal year is history and the next one has begun.

What's most galling is the transparency of this ploy to anyone but the most nearsighted of politicians. Does *anyone* actually take politicians' estimates of *anything* seriously? How could they? The revenue and expense projections for 1991, for example, were calculated during a recession, but budget writers audaciously assumed that the economy would nonetheless expand by about 3 percent — a healthy growth rate for a year when the economy is *not* in recession but far too optimistic for the real state of the economy that year. Actually, the economy, as measured by gross domestic product (GDP) — the value of all the final goods and services a country produces each year — declined in real terms by 0.74 percent. The politicians purposely practice fraud and deceit.

At the same time, they assumed that interest rates, which have a tendency to rise as the economy emerges from recession, would fall. They wanted it both ways — a strengthening economy with falling interest rates — but that's not the way the real world works. As it turned out, they actually got declining interest rates because GDP, the measure of how well the economy is doing, actually fell by almost 3 percent in the first quarter of 1991 and by 0.74 percent for the year. (A falling GDP indicates that an economy is in recession, which means that demand for capital is low. In turn, low demand for capital translates into lower interest rates.) Also, the Federal Reserve chairman, Alan Greenspan, responded to White House pressure and lowered interest rates in order to try to jump-start the economy. The differences between wishful projections and real experience in fiscal year 1990 amounted to $119 billion, more than one-third of the $338.8 billion budget deficit racked up that year (see the graph on page 56).

Year after year, Congress and the administration use the same maneuver with roughly similar results: The budgeted deficit is reduced by several billion dollars, while the actual deficit comes out at the end of the year that much higher. No one is fooled, the budget looks better, and the debt and the interest charges on it rise still. In the meantime, everyone manages or pretends to remain ignorant of our impending fiscal collapse.

These stunts — finagling growth estimates, delaying paydays, dropping items off the budget, and the like — pale in contrast, however, to the Social Security ruse. Here, as Everett Dirksen might say as he took another turn in his grave, we're talking real money — in the hundreds of billions of dollars. It works this way.

Some years ago, in 1983, Congress raised Social Security taxes and made other adjustments in the program supposedly to place it on an actuarially sound footing. The idea then was to collect in

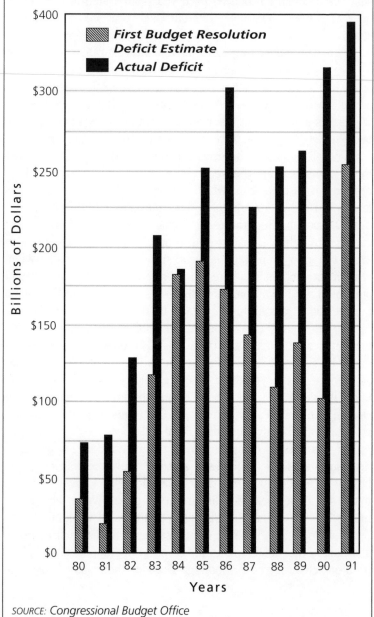

Annual Discrepancies between Government Estimated and Actual Deficits

Billions of Dollars

Years

Legend:
- *First Budget Resolution Deficit Estimate*
- **Actual Deficit**

SOURCE: Congressional Budget Office

current employment taxes the money that would be required to pay benefits to today's Baby Boomers later, when they have retired, because by 2010 the proportion of workers supporting retirees would have dropped from 20 to 1 to 3 to 1.

Consequently, the Social Security trust fund, where the money was supposed to be saved, has for some years been running a large surplus. In other words, more money is paid into the trust fund every year than is needed to pay current Social Security recipients. By the time the Baby Boomers were ready to retire beginning in 2010, the fund was supposed to have more than $1 trillion in assets. But instead of leaving the money to accumulate in the trust fund, as an individual saves in a retirement account and corporations are required to do in their pension funds, the government invests this money in its own securities — in effect, lending the surplus to itself. Congress replaces the real dollars that people pay into the Social Security trust fund with specially created, nonmarketable Treasury bonds. These are the federal government's IOUs to itself. Then they spend the actual money they have received.

Borrowing what amounts to current expense money from one's own savings account might be excusable if it were done infrequently and if some reasonable prospect existed that the IOUs could be repaid. But by now, 1993, the federal government has borrowed more than $1 trillion from Social Security and the other trust funds. Worse, though, the government doesn't even acknowledge that it is borrowing. In fact, it counts the surplus as revenue, thereby making the real deficit look smaller than it actually is. When Baby Boomers who are working today begin to retire, all they will find in the Social Security savings account is more than $1 trillion of the government's paper, which will undoubtedly have become worthless long before that time. (See Chapter 4 for more information on the Social Security scam.)

What the budget masters in Congress and the executive branch do to Social Security, they also do to other federal trust funds — military, postal workers, railroad, and civil service retirement;

Medicare surplus; and highways and airports trust funds. They borrow from these funds, and replace the money with IOUs. What's more, they count the money coming in as revenue, but they ignore the future liabilities on those funds — which makes the government's current books look better but guarantees bigger problems further out in time. It also distorts the true picture of the revenue stream. Without this gimmick, our real revenue increase is much smaller.

It seems to me pathetic that for all their posturing and deception, federal budget writers still have not been able to reduce the deficit — either the real one or the smaller one they cook up every year. Unable to stay within the original Gramm-Rudman-Hollings guidelines, Congress has resorted to pushing the balanced-budget target dates further into the future instead of facing the constraints of the law it passed. By the end of 1992, our deficit was 37 percent of our receipts, as the graph opposite shows. The trend has been moving steadily upward, and we'll later prove why this pattern will continue at an accelerating pace.

Legislators have delayed Gramm-Rudman reductions twice so far — once in 1987, when they moved the balanced-budget target date from 1991 to 1993, and again in 1990, when they realized the target dates were meaningless and chose not to set new ones. By doing so, they have illustrated their complete unwillingness to face fiscal reality. "We will keep our promises five years from today," they are saying to their constituents, "but in the meantime, it's business as usual." The law's original intent has been so subverted that Senator Ernest F. Hollings (D–SC) has publicly disassociated himself from the legislation that bears his name, and Senator Warren Rudman, a New Hampshire Republican, chose not to seek reelection in 1992, even though he had won his last race by a 70 percent plurality.

The electorate — that's us — is as much to blame for the budget failures of those who govern us as they are themselves, since we haven't held them to their pledges or punished them for their failures. Furthermore, we have continually and constantly pres-

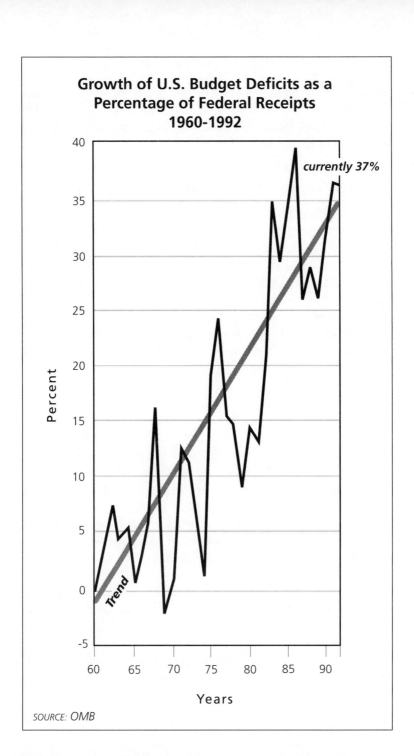

Growth of U.S. Budget Deficits as a Percentage of Federal Receipts 1960-1992

currently 37%

SOURCE: OMB

sured them for more and more money to pay for our pet causes. Surveys show that we have a strong distaste for Congress, but not our own representatives and senators. That dichotomy must change — *now*.

The Budget Reconciliation Act of 1990

The idea behind the Omnibus Budget Reconciliation Act of 1990, known as the 1990 budget accord, was sound enough: The federal government would reduce spending by $2 for every $1 it collected in new taxes. But this sound idea was soundly defeated by lawmakers and a president who would reach new heights of chicanery and doublespeak. The actual effects of the accord: Taxes soared and spending soared right along with them, to the point where the 1992 deficit topped $403 billion. Here's what happened:

Early in 1990, President Bush called an emergency meeting with Congress to address the hemorrhaging federal budget. No one, unsurprisingly, could agree on spending cuts. Finally, the president said he would break his "read-my-lips, no-new-taxes" pledge in return for deficit-busting legislation.

Congress, accordingly, passed the second largest tax *increase* in our nation's history. It authorized new or higher excise taxes — a 10 percent tax on boats and "luxury" cars, for example, which priced American products right out of the market; increased the top marginal tax rate from 28 percent to 31 percent; phased out a host of exemptions and deductions for higher-income taxpayers; and raised the maximum wage subject to a 1.45 percent payroll tax for Medicare from $53,000 to $125,000.

And the budget?

Our lawmakers relied on inaccurate estimates, twisted logic, and two enormous loopholes in order to continue running huge deficits.

For example, they came up with this clever idea: They would base any cuts made in the budget on reductions in projected *future* growth of government programs, not on actual spending for these programs in previous years. It worked like this: Say, in 1991, a program cost the government $100 billion. "In 1992," said our leaders, "with increases in the population, this same program will cost at least $150 billion. Now, we'll cut it." And they did. They sliced $10 billion from the $50 billion *increase* and announced that they'd saved the American taxpayer $10 billion. Of course, what they really succeeded in doing was increasing spending by $40 billion.

And those loopholes? The first loophole states that the budget agreement can be violated as long as a spending program is classified as an emergency. That's how unemployment benefits got extended, and that's how the federal government in 1992 was able to send emergency aid to post-riot Los Angeles. The second loophole states that spending estimates can be altered to reflect changing economic conditions or technical errors in calculating the costs of programs. You can imagine the effect of the recession on spending estimates. The loopholes, in other words, give Congress a free hand to violate the budget agreement at just about any time for nearly any reason.

It shouldn't come as a shock that revenues for 1992 came to $1.09 trillion, while estimated expenditures reached $1.38 trillion, or 27 percent more than revenues. And without counting trust fund surpluses as part of revenues (since the government should not be spending this money in the first place), expenditures exceeded revenues by nearly 40 percent.

Subsidies and Benefits Should Be Cut — All Except Mine

U.S. citizens have to realize that meaningful change requires some sacrifice by every American, and they must declare their willingness to accept their own share of the burden. It is time, in other words, for us to stop being a nation of special interests. There was a period in our country's history when people said, "I am an

American." We thought like Americans. We acted like Americans. We worried about what was good for the country. No more.

"Ask not what your country can do for you; ask what you can do for your country," President Kennedy stated in his inaugural speech. President Clinton, in his inaugural speech, told the nation: "It's time to break the bad habit of expecting something for nothing from our government." It's past time we all took those presidential words to heart, because this is the last opportunity we have to avert fiscal disaster.

Easy enough to say, critics counter. Tell that to doctors, farmers, Social Security recipients, single mothers, defense contractors, and Amtrak riders — all the interest groups who may have good cause to resist sacrificing their own benefits for the greater good.

How do you get those voters, not to mention the silent majority, to sacrifice?

I'm convinced that people will accept the pain of making adjustments short-term, if they think they'll have some gain long-term. So far, though, no one has been given any reason to believe that any benefit is in the offing. Moreover, a host of entitlement programs *could* be cut without hurting ordinary citizens — examples include subsidized loans to students whose parents can well afford their child's education; Social Security checks to wealthy retirees who continue to draw benefits well after they've collected every penny they contributed to the Social Security trust fund, plus interest; and federal military retirement programs that are periodically indexed upward and allow personnel to retire with a healthy benefit package as early as age thirty-eight.

Washington takes much of its lead from what it perceives to be the sentiment of the voting public. It's the public's responsibility to ensure that Washington understands it wants change and that the time for change is now. Voters must demand that the politicians they elected to office in 1992 stop spending money that the country does not have, and not come up with more programs for which we have no hope of paying. Citizens who can't see any further than their own little slice of our shrinking pie will keep encouraging politicians to equivocate, mislead, pander, and lie. And that's a sure-fire recipe for our national demise within a very, very short time.

4

The Great Social Security Scam

ALTHOUGH this is a story that could never happen, just suppose. . . .

What if the president of a very large corporation — we'll call him Ronald George — had to face up to the fact that his company was hemorrhaging money every year and that it fell to him to do something about it. So he consulted with his advisers, and together they concocted a simple, but ingenious, plan.

The scheme wouldn't stop the losses, but it would make those losses look a lot smaller. "Here's what we'll do," they said among themselves. "Instead of sending our employees' monthly pension-fund contributions to the fund, we'll use them to help cover the company's current expenses."

"We'll call it a loan," their lawyers said.

"Naturally, we'll pay the pension fund back when business improves," the president said with the best of intentions. Everyone laughed.

"While we're at it," one of the advisers suggested, "why don't we increase the employee pension-fund deductions? We could surely use the extra money."

"Agreed," said the rest of the advisers.

They congratulated themselves for coming up with such a clever solution to help alleviate the company's financial woes, which they had brought about in the first place. Then they called a press conference to make their raid on the pension plan appear legitimate.

"We have acted boldly to strengthen our employees' retirement fund by increasing the payments into it," the president said. But reporters started asking embarrassing questions. Eventually an investigation ensued, and the president and his advisers were hauled into court and charged with conspiring to defraud. "Guilty," the judge said, and off they all went to prison to join Michael Milken and Ivan Boesky, who had also defrauded lots of innocent people.

Except that it didn't really turn out that way. The conspirators didn't go to jail. In fact, most of them kept their jobs — because this isn't a fable about how justice triumphs; it's a true story about what President Ronald Reagan, President George Bush, and, now, President Bill Clinton and their respective U.S. Congresses have done and are continuing to do to the wage earners of this country. They're using your retirement savings — that is, the Social Security taxes you pay — to conceal large amounts of their deficit spending. What's more, they're replacing the money they use with IOUs in the form of government bonds that don't pay real interest, aren't likely to be paid back, and have no commercial value because they can't be sold in the marketplace. They simply add to the government debt. Michael Milken and Ivan Boesky should have been so clever and so brazen.

When President Franklin Roosevelt pushed the original Social Security bill through Congress in 1935, the system was designed as an auxiliary retirement plan. As Roosevelt said after he signed the bill into law: "The link between taxes and benefits gives the contributors a legal, moral, and political right to collect their pensions." The government, in effect, was forcing people to save for their old age and, in return, the government paid a fair rate of interest on the accumulating nest egg. In time, retirees would get back what they had put in, plus interest and accrued investment credit.

The Social Security system, in other words, was similar to a private insurance plan. Under an insurance plan, if you pay in X dollars over a long period of time, forty years, say, you'll eventually get back far more than you paid in. That's because the earnings from the money you contribute will allow the company to pay you X plus Y dollars at maturity.

The graph on page 67 shows how much a worker will have contributed to the Social Security fund during his or her employment years — and how much he or she will receive in benefits after retiring at age sixty-three. The numbers aren't surprising. They show that someone retiring today will get back more than he or she put in, while an individual who is now twenty-five to thirty-five years old will get back far less than he or she contributed. What's more, by the time these younger workers reach retirement age, the fund is likely to be empty anyway.

(Note: In the graphs that follow, "contribution" is the accumulated Social Security contributions of a worker and his employer, with interest, if the worker retires at age sixty-three; "return" is the amount of Social Security benefits that worker is entitled to collect.)

Initially, the government properly called Social Security a trust fund, because the government had an obligation to hold the money in trust until the wage earner began to be paid out when he or she retired at age sixty-five.

Then the Jesse James gang — also known as Congress — got itchy about all that money sitting around with nobody spending it. So in 1939, although they still called Social Security a trust fund, they really turned it into a "pay as you go" plan. With this plan, known as "Old-Age and Survivors Insurance" (OASI), tax payments from the current work force would finance the benefits of those already retired, which at that time was a ratio of about 50 workers to 1 retiree.

The new plan represented a fundamental change. What it meant

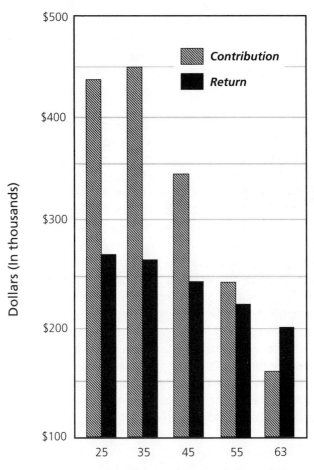

Social Security Benefits
Contribution and Return

Dollars (In thousands)

Employee's Age on July 1, 1993

Contribution

Return

SOURCE: *The Wyatt Company*

was that Uncle Sam dipped into Grandson Peter's current retirement payments in order to pay Grandpa Paul's pension, and it set up the later opportunities for a much greater fraud. With this shift in the law, any cash that happened to accumulate in the government's Social Security account lost its protection from congressional raids. Because as many as twenty workers were paying into the Social Security fund for every retired person receiving benefits, the account began accumulating a large surplus, but the money was not protected, as businesses that offer pension plans must do. You might as well have flashed a cash-filled billfold at the Pickpockets' Ball.

For a time, though, the new Social Security plan worked well enough. As in the past, employees and employers each paid the same percentage of the employee's wage into the system in the form of a payroll tax authorized by the Federal Insurance Contributions Act, or FICA. But far more people were employed and paying more into the fund than were retired and taking money out. The joint contribution required from employee and employer was just 2 percent.

Roosevelt's original idea had been to provide a supplemental retirement income for workers in commerce and industry only, but lawmakers kept adding beneficiaries, while at the same time increasing benefits to those already receiving Social Security. The problem was that no actuarial plan existed, so a person with only five years of covered employment could qualify for Social Security payments for the length of his or her retirement. Such an actuarially unsound plan isn't allowed in industry. But it does permit military and government workers to go to the private sector for a short time *and* double and triple dip.

In 1939, when Congress did away with the trust fund protection of Social Security, it also added benefits for the dependents of retired workers and insurance for retirees' survivors. Again, no actuarial provision was made for these added expenses.

In 1956, Congress added disability benefits for covered workers with no actuarial increase, turning what had originally been a straightforward old-age pension into what became known as OASDI (Old-Age, Survivor, and Disability Insurance). In 1965, with the creation of the Hospital Insurance (HI) and Supplementary Medical Insurance (SMI) funds, Medicare and Medicaid were added to the growing list of Social Security obligations (which were funded by separately established accounts). In 1972, benefits were indexed to keep inflation from chipping away at their purchasing power — that is, cost-of-living adjustments, or COLAs, were added to the basic benefit checks. Anyone familiar with pension plans knows there is no way to determine what pensions will cost when tying the programs to COLA indices. This fact alone makes the plan unsound for the future.

Our legislators made other changes, too. By 1962, the joint contribution of employers and employees had risen to 8 percent, thereby boosting taxes for wage earners who were making an average annual wage of $4,000 that year. Additional benefit packages, however, only increased the demands placed on Social Security funds. By 1983, the fund was paying benefits to retired military personnel (who already had their own generous pension system and had only to work an additional ten years in the private sector to qualify); farm workers; domestic workers; and government workers (who, like the military, were already covered under a separate pension plan), as well as to widows and widowers, orphans, the disabled and their dependents.

Nobody could argue with the good intentions underlying those changes, though no corresponding actuarial program existed to fund these many future financial requirements. The benefits were all paid from deposits of current workers and still are. Social Security checks, however, did indeed help millions of Americans — elderly and otherwise — escape or avoid poverty. In 1959, for example, more than one-third of elderly Americans had incomes below the official poverty line. Thirty-one years later, in 1990, due in large part to Social Security, only 12 percent lived beneath that income line. Today, for the poorest one-fifth of elderly Americans, Social Security payments account for 80 percent of their income.

The average older American receives 38 percent of his or her income from Social Security. And younger workers have benefited from these changes, too, since they have been partially freed of the burden of directly supporting retired parents or other relatives.

The trouble that's come about as a result of these changes didn't happen because Congress acted with bad intentions, but because it acted without fiscal foresight or responsibility. Between 1975 and the end of 1982, the theoretical surplus in the government's Social Security account started falling each year, which meant that the government was then paying out more in benefits than it was collecting from paycheck deductions.

With Social Security heading for the red, President Reagan appointed a commission that met and recommended — surprise! — higher FICA payroll taxes to bring in more revenues to support present and soon-to-be retired recipients. At no time was there any talk of proper long-term funding.

The commission's solution, speedily approved by Congress in 1983, put the bite on taxpayers in two ways. First, naturally, it accelerated implementation of previously scheduled FICA payroll tax increases, so that by 1990, the total joint employer and employee contribution would be 15.3 percent on the first $55,200 in income. Second, it made 50 percent of a recipient's Social Security benefits taxable when the individual's income exceeded $25,000 ($32,000 for couples).

But the new 1983 law also had a third effect that, in reality, was the cruelest: It led the public to believe that this large increase in Social Security taxes was going to fix the country's Social Security problem forever. Its supporters promised that huge surpluses would accumulate in the account, thereby assuring people, especially the large group of Baby Boomers, that plenty of money would be available to pay their benefits in the future. That was a cruel and dishonest hoax.

By 1985, the huge amounts of surplus cash that were accumulating each year gave elected officials permission to commit larceny on a much grander scale — a scale, in fact, that would have rapidly sent any private employer to prison. With the hike in payroll taxes, the government began collecting far more in Social Security revenues than it was required to distribute each year. Previously, the relatively tiny annual Social Security surpluses had virtually no effect on the size of each year's reported deficit. By 1985, however, the government was able to borrow vast amounts of this surplus cash and use the money to fund part of the annual budget deficit, which has been skyrocketing since 1982. By the end of 1992, the fund had accumulated nearly $320 billion in these IOUs. When a corporation does the same thing, the money involved is called an unfunded liability and the action is illegal. Corporations are bound by law to fund this type of liability.

The table below tells a sad story of fiscal greed and deliberate misuse of public funds. The first column lists Social Security's receipts each year — that is, the money paid into the system by employees and employers. The second column lists the annual total benefits and other expenses paid out by Social Security. The third column lists the amount by which Social Security receipts exceed outlays each year — in other words, it shows the surplus that should have been allowed to accumulate but which is instead being "borrowed" by the government to "reduce" its annual deficits. The last column shows the cumulative debt of the U.S. government to the Social Security account. You can easily see that in every year since 1985, the government has "borrowed" more and more of your Social Security nest egg to meet its current expenses. You can also see that the government's debt to the fund has grown larger each year, and that early in the next century, that debt will exceed $1 trillion. No wonder the politicians don't want to privatize Social Security and have the surplus properly funded and invested.

"Where," you might well ask, "will the government get the money to pay off these hundreds of billions of dollars in notes when they come due and when today's workers want to start collecting their benefits?" Good question. Nearly 80 million Baby Boomers

U.S. Government's Debt to Social Security ($ in billions)

Fiscal Year	Social Security Receipts	Social Security Expenditures	Surplus "Borrowed" Each Year by U.S. Government	Cumulative Debt of U.S. Government to Social Security
1980	$117.4	$118.5	0	$ 32.2 ±
1981	$134.6	$139.6	0	$ 27.2
1982	$148.0	$156.0	0	$ 19.3
1983	$170.3	$170.1	$ .2	$ 32.0
1984	$178.5	$178.2	$ .3	$ 32.2
1985	$197.9	$188.5	$ 9.4	$ 39.8
1986	$215.5	$198.7	$ 16.7	$ 45.9
1987	$226.9	$207.3	$ 19.6	$ 65.4
1988	$258.1	$219.3	$ 38.8	$ 104.2
1989	$285.0	$232.5	$ 52.4	$ 156.7
1990	$306.8	$248.6	$ 58.2	$ 214.9
1991	$322.6	$269.1	$ 53.5	$ 268.4
1992	$338.3	$287.5	$ 50.7	$ 319.2
1993*	$351.4	$304.6	$ 46.8	$ 366.0
1994*	$381.3	$321.6	$ 59.7	$ 425.7
1995*	$402.4	$338.8	$ 63.6	$ 489.3
1996*	$426.2	$357.3	$ 68.9	$ 558.2
1997*	$450.2	$377.2	$ 73.0	$ 631.2
1998*	$477.0	$398.2	$ 78.7	$ 709.8
1999*	$505.8	$421.0	$ 84.8	$ 794.6
2000*	$536.8	$445.9	$ 90.9	$ 885.5
2001*	$571.5	$472.8	$ 98.6	$ 984.1
2002*	$607.9	$501.1	$106.8	$1,091.0

* estimated
± fund balances accrued since 1939

should be asking themselves whether they will be able to collect the Social Security benefits they've been promised, because the answer is "probably not," unless the dollar hyperinflates and becomes substantially lower in value, or worthless altogether.

Between 2015 and 2020, under moderate economic growth, Social Security costs will exceed the amount of the system's income. From that point on, the deficit will grow increasingly wider, as the graph on page 74 shows. Other projections based on slower economic growth show a Social Security system deficit starting as early as 1995. So you know what Congress will do. It will raise the present contribution rate and the amount of an individual's earnings to be charged.

Something, clearly, is very wrong with the system.

Congress's ongoing system of handling cash flow is an elaborate piece of fiction to cover up its interest-free borrowing from your savings. According to this story, the Treasury does pay interest on the special bonds it issues to Social Security, but it does so only by issuing more bonds. In effect, the U.S. Treasury borrows from itself to pay the interest on its Social Security debt. Also, the "interest" it pays is only phantom income that is credited from one internal account to another. There is no money actually available to make benefit payments, and the whole dishonest scheme is yet another example of the blue-smoke-and-mirrors bookkeeping that Washington does so well.

Moreover, Congress's three-card-monte solution has created a huge problem that will become all too obvious in the years ahead. Right now, there are about 3.2 people paying into the Social Security fund for every one person receiving benefits. Remember, this is down from 20 to 1 in 1950 — and from about 50 to 1 in 1939. But, as the graph on page 75 shows, when the nearly 80 million Baby Boomers begin to retire, the number of people drawing benefits will climb steeply while the number of Social Security taxpayers will decline. Remember the Baby Bust?

In fact, in 2025 fewer than two workers will pay in for every beneficiary taking out. To cover this anticipated annual shortfall,

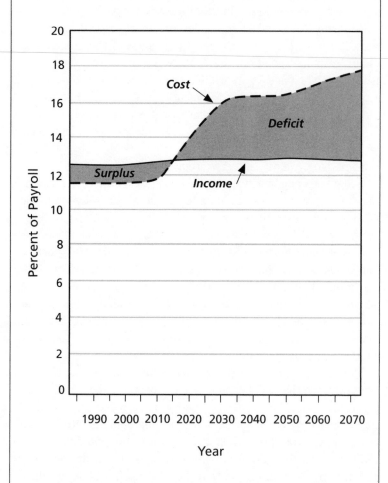

Projected Social Security Deficit

Percent of Payroll

Cost

Deficit

Surplus

Income

Year

Tax income represents payroll tax and income
tax receipts from taxing benefits

SOURCE: *1993 OASDI Trustees' Report*

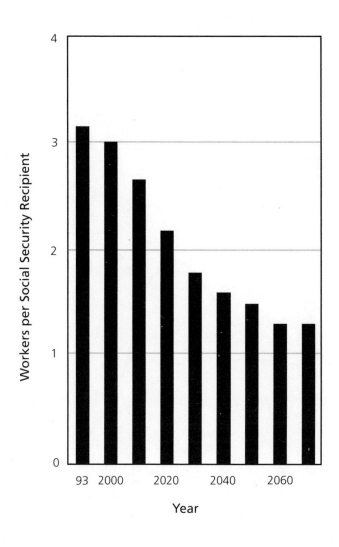

Long-range Ratio of Workers per Social Security Recipient

Workers per Social Security Recipient

Year

SOURCE: *1993 OASDI Trustees' Report*

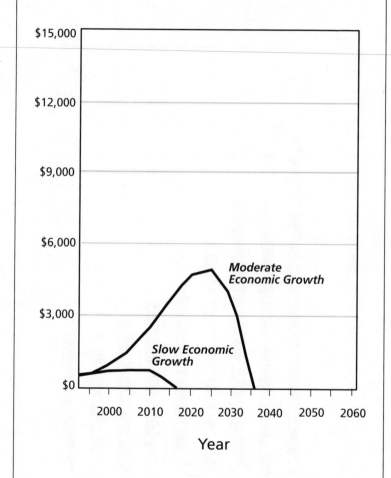

Projected Social Security Assets
(In Billions of Dollars)

Moderate Economic Growth

Slow Economic Growth

Year

SOURCE: *1993 OASDI Trustees' Report*

the Social Security fund needs to accumulate a real $7 trillion surplus by 2035. Will the surplus be there? No way. When today's Baby Boomers look for the money that was supposed to fund their Social Security benefits, they'll find just a pile of government IOUs.

As the graph on page 76 shows, the assets in the Social Security fund are projected to fall to zero within twenty to forty years. Assets will begin declining steadily after 2025 — about the time that today's thirty-one-year-olds begin to retire. By the time today's twenty-year-olds turn sixty-three, the fund will be empty. And that's if we experience moderate economic growth. If we experience slower growth, the assets could fall to zero as early as 2017, leaving nothing for anyone who is under forty today.

When Congress and the president were conspiring on the Social Security raid in 1983, were there no honest men and women left in Washington? Didn't anybody scream, "Stop, thief!"?

Senator Daniel Moynihan of New York called the 1983 amendments to the Social Security law a "robbery." Senator John Heinz of Pennsylvania said it was more like embezzlement. Moynihan even made a much-publicized effort to keep the government's hand out of the Social Security cookie jar, but to no avail. Dorcas Hardy, Social Security commissioner under President Reagan, wrote a book called *Social Insecurity* denouncing the scam. But they might as well have been scolding the masked gunman as he held up the corner grocery. As Mark Twain said, "There is no distinctly native American criminal class except Congress."

None of this is to argue that government should not, as a practical matter, be involved in helping — even forcing — people to put something aside for their own retirement. Some critics of Social Security have pointed out that if workers saved and invested the same amount of money weekly or monthly that they currently pay into the Social Security fund, the earnings on those savings would accumulate and reward them with a far larger nest egg than they will collect under Social Security. That's true.

But people assume incorrectly that their Social Security "savings" will provide them with some or all of the money they need for retirement. Partially because they are lulled into a false sense of security by their double-dealing government's empty promises, Americans lay aside far less per capita today than people of any other modern industrial nation. Our national savings rate has steadily declined from 7 percent a year during the thirty-five years after World War II to just 4 percent today. Without being forced to save, most workers — human nature being what it is — will spend any disposable income very soon. Then, when they retire with little or nothing put away, they are forced to join the welfare ranks. That's why the government's deceptions are so cruel.

Another criticism of Social Security is that it takes huge amounts of potential savings that could be invested in the stocks and bonds of private companies, thereby helping the economy to grow. Economist Martin Feldstein, former chairman of the Council of Economic Advisers under President Reagan, studied the subject and came up with a shocking statistic. Feldstein estimated that Social Security reduces America's private savings by as much as 40 percent. Not every economist agrees with the Feldstein findings, but no one denies that Social Security in its present form takes billions of dollars every year that could be invested in creating new jobs and a stronger economy and sends them to Washington instead. Furthermore, Social Security costs already amount to nearly 5 percent of our GDP, and are projected to soar to between 7 and 9 percent by 2065, as you can see in the graph on page 79. Compare those figures to the minuscule .02 percent of GDP that Social Security cost us in 1939, and you begin to realize the true price we pay now in lost opportunities for growth.

Would it be possible to set up a practical system that would ensure that workers have a decent retirement, that wouldn't allow government spendthrifts to hijack the people's savings, and that would keep those savings available for productive investment instead of government debt?

There actually is such a method, and it works. It's called the Individual Retirement Account (IRA). It allows taxpayers to save

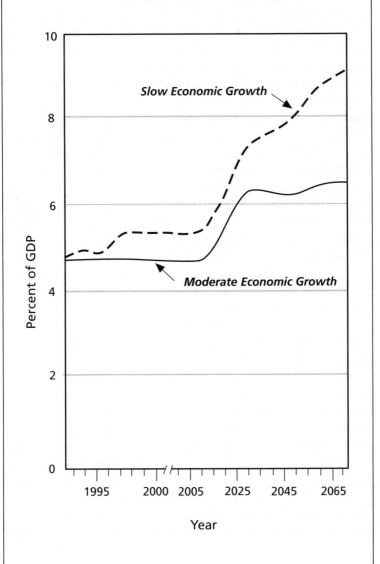

Long-range Social Security Costs as Percentage of GDP

Slow Economic Growth

Moderate Economic Growth

Percent of GDP

Year

SOURCE: *1993 OASDI Trustees' Report*

and invest a certain amount of money on which they do not have to pay income tax. The interest and dividends earned by those savings aren't subject to tax, either, until people begin to withdraw payments from the accumulated cash after age fifty-nine and one-half. IRAs encourage people to save for their own retirement without involving the government, and most of the money they save gets invested in the private economy, not in government debt.

Today, however, IRAs are of only limited value in solving our Social Security problem. First, they're not mandatory: No one is required to have an individual retirement account. Second, unlike in the past, most people — including anyone with retirement plans at their workplaces — can't deduct the amount of their IRA contribution from their earnings. Even those workers who can take advantage of deductible IRAs aren't allowed to contribute more than $2,000 each year ($2,200 for a married person filing jointly with a spouse who doesn't work outside the home). They actually fine you 6 percent if you try to put more than $2,000 a year into this tax-deferred savings plan. (Self-employed people have available a similar retirement savings opportunity called a Keogh, after the name of the senator who first proposed it. With a Keogh, the limits on how much you can contribute are much higher.)

But let's say we changed the law. What if we made IRAs mandatory and either eliminated the $2,000 limit or made it much higher? What would happen?

Just this: Every working person in the country would be able to save enough to finance at least a modest retirement. If you saved and invested $2,000 per year, for instance, and your investments earned, on average, a modest 5 percent annually, at the end of forty years you would have $241,600, which would give you a post-retirement income of $16,000 a year from age sixty-five to age ninety. To some, $2,000 sounds like a lot to sock away every year, but remember that you and your employer wouldn't be paying FICA, which today eats up $6,120 per year out of a $40,000 salary. If that amount were put away each year for forty

years at 5 percent interest, a saver would have accumulated well
over $600,000 for retirement.

Here's an indisputable fact: Hardly a worker in the country
wouldn't be better served by having his or her own IRA paying a
moderate rate of interest, than by contributing to Social Security.
Society would be better off as well for having that much more in
savings to invest in wealth-creating jobs. Of course, not everyone
can work, so not everyone can substitute an IRA for Social Security. What about the disabled children whose parents are deceased and others, who today draw one kind of benefit or another
from Social Security?

All we have to do to solve that problem is separate the retirement portion of today's Social Security system from the welfare
portion. Retirement will be taken care of through personal IRAs.
The welfare portion — the part that makes payments to widows,
orphans, the disabled, and others — would be financed like other
welfare programs out of general tax revenues. These payments
never should have been part of Social Security (which was designed as a supplementary safety net for retirement) in the first
place. Medicare and Medicaid, too, should be separated from Social Security and made an independent program.

The biggest scream of pain you would hear if such a plan were
seriously proposed would come from Washington, where lawmakers and the administration would have had $53 billion less of other
people's money to spend in 1993 alone. (The income from FICA,
or Social Security taxes, comes to about $255 billion and the cur-
rent Social Security annual benefits payout is about $202 billion.
The difference, $53 billion, is the amount government spenders
"borrowed" in 1993 to finance their excess spending.) Also, they
wouldn't have the money in Social Security to pay the $202 billion.

But consider the advantages: The amount added to private savings and investment every year would be one of the biggest economic stimulus packages in the history of the world. Not only
would your tax bill go down and your retirement income go up,

but the country would enjoy a tremendous economic boom, and we could update our manufacturing equipment at a time when new technology has made obsolete much of our existing equipment.

It isn't often that we have an opportunity to apply such an obvious and simple solution to so complex a problem. It benefits almost everybody in America — workers and business as well. It would benefit Congress and the administration, too — by forcing them to stay a little more honest.

There is little doubt that the government could reap a harvest from existing taxes — more than enough to make up for the lost Social Security funds — if the economy were stimulated by such massive yearly investments.

5

The Hockey Stick

WHEN I was still serving on the Grace Commission, I was handed two sets of numbers: One set gave a historic perspective of the U.S. debt and projected it to the year 1990, and the other projected our debt for the years 1985, 1995, and 2000. To establish annual numbers between 1985 and the year 2000, I had to plot the three points. First, to get the rate of change from year to year, I drew a line between the three points on semilog paper. Then, on regular graph paper, I plotted debt on the vertical axis; years along the horizontal, using the numbers obtained from the semilog paper for each year. The chart I ended up with stunned me.

From 1985 to 1994, the line I'd drawn curved steadily upward. In 1995, however, it became almost vertical. After rounding the turn, the line kept on going up, up, up, and up. Do you care about a line? No, but want to or not, you'll care about what the line represents: It shows that if present trends continue, by 1995 the deficit and debt levels will have driven us beyond the point of no return.

The Sherwood Division of Figgie International is the world's leading manufacturer of hockey sticks, and as I looked at the line

I had graphed, it came to me that that's exactly what it looked like: a hockey stick, as you see on page 85. I've called it the hockey stick curve ever since, and the sight of it always has the power to make me shudder.

But never more so than in 1991, when Gerry Swanson returned from a European fact-finding trip to give me, as he said, some good news and some bad news. I asked for the good news first, and he replied that the debt projections I had charted in 1985 for the next six years had been right on target. The bad news? That for six years debt projections had been right on target (see the graph on page 86). For a curve like this to be exactly on target for six years was almost inconceivable. It gave the remaining projections a high degree of authenticity.

For six years I'd been hoping I was wrong, but I wasn't.

Our debt is tracking right along the hockey stick, and 1995 is now just two years off. That year, when the debt heads straight up the handle, the country will, for all practical purposes, have become bankrupt, and the problems that beset Tom and Betsy Roth in Chapter 1 will descend on all of us. Control of our national economic life will pass out of our hands. You won't see Congress and the president arguing over federal budgets anymore. They'll be negotiating with our foreign creditors, asking permission to spend. How far the once mighty United States will have fallen — just like Russia, which fell very quickly.

With the hockey stick curve, I'm not dreaming up a scary warning against *increased* government spending. Not at all. On the contrary, the curve illustrates what will happen if the federal government just continues on its *present* fiscal course for only a few more years.

It's true that deficit spending on defense, interest, and social programs brought us to the point at which the curve starts bending upward. (See the graph on pages 42–43 to see how our deficits are projected to rise.) What will push us around the corner and start us up the handle of the hockey stick, however, isn't only more spending on programs but the compounding of the annual

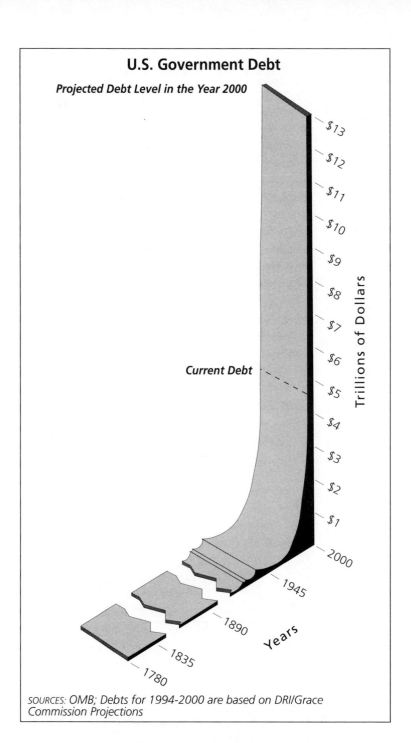

U.S. Government Debt

Projected Debt Level in the Year 2000

Current Debt

Trillions of Dollars

$13
$12
$11
$10
$9
$8
$7
$6
$5
$4
$3
$2
$1

2000
1945
1890
1835
1780

Years

SOURCES: OMB; Debts for 1994-2000 are based on DRI/Grace
Commission Projections

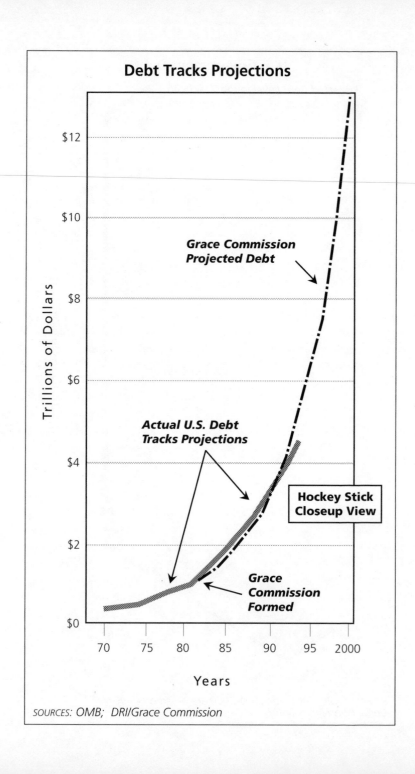

interest charge that we're adding into the debt. Ultimately, it will be interest charges, together with indexed entitlement spending, that will throw the United States into insolvency and onto the mercies of its lenders, who will be more concerned with recovering their money than with guaranteeing your or my liberty and pursuit of happiness.

The compounding of interest is useful when you're trying to save over a long period of time for retirement or some other major expense. If you leave the interest that you earn during one month in your savings account, the next month you earn interest on your original balance *plus* the interest. Just keep leaving the interest in the account, and the amount of interest you earn each month gets progressively larger and quite respectable.

For instance, you deposit $10,000 into an investment account that pays 8 percent annual interest, and you leave the interest you earn in the account. Your first month's interest won't be anything to gloat over — just $66.70. Five years later, the monthly interest on your $10,000 original deposit still won't be huge — just $99.40. But after twenty-five years, your original $10,000 will be earning $490 a month in interest — more than seven times the interest you received the first month you opened your account. Given enough time, compounding has a way of making interest grow into impressive amounts.

But what works to your benefit as a saver works to your detriment as a borrower — and the United States has been a heavy borrower now for more than thirty years. Each year we have added to our debt by additional spending and by borrowing to cover our interest payments. By spending more, which has to be borrowed, and by borrowing to make the interest payments, the U.S. government's debt and annual interest charges add up even faster than they would grow through compounding alone. The United States resembles nothing so much as a newly married couple with their first credit card. They find it easy to pay the minimum due the first month they get their bill, so the next month they charge more, and the next month more still. Finally, they've charged so much they haven't a prayer of paying off either the debt or the accumulated interest.

Looking at just a few years along the hockey stick illustrates how serious the country's problem has become. In 1964, the first full year of Lyndon Johnson's presidency, the national debt was $316 billion and the interest charge was just $10.7 billion. We could have paid the interest with just 14.8 percent of the federal government's revenues from personal and corporate income taxes that year. By 1988, the last year of the Reagan administration, the debt had climbed to $2.6 trillion and interest to $214.2 billion. It took 43 percent of the government's total income tax revenues to make the interest payment that year.

In 1992, the last year of the Bush administration, interest charges on the debt totaled $292.2 billion. Paying that amount alone ate up more than half of our personal and corporate income taxes. And in 1995, when the debt itself will have reached $6.56 trillion, the interest charge alone — some $619 billion — will amount to 85 percent of all income taxes and *more* than the government collects in taxes from individuals.

At that point, even if it eliminated most of the waste and questionable spending in its budget, the government couldn't save enough to pay the interest it owes. It would still have to borrow — and the next year, and the next year, and so on. Of course, the crisis will come before then, because no investor is going to continue to lend to a country that can't even make the interest payments on the amount it has already borrowed.

Here are a few facts you might want to ask your member of Congress to comment on the next time he or she is in the neighborhood.

- In 1992, the only budget item that amounted to more than interest on our debt was Social Security. That's right. The United States allocated more money to pay interest on the national debt than it did even for our national defense, and here's what taxpayers got in exchange for all that money allocated to interest payments: nothing.

- In 1992, the U.S. government spent more on interest than on the combined expenses of the departments of Agriculture, Education, Energy, Housing and Urban Development, Interior, Justice, Labor, State, Transportation, and Veterans' Affairs.
- In 1992, the federal government spent more on the three largest budget items — interest on the debt, national defense, and Social Security — than it collected in individual and corporate income taxes. In other words, more than half the money spent on education, environmental protection, crime fighting, and so on was paid for with borrowed funds.

Does this sound to you like any way to run a country, let alone the world's last remaining superpower? You can see what's coming next. Growing as they are, interest expenses will soon crowd even defense and entitlements such as Social Security out of the paid-for piece of the budget. Every dollar of tax revenue will go toward paying interest on the debt. And then what?

Once our debt begins its rapid climb up the handle of the hockey stick, there's no honorable way out of the situation. All that's left for us is to plead: America on its knees to its debtors.

Here's another way of looking at that same reality. Find the stub that was attached to your last paycheck and look for the box that says "Federal Income Taxes Withheld." That's money from your pay that you never see because it goes straight to the IRS. Well, in 1992, the equivalent of 61 percent of the amount in that box was spent on nothing more than paying interest on the debt that recent Congresses and presidents have accumulated in your name. In 1995, the federal government will pay more in interest than it collects from all of us in personal income taxes.

You might want to ask your member of Congress to explain *how* the government expects to pay any of its other expenses when everything it collects in personal taxes and more is needed to pay interest to debt holders.

Another thing you might ask your favorite politician is what he or she proposes to bargain away when our foreign debt holders — German, Saudi Arabian, Japanese, British — come demanding their money back. A government's ability to guarantee certain freedoms and liberties rests on that government's independence, which our government is close to giving totally away, if it hasn't already.

Already, rising debt payments have begun to interfere with the government's ability to budget its outlays. Politicians boast and posture about "controlling government spending," but can they? In 1992, more than 20 percent of the federal government's total budget — which, don't forget, included $400 billion of borrowed money — was spent on interest payments; another nearly 50 percent went to pay for entitlement programs such as Social Security and Medicare and Medicaid, in which spending can't be reduced except by cutting benefits to recipients or changing eligibility rules. Let's put that another way: These costs are built in and can be reduced only by not paying people — whether it's welfare recipients, Social Security recipients, or holders of U.S. bonds — money to which they are legally entitled. (The graph on page 91 shows the rise in entitlement expenses.) When you add these two categories of "uncontrollable" costs together, they represent almost 70 percent of federal spending. In other words, the U.S. government has already lost the ability to control about 70 percent of its expenditures and more than 85 percent of its revenues.

Do you know what seems most incredible to me as I lay this problem out? We did this to ourselves. We willingly allowed self-serving politicians to whisper reassurances in our ears while they robbed us — not to mention our parents, our children, and our grandchildren — of our financial independence and ability to make financial choices. Money that's spent paying off interest on a debt is money that cannot be spent on something else — anything constructive to help create jobs and restore our industrial base.

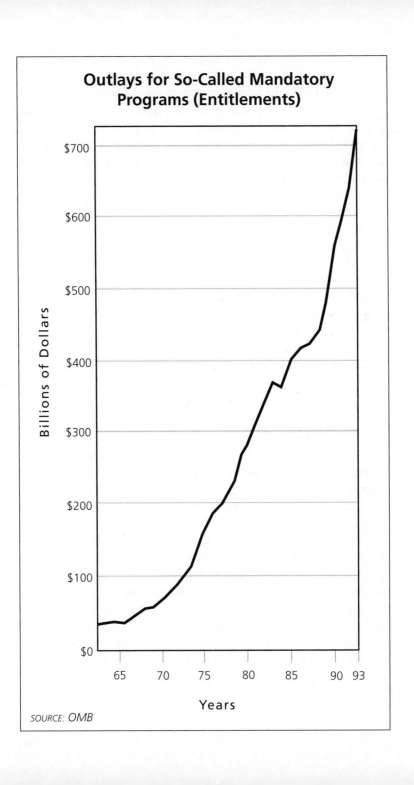

Outlays for So-Called Mandatory Programs (Entitlements)

Billions of Dollars

Years

SOURCE: OMB

Most of us like to have some choices over how we spend our money, because our priorities change from time to time. Could you afford to double your mortgage payment if it meant you could buy your dream house? Maybe you could, *provided* you were willing to give something else up, such as sending your kids to college or buying new clothes. What you decide to give up in order to buy the expensive new house is called the "opportunity cost" of buying the house. It's not just the money, but the opportunity to acquire or do other things that you must relinquish.

Hungary, to cite just one of the former Communist countries with this problem, spends about half its budget on interest payments. That necessity has seriously slowed and impeded the country's economic and industrial modernization. "What would we do," said one Hungarian banker to whom Gerry and his team talked recently, "if we didn't have to worry about servicing our debt? We could fix our disastrous health system, bring our transportation system into the twentieth century, equip and pay our police well enough to stop rising crime, improve public education, and create a modern banking system." Doesn't that sound suspiciously like the opportunity costs the United States is paying?

What could the U.S. government do if it weren't spending hundreds of billions of dollars each year on debt service? Fix highways and bridges? Easy. Fix schools? No sweat. Fund technical and medical research? Of course. Cut taxes? Absolutely. We could be spending our public funds on projects that would help make our industry more competitive in world markets, our people healthier and better educated, and our environment safer and cleaner. But we're not. We can't, until and unless we get the federal budget deficit under control. We can't afford to throw more dollars at any program, no matter how worthy it sounds, We are in deep, deep fiscal trouble. We pay a huge opportunity cost for having run up our debt, and this cost is only going to get bigger as interest charges grow. We already outspend our receipts by 27 percent.

At the moment, only one important difference separates the

United States and many of the Eastern European and South American countries that we think of as being poor or economically distressed. These countries receive financial aid from the International Monetary Fund (IMF), and the United States, ignoring reality, pretends that it is still rich enough to contribute money to the fund. Who is better off?

Those countries receiving IMF aid must conform to spending controls imposed by the fund if they want to keep receiving help. They must make the interest payments on their debt *and* meet all their other expenses *without* running an annual deficit. If they don't meet those conditions, they don't receive the IMF aid. The only reason American politicians can still spend money as if they had real money to spend is that no one has imposed similar limits on them. If this country had to live by the same rules as Hungary, Poland, or Brazil, the United States would literally be out of business. We could not qualify for an IMF loan. We must start to impose these world financial standards on ourselves before the world imposes them on us.

If the government of the United States were a corporation, such as Eastern Airlines or Pan American World Airways, and it didn't take drastic action soon to save itself, it would have to file for bankruptcy just like those companies did. It would be broken up and its assets sold off in partial satisfaction of its debts.

But I assure you that corporate bankruptcy would prove a lot cleaner and a lot less painful than what's going to happen in and to the United States when its government is found to be insolvent. If we wait much longer to fix our debt problem, the solutions that desperate politicians will propose and that creditors will impose will be so painful that we'll wish we could just close up shop and move somewhere else. But a whole country can't do that. Therefore, we must stop our debt from getting any larger, and we must stop it now. And we won't stop it without eliminating annual deficits and replacing them with positive cash flow. In fact, to become fiscally viable again we have to reduce it. Remember the once mighty Soviet Union and how quickly it disintegrated. The same can — and will — happen to us, unless we get our act together, and soon.

In the next chapter, we'll tell you what a country and its people lose when the debt structure they've been living on starts to crash.

6

Death by Debt

UNLESS the people's government in Washington, D.C., makes drastic changes in its fiscal policies now, the typical American family will be fortunate in the mid-1990s if it can feed and house itself, and, at that, it will not be in the manner to which it has become accustomed. Even if a business recovery and President Clinton's proposed tax hike boost government revenue for a short time, it will only postpone the inevitable.

Conditions could soon enough become grim:

- As many as 20 percent of American jobs — gone.
- Personal savings — eviscerated by inflation.
- Pension and Social Security payments — cut or eliminated by inflation and mismanagement.
- The American dollar — a joke, like the Weimar Republic marks hanging on my wall.

This is not an exaggeration. In fact, I may be understating the degree of calamity that will befall most Americans. It's going to be awful, and whatever you think I mean by awful, you can be sure that it's going to be worse.

While we can't be certain *exactly* how the tragedy of America's economic collapse will unfold, we can be pretty certain that the bottom will drop out of the American economy in either one of two ways or in some combination of both. In one scenario, which I call Death by Hyperinflation, prices spiral out of control and the dollar loses value — first by the month, then by the week, and eventually by the hour. In the other scenario, which I call Death by Panic, traders and investors on the world's financial markets literally put America out of business.

Probably, we'll get a taste of both hyperinflation and panic, but the shooting victim hardly cares whether he's dead of a .45- or a .357-caliber bullet. Hyperinflation or market panic or any combination will finish off America and Americans as we know them.

We saw in the last chapter how continued deficit spending by the federal government has raised the national debt to such a level that interest payments alone are already almost more than we can afford. Congress, the president, and the American people *might* wake up now and realize the size and seriousness of the problem that we all face. If this book helps play reveille, it will have done its job. As we saw in Chapter 3, our political "leaders" have already blown five chances. This is our last opportunity, and we can't afford to blow *it*.

But what if we don't wake up? After all, Americans have the attitude that they can get out of any crisis *after* it's occurred. This time, they are wrong. You can't recover from cancer once you've died. So what happens if we let the calamity develop? How do these two scenarios — Death by Hyperinflation and Death by Panic — play themselves out? Some of what follows is speculation, of course, but none of it is implausible, and if it doesn't happen in exactly the way we've laid it out here, it will happen nonetheless and in some other way that's just as unpleasant. Remember, we've spent more than seven years studying just such effects around the world.

Both scenarios begin in the present with the White House blaming the Congress and the Congress blaming the White House for everything that ails us. Neither of them wants to speak the truth, and we, the electorate, keep electing the people who are best at telling us only what we want to hear — and how much they are going to do for us or some part of "us."

Besides, our leaders help us find plenty of outside devils to blame for the slowed economic growth that, over the next few years, will just continue and for the joblessness that keeps getting worse. We can hate the Japanese and Germans, who we think are greedy and arrogant, because they keep buying our companies. We can damn the Mexicans, who we believe will work for peanuts and continue taking our jobs. We can resent the Saudis, who control the price of oil.

Meanwhile, here's what's happening behind the scenes. Every year the U.S. Treasury borrows more and more money to pay the ballooning interest on the growing debt that the politicians create, and every year the notes, bonds, and bills that the Treasury sells to raise this money are getting harder and harder to peddle to wary investors. A good friend of mine, Dick McConnell, who is a prominent investment adviser, recently said to me, "Harry, who in their right mind would invest in Treasuries?"

McConnell and other prudent investors are worried about the government's ability to continue to service this swelling debt burden. The only way the Treasury can continue to find buyers is to agree to pay higher and higher interest rates, which, of course, only makes the government's payment problems worse. Or, the Treasury can sell some or all of its debt to the Federal Reserve, which has the effect — I'll explain how later — of *creating* the money the government needs to service its debt. Both alternatives involve unpleasant costs, and the choice poses a dilemma to the people at the Treasury and the Fed. They have to decide whether investor revolt or inflation is the greater immediate risk. Let's suppose that they decide to keep on pushing American debt to investors in the market. That's the Death by Panic scenario.

Warning: The picture we're about to show you isn't pretty.

Death by Panic

In 1992, the Bush administration racked up a $403.7 billion budget deficit, the largest gap between revenue and spending ever recorded by any nation in the history of humankind. Four hundred billion is, as Ross Perot has pointed out, more than we spent to fight and win World War II. Was the president worried? No, sir. To admit to worry would mean showing weakness, and this country and its then president were tough. "The United States is," Bush liked to stress in his speeches, "the richest country and the only superpower on the face of the earth." To show how rich we were, Bush pushed Congress to give $12 billion in aid to Russia, which is a country with an admitted problem. Few people pointed out to the president that the United States didn't have $12 billion of its own to give away — that, in fact, we couldn't afford right now to give *any* money away. No one wanted to look like a wimp.

Now our Death by Panic scenario really starts rolling.

Year One

The American national debt at the start of year one has climbed to $4 trillion, and the interest on that debt has jumped to some $300 billion — more than the country spends on education, justice, housing, and the environment combined. Investors keep buying American debt, so the Treasury keeps selling it, although interest rates have crept up a bit. Whereas in 1991 the government paid an average of 7.5 percent interest on the long-term Treasury bonds it sold and an average of 5.0 percent on short-term T-bills, by the middle of year one, long-term rates had inched up to 8.5 percent; short-term rates, to 7.5 percent. A little more expensive, but not to worry.

The deficit sets a record and goes to $640 billion, in part because the higher interest rates increase the government's interest payment and in part because Congress and the president still can't agree on spending cuts and entitlements continue to rise 12 percent annually. Government debt climbs to $4.98 trillion, 80 percent of the value of all the goods and services sold in the country during the year. Just the interest charges alone are now larger than any other government expense. The world's investors are getting edgy, and foreign political leaders begin to drop the polite tones from their insistence that Washington get its fiscal house in order. You *must* start to reduce the deficit, the Europeans and Japanese say, but American presidents don't like taking suggestions from countries that aren't superpowers, countries that we whupped in the last big war. Nor do they like listening to countries that, unlike us, are fiscally responsible.

Short-term interest rates on T-bills jump, which naturally causes the interest rates that other borrowers — businesses and individuals — must pay to climb as well. Members of Congress condemn American and foreign bankers as greedy and denounce the currency speculation taking place on financial markets.

Year Two

Year two starts out as a replay of year one. Interest rates are rising steadily now, far beyond the ability of most private borrowers to pay them, which means that hardly anyone is taking out mortgages, and the housing industry has collapsed. Only a handful of businesses are borrowing, which means that most are not expanding or modernizing. We're in deep recession again. Congress remains deadlocked over the deficit, with Democrats vowing to raise taxes, Republicans determined to lower them, and the president promising to veto any legislation that includes too large a cut in his pet programs. No one goes after the entitlement programs or tries to prohibit the adoption of new domestic programs. And we substantially increase foreign aid to needy nations around the world.

By the end of the summer, interest rates have zoomed to worrisome heights. In a T-bill auction, the government has to pay 14 percent to attract buyers, which matches the rate it paid in 1981.

The interest charge on the national debt for all of that year comes to $517 billion, more than half of what the government spent on everything else combined.

Even if they could afford the interest rates, American companies are crowded out of the credit markets by this massive government borrowing. In any economy, there is only so much money to lend, which is determined, in part, by the amount of money that people and companies have saved. When all of the savings are loaned out, there's little left to lend. Loans to the government have practically depleted the country's pool of savings, and foreign investors are wary of lending more to the United States, no matter how high the rates.

Heads of other governments continue to insist that Washington act to reduce its still growing indebtedness. Our leaders continue to ignore them.

The Fed is hanging tough, though, despite haranguings from the administration that it should buy some of this debt itself, thereby increasing the money supply and easing the recession. "No," the Fed chairman responds, "if we start down that road, inflation will only get worse. You, Mr. President, and the Congress have to get the deficit under control."

Fat chance of that happening.

Meanwhile, businesses and citizens are beginning to get seriously hurt. Older Americans living on pensions have seen the value of their incomes drop steadily. That's because as interest rates have climbed, the value of the fixed-income assets held by their pension funds has dropped in proportion. Some pension funds have been declared insolvent, along with many insurance companies that were paying annuities to retirees.

Cities, towns, and states, cut off from federal aid and facing reduced business-tax revenues as company after company closes down or moves overseas, have no choice but to increase property tax rates, sales taxes, and state income levies. More and more citizens are simply refusing to pay their taxes. Municipalities begin to default on their bonds.

Bank failures have become epidemic as customers withdraw deposits in order to invest them at higher rates in money-market funds. The banks can't pay those higher rates, because the earnings from their own portfolios of fixed-interest mortgages and variable-interest mortgages that have reached their lifetime interest-rate caps don't generate enough income. Most banks have canceled credit cards as market interest rates have climbed above the limit the law allows them to charge cardholders.

Consumers had unwittingly started this spiral by getting some good news. When interest rates first began their climb, the value of the dollar on foreign currency markets rose, too. If they wanted to earn those high U.S. interest rates, foreign investors first had to buy dollars, which they could then invest in Treasury securities, so the demand for dollars — and their value — went up for a while. Consequently, for a time at least, the prices of foreign-made goods in the United States went down.

Consumers found that they could buy Japanese electronic goods and German automobiles for less than they would have spent the previous year. Zenith, meanwhile, dropped completely out of the television manufacturing business, and General Motors permanently closed its Oldsmobile division. The appreciating dollar also made it harder for American companies to sell their products overseas, so export sales fell off as these companies gave up business to foreign competitors. Lots of workers lost their jobs.

When interest rates on Treasury debt began to leap upward, however, the value of the dollar began to weaken. Some aggressive foreign investors still lusted after the high earnings they could collect on U.S. government securities, but more became nervous about holding the currency of a country that was so clearly in trouble. If anything happened and the value of the dollar were to drop quickly, they reasoned, they'd be left holding securities that would then be worth a great deal less when the dollar was converted back into yen or German marks. The currency loss could wipe out all the interest income they had earned on the securities.

On the other hand, with the decline of the dollar American companies started to look even cheaper to foreign corporations and investors, who could now afford to buy whole businesses just to get the technologies or the real estate or the equipment they wanted. They didn't need the workers and the production, so they bought the companies, broke them up, and shut them down. More than a million more American workers lost their jobs.

Year Three

Now it's late winter, year three, and the days are short, dark, and cold. On one particularly miserable afternoon, with sleet falling outside, the respected central banker of a European government — it could be France or Germany or England — gives an interview to a major newspaper. The reporter isn't buying the usual eyewash.

"Isn't it true," he finally demands of the banker, "that in reality the United States of America is insolvent?"

"Well," begins the banker.

"Sir," interrupts the reporter, "couldn't you manage a one-word answer to my question? Is the United States government insolvent?"

The banker looks blankly at the reporter for a minute. When he finally begins to speak, his throat is dry, and he has to swallow. In a low voice, he says, "Yes."

The banker has finally spoken the truth that no central banker has dared to say plainly and publicly before. He has acknowledged as fact what lots of people have known but couldn't as yet accept. Having said the word, however, the banker feels no further need to hold back. He goes on to tell the reporter that he doesn't believe that the United States will be able to service its debt. He says that all those billions of dollars in American IOUs that investors and governments around the world hold will probably never be paid back dollar for dollar. He says, in colossal understatement, that what he has just said may cause the holders of this debt to be upset.

The next day financial markets all over the world shut down

under the onslaught of sell orders. The panicky holders of hundreds of billions of dollars of Treasury securities decide to sell them, but few buyers show up. The value of those securities plunges. You could buy them, if you wanted them, at 9:00 A.M. for 90 cents on the dollar, at 10:00 A.M. for 80 cents, and at 10:30 A.M. for 75 cents.

The next day, the sun is bright but millions of Americans find they have no jobs, no prospects, and no savings. They have no savings, because the banks have no cash, only IOUs, such as mortgages and government bonds — and those have now become worthless. Now, phase two, the depression, begins.

European and Japanese finance ministers call an emergency meeting. They'll impose strict limits on spending by the American federal government in exchange for an agreement to hold another series of meetings on restructuring American debt. They are insistent that the United States not be allowed simply to walk away from its obligations.

Within the week, the government announces plans to cut the armed services by half. The other half will be kept on, at half pay, to quell the uprisings that have begun in cities and suburbs alike. Riots become commonplace throughout the country. Congress passes emergency legislation eliminating Social Security benefits for anyone earning more than $10,000 a year and cutting benefits to remaining qualifiers by 75 percent. Medicare and Medicaid are "temporarily" suspended. With no prospect of receiving these payments, hospitals begin to curtail, and in some instances eliminate, treatment for what are now charity cases. Many hospitals begin to show signs of failure, and some, in fact, fail. Doctors' incomes plummet, many cancel their malpractice insurance, and the medical profession, as a whole, drops into the abyss.

Many stores close, since consumers have no cash because by now most banks have failed. No one honors credit cards, but some entrepreneurs soon set up barter exchanges. People trade their new stereo televisions for a week's worth of groceries, but they hold on to the Audi against the day when gasoline might be available again. In Lower Manhattan, pedestrians run the risk of being struck by plunging suicides, and in California a nonpartisan committee called RAG (Restore America's Greatness) is organized to draft Ronald Reagan in the 1996 presidential election campaign. "Here I go again," responds the Gipper.

That's one way — financial panic and its consequences — that the United States economy might collapse under the debt load that it's building up.

Death by Hyperinflation

The other plausible scenario is Death by Hyperinflation. For our purposes, hyperinflation is inflation that is severe enough to cause people to lose faith in our currency. Hyperinflation isn't so abrupt as panic, but the long-term results are much the same. It is the reason former Senator Warren Rudman says "our money will be worthless by 1997."

We could succumb to hyperinflation instead of panic if, instead of selling all those government securities to other investors, the Treasury sells its securities to the Federal Reserve. That's called "monetizing" the government's debt.

Here's what that means and how it works. When the federal government needs more cash to cover expenses — to erect new office buildings named after former pork-barreling members of Congress, for instance, or to pay interest on the debt — the Treasury Department prints up some new IOUs (Treasury bonds, notes, or bills) and sells them. In the last scenario, the Treasury sold those IOUs to investors of one sort or another — to you, for instance, or to the Saudi Arabian government, say. You and the other investors used *real* money to pay for those securities, so it was real money — yours and cash from other investors — that the government used to pay for its new buildings.

But instead of selling the securities to you in exchange for your money, the Treasury, which provides our government with the funds it needs, could have sold them to the Federal Reserve. To do that, the Fed, whose primary role in our economy is to control the money supply, simply writes a check to the Treasury Department, which deposits the check in a bank somewhere. At the instant the Treasury makes that deposit, brand-new money is created. How?

In reality, the Fed didn't have any money to back up the check it wrote, but the commercial bank honored it just the same. The Fed doesn't have to have money. It just creates credits for commercial banks to draw against when they make loans. So the checks from the Fed that the Treasury deposits into commercial banks get turned into dollars when the banks lend them out. In effect, new money has been created.

Selling Treasury debt to the Fed is certainly handy for the government, but it does have a drawback. Creating new money without any accompanying economic growth breeds inflation, since it just adds money to the economy without increasing the amount of goods or services available to spend it on. When people have more money to spend but no additional products or services to spend it on, the prices of existing goods and services rise. More money chasing the same amount of goods and services is one of the classic causes of inflation.

So, here's how the Death by Hyperinflation scenario goes.

Year One

The financial markets, here and abroad, notice the Fed buying some of the government's debt. "Hey," they say, "this is going to be inflationary. We'd better prepare ourselves." So banks and other lenders raise their interest rates to protect themselves against the anticipated loss of value in the dollar. After all, what's the use of charging 4 percent interest on a loan if the inflation rate will climb to 10 percent — if, in other words, the dollars you get back are worth 10 percent less than the dollars you loaned. If that is the case, the lender would actually lose 6 percent on the transaction. So, if lenders think inflation will rise to 10 percent, and they want to earn 4 percent *real* interest, they'll raise their *nominal* interest rate to 14 percent. Higher rates mean that it costs the government even more to service its old — and new and growing — debt, thereby increasing the deficit. That's why it's foolish for the government to be shortening its debt instruments, while industry is lengthening theirs.

Meanwhile, of course, the value of the old securities that people hold — those that were issued at low rates of interest back in the good old days of the late 1980s and early 1990s — have plunged. Nobody wants them, since they earn at a rate lower than inflation. People sell them for whatever they can get, but they don't save the cash from the sale. With inflation, a dollar saved today could be worth 99 cents tomorrow, so when people get cash, they want to buy something with it, something like an oriental carpet or vacuum cleaner, whose prices will be higher tomorrow than today. Naturally, this strong demand for goods only drives their prices higher still. That's one of the insidious characteristics of inflation: It promotes itself.

Year Two

By late in the year, the annual inflation rate has climbed to 22 percent and is rising by a point or more a month. Interest rates are running at 30 percent and more. When the government tries to raise cash to cover its deficit, which by now is almost as large every month as it used to be every year, investors refuse to buy the fixed-rate notes because of their uncertainty about future inflation. When it can't sell any of its debt, the Treasury has to sell it all to the Fed, which only exacerbates inflation.

Year Three

Sometime in year three, corporate profits vanish, submerged by inflation, and no individuals or companies are able to borrow. The home construction industry dies. Manufacturing productivity goes into decline as plants deteriorate. Many companies can't generate enough new working capital to sustain themselves, so they gradually slide into oblivion.

Overseas, the dollar is virtually worthless, but foreign corporations can pick up American industrial plants and operating facilities easily if they pay in Japanese yen or the new Euro-currency. So foreigners buy U.S. companies in order to acquire technology or other assets and, often, shut the operations down and move them out of the country. American companies also face shutdown simply because banks have cut off their credit, and foreign companies move in like buzzards on carrion. *C'est la vie.*

By the end of the year, banks cancel consumer credit cards, because they can't collect the debt fast enough to keep pace with the declining value of the dollar. Accounting systems break down, and people stop paying taxes because no one can keep track of the numbers anymore. Bookkeeping computers are overloaded with zeros. The deficit, as near as anyone can figure it, seems entirely out of control. Hyperinflation is pushing the economy, along with public morale, into a hopeless and major depression. Black markets are springing up all over the country. The middle class begins to disappear. In California a nonpartisan committee called RAG (Restore America's Greatness) is organized to draft Ronald Reagan in the 1996 presidential election campaign. "Here I go again," responds the Gipper.

Early Warning Signs

Those are two ways that the U.S. government's mounting debt might end up killing the American economy — that is, by driving it by one route or another into deep, deep depression. I don't say that this will happen exactly one way or another, but that it's going to happen somehow in the absence of quick and dramatic remedial action by the federal government I am absolutely certain. We have frittered away a decade when we could have done something about our problem without too much pain. Now we have an emergency.

You can look for three warning signs that one or the other of the pictures we've painted — or another one just as dismal — is about to come to life. These are signs that would alert savvy investors in this country and overseas that U.S. government securities are no longer rock-solid safe.

- **The federal government can no longer collect enough tax revenue to service its debt.**

When a bank evaluates a loan application, one of the factors it examines is the applicant's ability to make the payments. The question is: Does he or she have enough income to service the loan *and* meet other financial obligations? A bank will usually not grant a mortgage, for instance, if the mortgage payments are going to exceed 28 percent of the applicant's income.

In 1993, the annual debt service — the interest charges, that is — on the federal government's debt is expected to reach 42 percent of the total revenue the government collects, not including Social Security taxes, which are intended to cover future Social Security obligations. In 1994, it will eat up 66 percent of such government tax revenues. By 1997, interest on the federal debt will require virtually every cent of personal and corporate income taxes the government collects. Before that happens, investors will begin reevaluating the safety and security of U.S. government debt securities.

You'll see this warning sign in news reports comparing the deficit with the government's interest expenses, but you may have to read closely to find the numbers.

- **The Federal Reserve begins to buy substantial amounts of the government's debt.**

The Fed constantly buys and sells government debt on the open market in order to effect small changes in the money supply. This is called monetary policy (as contrasted to fiscal policy, which is the government's collection of taxes and spending of tax revenues). No one gets nervous when the Fed buys just enough of the federal debt to keep the money supply growing at a rate that matches production growth in the economy. But when big-time investors with millions and billions of dollars floating around in the financial markets see the Fed buying increasing amounts of the government's debt, they get nervous about inflation. Interest rates begin rising in anticipation of inflation, and the process builds on itself. To keep an eye out for this warning sign, watch the newspapers again. You'll begin to see stories about bankers and economists fretting about the expanding money supply.

- **Congress and the administration, while they talk a good game, avoid taking the bold actions needed to bring down the deficit.**

Don't pay attention to what the politicians *say* about the deficit. Note carefully what they *do* about it. You've noticed, perhaps, that it's not enough? That warning sign tells us that we're already headed for trouble at a rapid and accelerating pace.

7

Yes, It Can (and Will) Happen Here

IF you were to lay all the economists in the country end to end, the after-dinner speaker's joke goes, they would never reach a conclusion. For every opinion held by one of these practitioners of the dismal science, three more will take different and conflicting points of view. Some will even defend the indefensible: the federal government's continued deficit spending.

Economists of both liberal and conservative stripe each can cite their respective reasons why deficits don't matter or, if they do matter, why America's case is special.

Politicians usually seize upon whichever economist's argument suits their needs at the moment. Ronald Reagan was beguiled by a faction that argued that cutting taxes would create so much economic growth that government revenues would increase and the debt and deficit would vanish. Reagan proposed and got tax cuts through Congress, which did prompt some economic growth, but the disappearing deficits that this merry band of supply-siders promised were never realized, because the revenue growth was both vastly overestimated and insufficient and the promised reduction in government spending never occurred and, in fact, increased.

This book doesn't use complicated mathematics or computer-generated economic models to make its own case. I believe that clear eyes, well-researched facts, good sense, and lessons drawn from the historical experiences of other countries are all the tools one needs to come to some basic conclusions about the economy.

Since others will disagree, however, and take issue with my conclusions, you should know why I believe their arguments are wrong. In this chapter, you'll get a brief summary of these differing and conflicting opinions and then an explanation of why I think they're incorrect; a number have already been proven so.

I'm not going to equivocate over fine points of theory or quibble at the margins of argument. The country's impending financial crisis is nearly upon us. The time for polite debate has passed. It is time to act. Deficits *do* matter, and our national debt crisis *can* and *will* bring the United States to its knees — no matter how good a game the economists and politicians talk.

Herewith, the economists' arguments on why our mounting debt and annual deficits won't hurt us, and my responses to same.

ARGUMENT: *Even if the debt is growing from year to year, so, too, is our economy. The United States' gross domestic product (GDP) nearly doubled in the past decade, and it's still one-quarter greater than Japan's and Germany's combined.*

ANSWER: The gross domestic product is the value of all the final goods and services a country produces in a year. It is, in effect, a nation's paycheck.

Why is GDP important in relation to debt? It's as simple as Personal Finance 101. Just as a person who pockets a hefty pay raise can afford to charge more on his or her credit cards, a country whose GDP is expanding can safely take on more debt. But there's a caveat to this contention that many people neglect to mention. Debt must remain in some reasonable ratio to income if a person wants to remain solvent.

As long as debt as a percentage of the country's GDP remained constant or declined, the United States could afford to borrow. We got ourselves into trouble in the 1980s when our debt began to grow faster than our GDP, which is the alarming situation we still face today. It's true that in the past decade our GDP almost doubled, but our debt was climbing faster yet.

To understand what's happened, let's look at a little recent history. The country borrowed heavily to pay for World War II, and at the war's end, our debt was 128 percent of our GDP. But from 1946 until 1974, our debt as a percentage of GDP steadily declined to 35 percent. Since 1982, though, the percentage has increased dramatically. In 1982, America's debt stood at 36 percent of GDP. In 1991, it was 64 percent. At the end of 1992, it was 68 percent. By 1996, the national debt is projected to be larger than GDP (see the graph on page 113). What is happening is that our debt is growing three times faster than the size of our economy. That is why we're in deep trouble and going to go deeper.

ARGUMENT: *Other major industrialized nations tolerate high levels of debt relative to GDP, and so can we.*

ANSWER: Not true. Our debt as a percentage of GDP (see the graph on page 114) is higher and growing faster than that of most industrialized nations in the world. It is also indisputable that no government — anywhere, ever — has operated for long under these circumstances without its citizens eventually paying a ruinous price, and nothing about the United States suggests that we're in any way exempt from this rule of history. As we'll see in chapters 8 and 9, countries such as Argentina, Bolivia, and Italy offer proof that no country can indefinitely get away with spending more than it produces.

ARGUMENT: *The debt doesn't matter because we owe most of the money to ourselves.*

ANSWER: True, American citizens and institutions are the biggest buyers of U.S. Treasury securities, but the total amount we

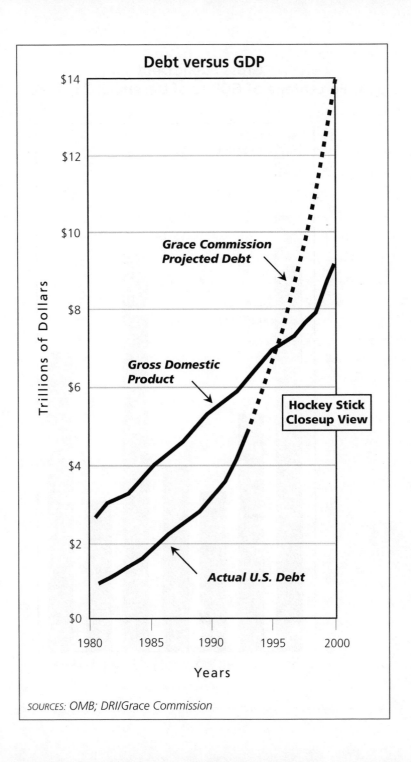

Debt versus GDP

Trillions of Dollars

$14

$12

$10

*Grace Commission
Projected Debt*

$8

*Gross Domestic
Product*

$6

**Hockey Stick
Closeup View**

$4

$2

Actual U.S. Debt

$0

1980   1985   1990   1995   2000

Years

SOURCES: OMB; DRI/Grace Commission

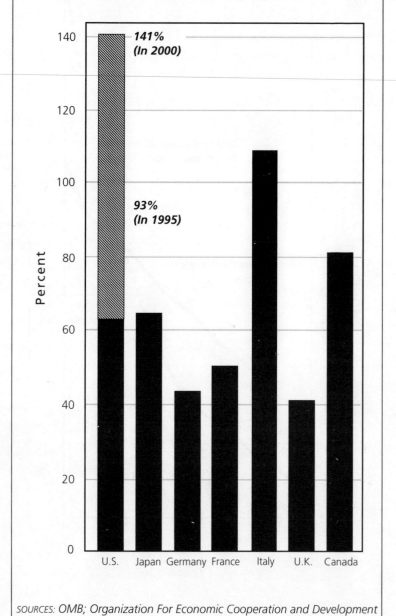

Gross Public Debt
As Percentage of GDP as of December 31, 1992

141%
(In 2000)

93%
(In 1995)

Percent

140

120

100

80

60

40

20

0

U.S.　Japan　Germany　France　Italy　U.K.　Canada

SOURCES: OMB; Organization For Economic Cooperation and Development

owe to foreigners has soared. The United States, like any garden-variety developing nation, is now in hock to the world. A creditor nation is one that has more invested abroad than foreign countries have invested in it. A debtor nation is just the opposite — foreigners have more invested in it than that country has invested abroad. In 1975, we were the world's largest *creditor* nation. By 1986, we had become the world's biggest *debtor* nation, an ignominious position we still hold.

We now owe more money to foreigners than any other country on earth. Today, 12.3 percent of our Treasury securities are in the hands of Japanese, Saudis, Germans, and other foreigners. Twelve percent may not sound alarming, but the figure is misleading. The issue isn't the percentage of our debt that's held by foreigners; it's the total *amount* that we owe them.

A few numbers sketch the situation: Twelve percent of $4.1 trillion — our total debt at the end of 1992 — or a total of $504 billion in U.S. securities are in foreign hands. At the end of 1982, by contrast, we owed foreigners only $142 billion. In just ten years, then, we have had more than a threefold increase in the amount of debt held by foreigners.

The amount matters, because that's what we pay interest on. If we fork over, say, an average of 8 percent interest on the national debt, we'll send foreign creditors more than $40 billion this year — wealth that we and our children may never see again.

The graph on page 116 shows precisely how much we owe to foreigners.

Moreover, debt securities form the core holdings of U.S. banks and pension funds, including the pension funds of state and local government employees. If the federal government defaults on its debts, we will devastate these accounts.

ARGUMENT: *Our indebtedness to foreigners won't cause us to lose our economic sovereignty.*

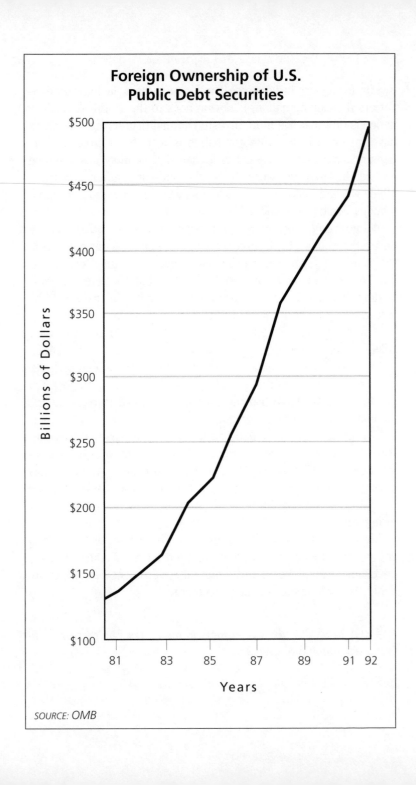

Foreign Ownership of U.S. Public Debt Securities

Billions of Dollars

$500

$450

$400

$350

$300

$250

$200

$150

$100

81   83   85   87   89   91 92

Years

SOURCE: OMB

ANSWER: Wishful thinking. The degree of our indebtedness means that we *must* dance to the foreign investors' tune, or they'll stop lending to us. If foreigners stop buying new Treasury securities, we won't have the money we need to run the country.

Why would foreign investors stop buying our debt? They could lose faith in our creditworthiness. In fact, their faith began to crack several years ago in the wake of the 1987 stock market crash. Also, foreign investors could be tempted by higher rates of return in their own countries or elsewhere.

If foreigners become reluctant to buy our debt, we would have to increase the interest rates we pay in order to make Treasury investments more attractive — a move that would have dire consequences for the economy. It's already happened. One week in the spring of 1992, for example, the interest rate on long-term Treasury securities was bumped up a full point, because the government was unable to attract enough investors at lower rates. Remember, high interest rates mean higher interest payments on the debt and higher deficits. It's a vicious cycle. Scary, isn't it?

Here's another question to ponder: If foreigners decide to cash in their Treasury securities, what will they do with the dollars they receive? Chances are good that they'll use them to buy productive assets, such as factories and entire companies, in this country. In fact, that's already happened, too. Today, foreigners own more than $2.3 trillion in U.S.-based assets (see the graph on page 118), including such American icons as Rockefeller Center, Burger King, Brooks Brothers, Holiday Inn, and Columbia Pictures. Foreign ownership of U.S. assets has more than quadrupled since 1980. If the trend continues — as it assuredly will if we fail to rein in our debt — we will have transferred control of most of our productive assets from ourselves and our children to foreign owners. With ownership will go the stream of profits that was to serve as our children's inheritance, and job security will be minimal at best.

ARGUMENT: *The debt isn't a burden on future generations, because they will benefit from the investments we make now.*

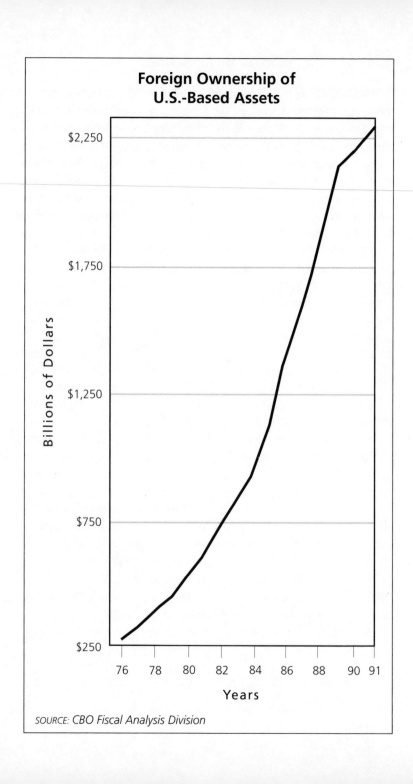

Foreign Ownership of
U.S.-Based Assets

Billions of Dollars

$2,250

$1,750

$1,250

$750

$250

76 78 80 82 84 86 88 90 91

Years

SOURCE: CBO Fiscal Analysis Division

ANSWER: The problem with this argument? We aren't using the money for investments. We're using it to pay our current expenses. We're not borrowing to build highways or bridges or repair the crumbling infrastructure of our cities, as we did in the past (see the graph on page 120). In the nineteenth century, we used foreign money to construct railroads, factories, and other long-term productive assets, and our borrowing helped us become an industrial powerhouse. In the late twentieth century, we're borrowing to pay our current bills, such as the interest on the national debt, the bailout of the savings and loans, and defaults on student loans. Capital investment continues to plummet.

Compare our nation's situation to that of a family who borrows from the bank to pay its day-to-day expenses — groceries, gasoline, clothes, and so on — rather than using its borrowing power to purchase a long-term asset, such as a home. Will it have anything to pass on to its children? The answer is no, and neither will our nation. We will have nothing left to pass on to our progeny.

ARGUMENT: *Borrowing from Social Security and other so-called trust funds to finance the deficit is okay, because it keeps interest rates low and limits our need to borrow from foreigners.*

ANSWER: It *would* be okay if there were any prospect that the U.S. government will be able to repay those loans when Social Security and the eight other federal "trust" funds — such as military, postal workers, and railroad retirement — need the money themselves to pay benefits and meet their own obligations. But where will the cash come from?

Borrowing to meet today's expenses from monies that we're meant to set aside for the future is a cruel trick. When retiring Baby Boomers look for their Social Security benefits twenty or thirty years from now, all they'll find in the Social Security account is a bunch of paper IOUs from the federal government. When retiring postal workers, military personnel, civil servants, and railroad employees look to their government-run pension funds for

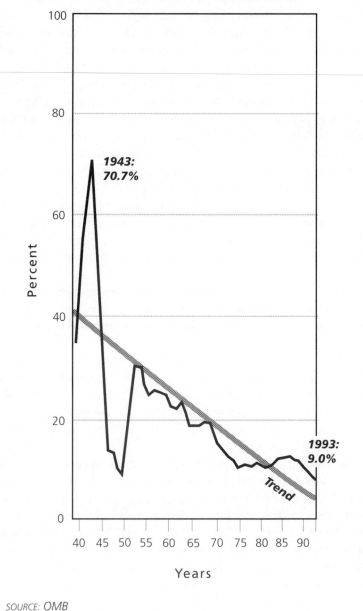

Capital Investment Outlays
As a Percentage of Total Outlays

1943:
70.7%

1993:
9.0%

Trend

Percent

Years

SOURCE: *OMB*

monthly checks, the money supposedly set aside to pay those checks won't be there; just those paper IOUs. When we want to build a new highway or mass transit system in the future, the highway "trust" fund will be stuffed with government paper. Sorry, they'll say, but walking is good for you.

In effect, we're keeping interest rates temporarily in check now by loaning these fund surpluses to the Treasury to finance some of our government operations. If the government did not borrow from those sources, it would have to go into the marketplace and compete against other borrowers for funds, thereby driving interest rates higher. But we're using this strategy at the expense of our own future retirement incomes, our government employment system, and our highway systems.

ARGUMENT: *The debt hasn't caused interest rates to rise.*

ANSWER: Not yet, but it will. It's true that in the past two years our debt has reached alarming proportions without triggering the higher interest rates that we predict for the future. (The graph on page 122 shows the change in real interest rates.) There's a simple reason for this seeming contradiction: Right now, there's plenty of money for the U.S. government to borrow.

One reason there is so much capital available is that the United States and other nations are experiencing slow to no economic growth. During such periods, businesses reduce their borrowing, so the demand for capital in the private sector is low, leaving more money available for the U.S. government to borrow.

A second reason is that the Federal Reserve has pumped billions of dollars into the economy in an effort to shore up the banking system in the wake of the savings and loan scandal and to ease the economic slowdown by stimulating borrowing. Many banks, however, are choosing not to loan that money. Rather, they're investing it in government securities to help revive their own balance sheets. There's a third reason that rates have not yet climbed: The Fed has kept them artificially low in order to spur

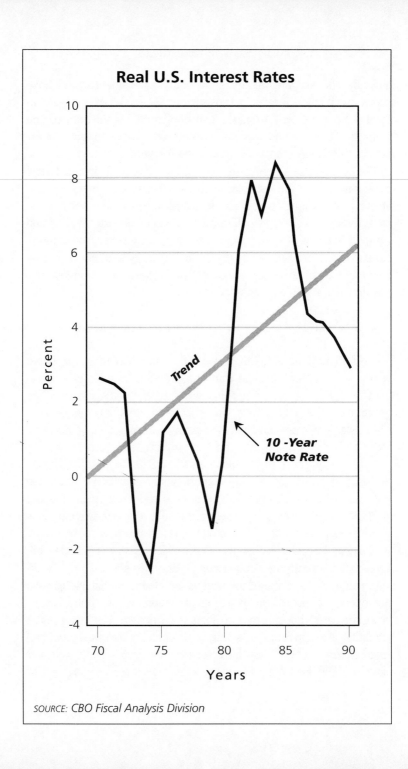

Real U.S. Interest Rates

Trend

10 -Year
Note Rate

Percent

Years

SOURCE: CBO Fiscal Analysis Division

economic recovery, a recovery that to date has been sporadic and unimpressive.

But as economies here and abroad begin to recover in earnest, the private sector's demand for money will grow, and the competition for capital between industry and the U.S. government will heat up. The government *must* borrow whatever amounts are necessary to cover its shortfalls, so it will pay whatever rates investors demand and, sooner or later, interest rates will soar.

Recent situations in Brazil and Argentina illustrate the point. In the 1970s and 1980s, the governments of those two countries had to pay interest rates as high as 45 percent above the rate of inflation to attract capital. In November 1986, businesses fortunate enough to find credit paid 90 percent annual interest to borrow. Three months later, the annual interest rate for nongovernment borrowers had climbed to 550 percent. Yes, you read that right — 550 percent. As you might guess, there's no such thing as long-term mortgage money in those countries. Homes, if they sell at all, go for cash.

ARGUMENT: *The debt hasn't caused investment in American industry to decline.*

ANSWER: Yes it has. Since 1980, investment in plants and equipment as a percent of GDP has been plummeting. (See the graph on page 124.) In 1980, it was 13.4 percent of GDP, and in 1992, it was 9.2 percent with a sharp downturn continuing. The shortage of capital caused by the federal government's insatiable need for funds will continue to be a main cause of reduced investment in the private sector. Want proof? Consider Italy.

Italians save at an unusually high rate, but the country's public sector eats up some 80 percent of these domestic savings, effectively crowding the private sector out of the domestic credit market. Italian companies have to look elsewhere for much of their funding, but whether they borrow at home or abroad, they pay exorbitant interest, because they are competing with their own

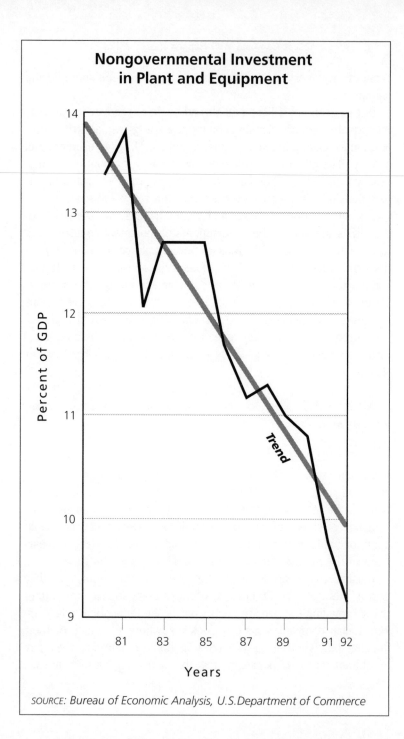

Nongovernmental Investment in Plant and Equipment

Percent of GDP

Years

SOURCE: *Bureau of Economic Analysis, U.S. Department of Commerce*

government. At the end of 1991, for example, with inflation at 6.4 percent, the Italian government was selling long-term bonds paying an interest rate of 12.9 percent.

"The deficit is drawing resources away from productive activities," an Italian manufacturing executive told us. "We don't have the money to finance private-sector activity, because it's costly and difficult for Italian firms to borrow money." Consequently, employment and economic growth in that country have stagnated.

ARGUMENT: *The debt hasn't caused our standard of living to suffer.*

ANSWER: Wrong. Since 1985, real U.S. per capita economic growth has lagged behind that of other major industrialized nations, and in 1990 the United States was one of only two major industrialized nations to show a drop in this measure. The real net worth of U.S. households — the value of their assets minus their debts — actually fell by 4.3 percent from the end of 1989 to the end of 1990. Many polls already show that many Americans no longer expect even to be better off than their parents, as they traditionally have.

What's more, even the paltry economic growth we're experiencing now is a result of more work and longer hours, not productivity gains. Instead of working smarter, we're working harder, as a study by the Federal Reserve Bank of Cleveland shows. (See the graph on page 126 for changes in hourly compensation.)

The strain on American living standards is already evident: The proportion of two-parent families in which only one parent works is shrinking; the amount of leisure time available to the typical worker is falling; the percentage of Americans who own homes is dropping; and the age at which first homes are purchased is rising. Moreover, the personal bankruptcy rate is nearly triple what it was in the 1960s and 1970s; the cost of higher education exceeds

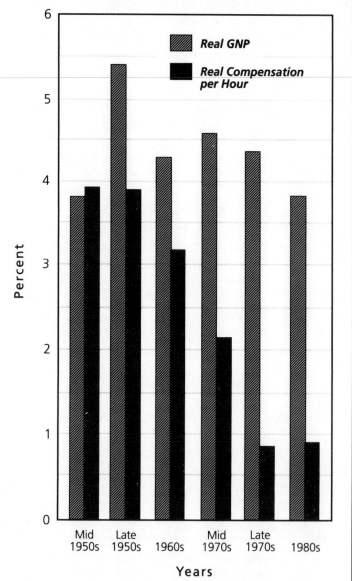

Worker Compensation
Annual Percent Change

Real GNP

Real Compensation
per Hour

Percent

| | Mid 1950s | Late 1950s | 1960s | Mid 1970s | Late 1970s | 1980s |

Years

SOURCES: *U.S. Department of Commerce, Bureau of Economic Analysis;*
U.S. Department of Labor, Bureau of Labor Statistics

the means of a growing number of families; and we have one of the industrialized world's highest infant mortality rates.

Do you still think our standard of living isn't declining?

ARGUMENT: *Some deficit spending is good for the economy. A little extra government spending on roads and other projects can boost the economy out of recession.*

ANSWER: That can be true under some circumstances, but it isn't true now.

It was John Maynard Keynes, the once-radical British economist, who first proposed in the 1930s that governments could help rev up their economies by deliberately overspending.

Keynes said that deficit spending *per se,* whether it was money spent on hiring the unemployed to rake leaves or on buying new limousines for cabinet secretaries, was an effective recession-fighting technique. By spending more than it collected in taxes, the government would, in effect, be creating new money. This extra cash in the hands of businesses or consumers would increase the demand for goods and services, causing companies to hire more people and, in effect, helping jump-start a sluggish economy. The government could create the new money either by increasing its spending while leaving taxes unchanged, or by cutting taxes while leaving spending alone. Either action would add money to the economy. John F. Kennedy relied on Keynesian theories during his administration, and they worked.

Once a recession ends, though, Keynes preached that deficit spending should stop. And that's precisely where we've failed. We've run a deficit in good times and in bad, and now we have basically operated the government for more than three decades with an ever-increasing deficit. By making deficits business as usual, we've created additional interest burdens for ourselves as well as for future generations. That we will end up paying for our excesses is certain — and soon.

ARGUMENT: *The debt won't cause inflation.*

ANSWER: Wrong again. The debt *will* cause inflation, and here's why. In order to finance the debt, the U.S. Treasury has only two choices. It can borrow money by selling securities to private investors either here or overseas. That's what it has been doing. Or it can "monetize" the debt — which simply means it can create new money and use that to cover the deficit, as we saw in the last chapter.

As you recall, the government creates new money by selling its securities to the Federal Reserve, which hands the Treasury a check that it can deposit in any commercial bank. There's no real money behind the Fed's check — just the commercial bank's faith that the Fed will make good. The problem is that the commercial bank can lend this money to borrowers just as it lends any other deposits. Now we have new money out in the economy, but no one made anything or performed any service to produce it. When you have more money but the same number of goods and services in an economy, the price of those goods and services tends to go up. That's inflation.

The only thing standing between us and inflation, then, is the government's willingness not to monetize its debt. But every government that has ever had our government's deficit problem sooner or later is tempted to take that course, and there's no reason to believe that it won't happen here.

ARGUMENT: *Calling too much attention to today's debt is wrong, because it dampens consumer confidence.*

ANSWER: Raising the alarm about our national debt isn't what's causing consumers to lose confidence in the economy and the nation. Confidence is waning because people are smarter than our so-called leaders think they are. Americans understand that countries can't live beyond their means indefinitely. Consider: U.S. consumer confidence rose just after the 1992 presidential election because many people believed that President Clinton would at last tackle the deficit and debt. By his fifth month in office — after a lot of talk, but no serious action on the deficit — consumer confidence levels were lower than they were before the election. Consumers' lack of confidence isn't caused by the debt and deficit *per se*, but by the mistrust they have in Congress and the administration's ability to solve it.

If Congress and the administration ever did tackle the deficit and reduce government spending, consumers would feel better about our country's economic future and spend more. Similarly, business confidence would increase once businesspeople were convinced that our government was charting a fiscally sound path. Foreigners who have invested in our debt would also feel more comfortable about their prospects for repayment and begin to relax.

ARGUMENT: *We don't need to worry about the debt and deficit, because Congress will ultimately solve the problem.*

ANSWER: Right now we have two chances of that happening — slim and none. Need we say more?

8

The Price We Pay for Deficit Spending

AS the United States is about to find out for itself, people and countries get little respect when they're so far in debt that they can't pay back what they owe. The debt we're building will deprive us of our wealth, to be sure, but it's also going to cost us our prestige and influence in the world and take a large bite out of our self-respect.

You only have to half-read the newspapers to know that the United States has already lost much of its ability to compete commercially and diplomatically with other nations, particularly Germany and Japan. We don't have the same policy clout we used to have overseas, and we can't even take care of the social problems we have at home. A country can put things on the tab for only so long before it starts paying a price, and we're about to start paying it. How?

Let me list the ways.

Higher Inflation

The politicians won't warn you about this one, because they don't want you worrying; they want your vote the next time they run for office. But you'd better worry, because the United States is about to see the return of inflation. *Real* inflation.

"Inflation," says a Brazilian executive we interviewed, "is when you go to the same restaurant each morning, order the same breakfast, and each time have to ask how much it costs." That's the kind we're going to get.

Inflation can reduce the real value of a nation's debt — or even whittle it down to close to zero as happened in Germany after World War I. That's why governments tend to resort to it as they pile deficit upon deficit. The problem is that inflation treats the disease by destroying the patient. Paying off debt with inflated money slashes the amount that a country owes, but it turns a nation's currency into worthless paper and its economy into shambles.

If you don't think that even a little inflation can knock you for a loop, consider this: Say you have a bond that cost you $10,000, and the inflation rate that's now around 5 percent doubles to 10 percent. Do you know what the value of your bond would be if you have to sell it prior to maturity? It could fall to about $6,000. That's what inflation could do to people's investments.

Debt-ridden South American nations have suffered under some of the worst inflation rates of the twentieth century. In the late 1980s, one of our researchers bought a loaf of bread in Argentina and found that the price marked on it had risen by the time he reached the checkout counter. In Bolivia, in the spring of 1985, inflation reached an annualized level of 50,000 percent.

The nations of Eastern Europe have also experienced punishing price increases. In Poland in 1990, inflation topped 500 percent. Economists usually express inflation in annual terms, but not the average Pole. "When I say 3 percent inflation, I mean 3 percent a month," a Polish banker said as he tried to explain what he considered a reasonable inflation target. Three percent a month is an annual inflation rate of about 42 percent.

Individuals suffer in inflationary economies because wages, while they often rise rapidly, don't climb as fast as prices, so consumers lose purchasing power. Poland, for example, penalizes businesses if they grant their workers raises that exceed a monthly limit, which the government sets at 60 to 80 percent of inflation. In other words, by law, Polish wages trail inflation by 20 to 40 percent a month. Imagine you wanted to buy an automobile or a television or a new suit — or even go out to a restaurant. Each time you saved $100 toward your goal, its price would shoot up by $20 or $40. That's what life's like for people in countries with high inflation rates. They're running after a carrot on a stick with little chance of ever getting a bite.

That's bad enough, but there's worse: Polish workers' wages usually aren't adjusted weekly or monthly. Instead, they collect their cost-of-living raises at the end of the year. That means they have to suffer through twelve months of rising prices and falling purchasing power before their paycheck is adjusted, however inadequately, for inflation. "Inflation can help you solve a company's personnel problems," joked an Argentinean banker with whom we spoke. "All you do is not adjust workers' wages for inflation and eventually you're paying them nothing."

Businesses suffer, too, because companies can't charge enough for their goods or services to compensate for their own higher costs. This is particularly true for businesses trying to compete in world markets. Companies in Eastern Europe, for example, are currently getting squeezed in a vise of higher internal costs on the one side and the need to remain price competitive in world markets on the other. Many businesses in that part of the world won't sign a contract unless it contains a clause stating that the price of the goods they're selling will rise with inflation.

Inflation-adjusted contracts make sense when you consider it can take years to fill some orders. This is a lesson I learned first-hand. Because of a backlog in orders, one of our subsidiaries required two years from the time an order was placed to produce a fire truck. During the high inflation of the 1970s, we were required to quote a city or town a fixed price for a truck, but by the time we made delivery we had spent more to produce the truck than we were going to get. We lost significant amounts of money in honoring our contracts, and so would any company that sells products with long lead times.

In Argentina in the late 1980s, most companies wouldn't sell goods by catalog price. That's because the prices published in a catalog more than a week or so old were already out of date and too low. Customers had to call the seller to get current prices.

Don't think inflation has to hit 100 percent or 1,000 percent to wreak havoc in the United States' economy. An inflation rate of 18 percent would *double* the prices of goods and services in only four years. Our businesses would find it impossible to pass on that much of an increase in costs to buyers in world markets. Likewise, the same inflation rate would chop the purchasing power of an elderly person's fixed income in half in the same amount of time. Everyone suffers with high inflation in an economy — sellers and buyers alike.

Higher Taxes

Read my lips. If Congress and the president don't get the deficit under control now, we *will* get higher taxes in the United States. Sooner or later, to cope with mounting deficits and expanding entitlement programs, this government, like every other spendthrift government, will try to bail itself out of its dilemma with tax hikes. Witness Clinton's call for new taxes.

They might call a spade a spade and raise tax rates, which anyone can see is a tax hike. But they don't have to. They can raise the tax burden by expanding the tax base, sneaking in hidden taxes on goods and services, or by reducing and eliminating deductions and exemptions. The American people have already been hit with a huge tax increase, thanks to the Budget Reconciliation Act of 1990, which included a smattering of all these elements. (You'll find the details in Chapter 3.)

Higher taxes have an obvious cost — which is that people have less money in their pockets. But there are other, not-so-obvious costs as well.

Noncompliance, for one. High tax rates encourage tax avoidance and tax evasion. People go to elaborate lengths to avoid, legally or illegally, paying their fair share. In Hungary, for example, where employers pay a 43 percent social insurance tax (the equivalent of our Social Security tax), and employees pay progressive social insurance taxes of up to 10 percent and progressive income taxes as high as 50 percent, some pretty big companies have no employees at all. That's strange, since a lot of people seem to be working in these businesses. Those workers are "independent contractors," explained the manager of one professional services firm. That way, the firm doesn't have to pay payroll taxes and what the employees — oops, independent contractors — report as earnings is up to them. Many Hungarian employers reduce their tax bite by paying a portion of wages under the table. That means billions of dollars in revenues are lost to the so-called underground economy, a phenomenon that's not unfamiliar in this country.

The Polish government, in an attempt to lure foreign capital into the country despite its high tax rates, rescinded some taxes for corporations with foreign ownership. Suddenly, thousands of Polish businesses acquired foreign "partners," most of whom are lawyers in Berlin or someplace else, who act as partners for a fee.

In Italy, the only major industrialized country in the world whose debt is more than 100 percent of its GDP, taxes, especially indirect taxes, have risen steadily in recent years. The fuel tax, for example, now accounts for more than 75 percent of the pump price of gasoline. Not surprisingly, Italian compliance with tax laws is among Europe's worst. Estimates of personal income tax receipts lost to evasion range from 37 to 68 percent of actual taxes owed and revenue collected from the country's value added tax, or VAT, is only half of what it should be.

Besides encouraging noncompliance with and disrespect for the law, higher taxes reduce incentives for people to work, invest, and save. Especially work. One reason Ronald Reagan embraced supply-side economics was his belief that high taxes were discouraging productive work. In that, he was probably on the mark.

In the late 1970s, before Reagan entered the Oval Office, a lot of people were beginning to notice that while they were taking home a fatter paycheck, the extra cash wasn't doing them any good. The reason, they discovered, was "bracket creep," otherwise known as "taxflation." Every time they got a raise, they would get thrown into a higher tax bracket, despite the fact that their raise was only keeping their purchasing power even with inflation. The more taxes the government takes out of the next dollar a person earns, the less inclined that person is to go to the trouble of earning the next dollar. As taxflation pushed Americans into higher and higher tax brackets, they became less interested in productive work and more interested in looking for ways to beat the tax system. Consider the excesses of the 1980s, when many investments in areas such as real estate were made more with an eye toward piling up tax-deductible losses than producing long-term value.

Businesses and tradespeople who ask for cash payments aren't doing it because they don't trust your check. They're doing it to avoid paying taxes on that revenue, just as people who work "off-the-books" are willing to accept employment with no fringe benefits or legal protections so that they can avoid paying their share of the public's expenses. No one really knows how much income isn't reported to the Internal Revenue Service, but estimates are that the country loses as much as $127 billion in revenues annually. That's one of the prices you already pay for high tax rates, and if tax rates go higher, honest taxpayers will suffer even more from the cheats.

Rising Interest Rates

Probably the first thing many people notice when interest rates start to climb is that they no longer qualify for a mortgage or that they can't afford the house they want — or that the monthly payment on the variable-rate mortgage they already have starts going up. When interest rates head up, the first thing that heads down is the housing market and home construction, which not only keeps people from buying houses but puts lots of people who build them out of work.

Likewise, rising interest rates give the auto market a flat tire. People can't afford auto loans, so they don't buy new cars, which puts the workers who build them and everything that goes into them — electronics, brakes, upholstery fabric, hose clamps, tail lamps — out of work.

People with money invested in bonds — which includes lots of people saving for retirement or already retired — lose money if they have to sell their bonds before maturity, because as interest rates climb, bond prices fall. Even if bondholders don't have to sell their bonds at lower prices, they are nonetheless locked into relatively low rates of return, which could, in fact, turn negative. As inflation rises, so do interest rates, and bond income can quickly become a losing proposition. When inflation hits 10 percent, the holder of a bond paying 8 percent interest is actually receiving a *negative* real return. In other words, he or she is losing 2 percent a year. Moreover, the original bond is losing value, because at the time of redemption, the purchasing power of the money originally invested in the bond will have been eroded.

American companies and their employees lose if rising interest rates also cause the dollar to rise in value as compared to other currencies. In the 1980s, our high real interest rates caused the value of the dollar to soar relative to other countries' currencies. When the dollar is stronger, the goods that U.S. companies export become more expensive overseas, while imports become less expensive in the United States. Consequently, American companies lose sales and market share both at home and abroad — and with lost sales goes rising unemployment.

Moreover, higher interest rates undermine the value of loans held by banks, businesses, insurance companies, and individuals, potentially endangering their stability. In the 1960s and early 1970s, for example, savings and loans issued low-interest fixed mortgages. As inflation forced interest rates up, the S&Ls found themselves in a fix. They had to pay high interest to their depositors, while receiving relatively little income from the mortgages they held. As a result, many S&Ls failed and learned a hard lesson: You can't survive in the real world when the income interest you receive is less than the interest you must pay your depositors. It was widely predicted at the time that banks would never again issue fixed-rate mortgages, but they did — and now they're getting into trouble once more.

If you're getting the impression that rising interest rates caused by huge federal government borrowing are bad for most people and are to be avoided, you have the right idea.

Credit Shortages

When governments have to borrow huge sums to cover their deficits, they not only raise the cost of capital — interest rates, in other words — but they can dry up its supply. Meaning? You won't be able to borrow. Neither will the company you own or work for.

Government borrowing has effectively crowded many private borrowers out of the credit market in Italy. In Eastern Europe and in South America, the credit squeeze for businesses and individuals is almost total. It is difficult for Hungarian enterprises to borrow at all, and if someone will lend them money, it's only for a short time. The same is true in Brazil, which is one reason why most business there is transacted in cash. Major purchases, such as automobiles or even houses, are made with a cash down payment of at least 50 percent.

Hungary and Poland have no formal consumer loan market, so most Hungarians and Poles operate entirely with cash. To finance large purchases, many Hungarians join credit circles, which are also common in South America. Two hundred families, for example, will pool their money to buy two automobiles, which are then distributed by lottery each month. It's hard to imagine this happening in the United States, but people adapt to the circumstances they find themselves in.

In Great Britain in 1976, the government couldn't borrow enough to finance its deficit. It was forced to act like a developing nation and turn to the International Monetary Fund (IMF) to bail out its bankrupt economy. Many British believe this event finally awakened the country to the seriousness of its economic problems, and paved Margaret Thatcher's way to victory in the next election.

The U.S. government also consumes a huge portion of its domestic credit market, as the graph on the next page shows. Other countries aren't anxious to see U.S. interest rates rise much, because they fear for their own ability to borrow. The United States is such a huge consumer of debt that it can suck the money out of world capital markets, leaving other governments, as well as business, short of capital — that is, until foreign investors wake up to our fiscal folly. At some point, no one with any sense is going to want to loan money to a government that hasn't a prayer of paying it back.

Reduced Economic Growth and the Wrong Kind of Growth

The curses of large deficits — inflation, high taxes, climbing interest rates, and capital shortages — are a drag on an economy's growth, but they also promote the wrong kind of economic activity.

Individuals and businesses will try to make money the best way they can. Can you blame them? So, if a business can generate more profit by using its capital to speculate in currency markets than by building a new manufacturing plant, it will speculate. And the people who might have gotten jobs in the new plant will stay unemployed. If individual investors can make money by buying and

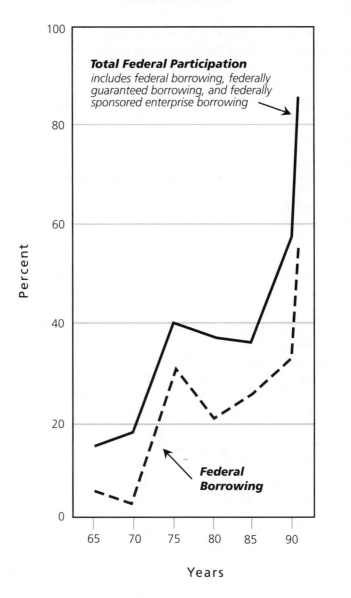

Federal Consumption of Domestic Credit

Total Federal Participation
includes federal borrowing, federally guaranteed borrowing, and federally sponsored enterprise borrowing

Federal Borrowing

Percent

Years

SOURCE: OMB

selling, say, antique oriental rugs than by investing in corporate stocks, they'll buy the rugs, and business won't have access to that money.

In South America, many companies halt production entirely during periods of particularly high inflation and join other investors in nonproductive speculation. The economic instability created by large deficits in one country encourages both businesses and investors there to invest their capital someplace else. When that happens, investment and economic growth aren't just delayed, they're lost altogether.

Reduced Standard of Living

The numbers and statistics that I've just cited aren't just figures from a record book. They have real effects on real people's lives. When companies and individuals don't invest, daily life gets harder. Just one example out of the thousands that you'd begin to notice: Telephone systems break down, and calls that used to be easy become impossible. A Hungarian executive asked one of our researchers to call someone else for him in Hungary. It would be easier to make the call from the United States, he explained, than from within the same country, which, because of its debt, can't afford to modernize its communications systems.

In truth, all of the amenities that have made middle-class life in the United States the envy of most of the world — our housing, cars, highways, and health care; the access we have to supermarkets rich with a variety of quality foods; our vacation and recreation resources in national parks and forests and on seashores; the convenience of ATM banking; the richness of our entertainment and communication media from movies to live theater to MTV; all of the products and services that make life in these United States a far more pleasant experience than is available to most of the world's population — we risk losing by piling up debt at an unprecedented rate.

We also diminish our ability to help our neighbors and fellow citizens who aren't as fortunate as most of us. When the economic pie is getting larger, no one minds sharing his or her expanding slice with the recipients of charity or government-provided assistance. We're less generous when our own share is shrinking.

Imagine what we might accomplish as a nation — the new Mag-Lev train system we could build or the environmental damage we could clean up or the housing we could construct — if we weren't spending more than $296 billion this year on interest payments.

It is very important to recognize that little of our deficit spending has gone into building the future, only into paying for current consumption. Americans have always looked forward to the future; that's what our country has been all about. Today, we've begun to dread it. Whether our political leaders acknowledge it or not, most of us have a visceral sense that we've already spent a good portion of our own and our children's futures. Many of us no longer expect to live as well as, never mind better than, our parents did. The houses we grew up in may be the best houses we'll ever live in. Our parents' cars may be the best we'll ever drive. Our children won't get the educations we got.

Since 1985, real per capita economic growth in the United States has lagged behind that of the other most industrialized nations by more than 43 percent, and in 1990 the United States was one of only two major industrialized nations whose economy shrank on a per capita basis. That year, the net worth of the average American household dropped by more than 4 percent.

It is not a happy prospect we face, and it's coming at us with the speed of light.

Loss of Control over Domestic Economic Policy

Huge deficits and debt rob the government of any flexibility it might have had in controlling the domestic economy. Normally, when the United States suffers a recession, the government can spend more to help get things moving again. Not now. The government is already spending 27 percent more than it takes in, and adding to that deficit will hurt, not help, the economy. Yet Clinton wanted to spend money on several new programs, starting with the so-called jobs bill proposed in February 1993 in the form of a $16 billion stimulus package.

Monetary policy also gets derailed by debt and deficits. Governments usually try to keep interest rates low in order to promote investment and consumption and fuel economic growth, but continually financing our large deficits will require the government to keep interest rates high enough to attract the capital, especially foreign capital, that it needs to finance its debt and deficit.

In other words, the government has already lost its ability to use fiscal policy — government spending and taxation — to keep the U.S. economy on a more-or-less even keel, and it has diminished its capacity to use monetary policy — control of the money supply — for the same end. What's coming next is external control, that is, other nations telling us what we may and may not do, just as the IMF now gives developing nations their marching orders. We can cure our deficit, or the countries that hold our debt will take control of our economy and cure it for us whether we like their methods or not.

Foreign countries haven't yet pressured us as hard as they might to mend our ways, because we still play a powerful, if reduced, role on the world stage as protector of the free world. Moreover, some nations, though they may publicly state otherwise, wouldn't be unhappy if the American dream collapsed and they could step in as the new, dominant world power.

Nonetheless, our allies have been lecturing us about our deficits for more than eight years. Japan points to the United States' deficits as the cause of our trade imbalance. When our debt reaches such proportion that we may no longer make the interest payments due, as it will in the mid-1990s, then the holders of our debt — probably a group of nations — will dictate terms of settlement to us. We'll be in the same situation as many South American countries, Poland, Russia, Ukraine, and other developing nations. As a recipient of IMF and World Bank support, Poland has no choice but to abide by strict limitations on its fiscal and monetary behavior. That nation has recently negotiated a debt-reduction package with the "Paris Club," a forum in which debtor nations can negotiate with their creditor nations and that now holds some 70 percent of Poland's external debt. The government is further restricted on how much it can borrow and how much it can spend. Poland has strict limits, for example, on the size of its budget deficits, the amount it can borrow from foreigners, the amount it can increase the wages of state employees, and the rate at which people can exchange the country's currency.

We're already in the same dismal situation as Italy, which, after paying for its debt service and entitlement programs, can control just 30 percent of its budget. "The deficit ties the government's hands," complained one Italian economist. "It's difficult to cut spending because debt interest is such a big part of it, and we have the same problem with entitlements the U.S. has — they are difficult to reduce. The need for revenues makes it impossible to control inflation — as soon as they raise taxes to lower the deficit, prices go up."

"Prayer," said an Italian banker, "is a key tool of our monetary and fiscal policy. Don't forget, the Vatican is only a couple of kilometers from our central bank." It's probably as good an economic tool as Washington has these days as well.

Loss of World Power

Throughout history, the world's great powers have been exporters of capital — sixteenth-century Spain, seventeenth-century Holland, and nineteenth-century Britain, for example. As those nations became debtors, however, they lost their ability to influence world affairs to their own advantage. That is, in commerce and in diplomacy, they then had to play by others' rules and they didn't win as often.

Our massive economy allowed us to exert our will around the globe for much of the twentieth century. We were able to build the world's most powerful armed forces and to influence the behavior of other nations by applying our considerable economic leverage. When President Kennedy told Secretary General Khrushchev in 1962 that the Communist leader could not put Soviet missiles in Cuba, Khrushchev ordered his ships to reverse course because he knew Kennedy could enforce his demand. A lot of things went our way in the world, not because we used military, diplomatic, or economic force, but because we *could.* Debtor nations don't have that kind of clout, and we'll have to revise our behavior and our self-image accordingly.

After World War II and the Korean war, the United States was able to play the leading role in rebuilding the economies of West Germany, Japan, and Korea. We spent $13 billion (not adjusted for inflation) between 1948 and 1951 on the Marshall Plan alone. By the end of 1991, however, Congress had appropriated less than $450 million in direct aid to Eastern Europe, in contrast to West Germany, which had pledged or sent $66 billion in cash and credits by February 1992. Because we are broke, we are able to offer the former Soviet republics little help in their economic transition. Our inability to act will cost us diplomatic as well as economic advantages in these parts of the world. It will make it difficult for our businesses to compete in these expanding markets.

Hungary and Poland, starved for foreign capital, are attempting to sell off vast state holdings to overseas investors. Poland, for instance, intends to put 25 to 30 percent of its state enterprises into foreign hands.

The United States hasn't announced a fire sale of its productive assets yet, but we might as well. It's going to start happening as foreign investors eventually stop buying our debt, start selling the large number of U.S. bonds they hold, and use the proceeds to buy our factories and other resources. When that happens, most of us will be working for companies whose executives and shareholders live somewhere else. Like China and the Chinese in the nineteenth century and Russia and Russians today, we'll be a huge, populous country that has allowed itself to become powerless to make its own choices.

9

What Others Can Teach Us

IF the United States were the first country in history to experience the crisis that our debt and deficit are about to bring down on us, government officials might have some excuse for what they've done. "Gee," they could say, "we didn't know it would come to *this.*"

One of the most exasperating characteristics of our problem, however, is that our so-called leaders started us down this road knowing exactly where it would lead.

Or, if they didn't know where they were taking us, they *should* have known, because the historical precedents are legion. Sooner or later, every country that has spent beyond its means has collided with disaster. The crash that we are about to experience has been experienced many times before.

Why, for instance, did Rome fall?

Three successive emperors — Caligula, Claudius, and the fiddler Nero — emptied their treasuries to pay for lavish ceremonial feasts, luxurious villas, elaborate temples, no-show civil servants, and bribes to the army and Praetorian Guard to ensure their loyalty. When they ran out of cash, these arrogant rulers raised taxes, seized the assets of wealthy citizens, or expanded the money supply by reminting old coins using more base metal and less gold and silver.

What they got for their trouble was severe inflation. In one thirty-year period during the third century A.D., for example, the price of wheat rose 100,000 percent. A loaf of bread that cost the equivalent of $2 at the start of the period cost $2,000 at the end. By the time Rome collapsed, high taxes had already destroyed Roman commerce. Cities and towns were reduced to ruin by lack of investment in their maintenance, the population was impoverished and dwindling, and riots and rebellion were commonplace.

Fourteen hundred years later, in the 1600s, Spain, which had been one of the mightiest countries of Europe, began running huge deficits to pay for wars, a bloated civil service, and endemic corruption. By the end of the seventeenth century, revenues covered only half the state's spending. Sound familiar? Repeated currency devaluations, growing inflation, and a murderous tax burden killed off Spanish industry and agriculture. Impoverished, Spain lost its global influence as its empire contracted to a fraction of its former size.

If history that old seems too remote to you, travel no farther back than our own century. After World War I, Austria and Germany were devastated, because, along with the debt they accumulated to pay for the war, they had to make massive reparation payments to the victorious Allies.

In the years from 1919 to 1922, Austria's budget deficits typically amounted to more than 50 percent of total government spending. The government financed these deficits largely by selling its debt to the central bank, which rapidly expanded the money supply. You know by now what that brings: inflation. The Austrian inflation rate rose 6,990 percent in the eleven months from October 1921 to August 1922. The exchange rate, which stood at 17 crowns to the U.S. dollar at the start of 1919, dropped to 71,000 crowns to the dollar by December 1922.

To get its currency and economy under control again, the government agreed to balance its budget by slashing the number of government employees, raising the prices of government-sold goods and services, increasing taxes, and improving the efficiency of tax collection. That worked, but Austrians suffered terribly for their government's earlier sins. Unemployment jumped tenfold in one year and continued to climb for the next several years.

In Germany, the fiscal situation was even worse. In 1920, the German government borrowed more than 60 percent of its revenues. By 1923, the deficit had risen to 88 percent of revenues, and the government financed it almost entirely by printing money — so much money that the Weimar government had to requisition printing presses from German publishers to keep up with demand for new, large-denomination bills. The number of currency notes in circulation surged from about 67 million at the start of 1921 to an incredible 496 billion by December 1923. The six Weimar Republic notes I found during World War II and that now hang, framed, on my wall were among the billions printed that year.

While Austria got inflation, Germany experienced hyperinflation — a 1.02 *trillion* percent increase in prices during the sixteen months from August 1922 to November 1923. The price of a loaf of rye bread rose from 0.29 marks just before the war, to 1,200 marks during the summer of 1923, to 428,000,000,000 marks by November of the same year. Germans needed baskets of cash just to buy food for dinner.

The Germans either had to break this inflation or see their country dissolve into complete anarchy. Accordingly, the government slashed its own employment rolls by 25 percent and pledged not to spend a pfennig more than it took in. The strategy eventually restored financial stability, but the misery that hyperinflation had inflicted was branded on the nation's memory and was one factor that led to Hitler's taking over the government. Even today, almost seventy years later, the experience affects the German attitude toward public debt. Indeed, the Germans have a constitutional provision that states that deficits should be incurred only for productive investments.

But we don't have to hire historians to see where deficit spending will take us. We have only to look around now. At South America. At Europe, East and West, and certainly at Russia.

Since the end of World War II, some of history's greatest national disasters have taken place right here in the Americas. North Americans used to laugh or shake their heads at the economies of the south that seemed always on the brink of collapse. Banana republics, we derisively called them. We're not laughing now, and we ought to be studying their experience.

- In 1985, just before Bolivia suffered a few months when inflation reached record annualized levels of 50,000 percent, the country's tax revenues covered only 15 percent of government spending. (U.S. tax revenues covered only 79 percent of *all* our government's 1992 spending. However, if we exclude Social Security taxes, revenues covered only 49 percent.)
- Argentina's deficit reached 11 percent of its gross domestic product in 1985, resulting in an annual inflation rate of about 672 percent. When the deficit is such a high percentage of a nation's GDP, government borrowing absorbs all the savings of the country and more. The only choices left are to borrow from foreigners or print money. Argentina chose the latter course. (The U.S. deficit in 1992 came to 7 percent of our GDP, up from only 2.7 percent a decade age. In 1995 it will reach Argentina's 1985 level of 11 percent.)
- In 1988, after amassing deficits equal to one-third of its GDP over a three-year period, Brazil had nearly 1,000 percent inflation. (The United States' projected deficit for the years 1993 through 1995 is nearly 30 percent of our estimated GDP for 1995.)

The charts we've reproduced on pages 149 to 151 show that in all three countries hyperinflation was preceded by a period of

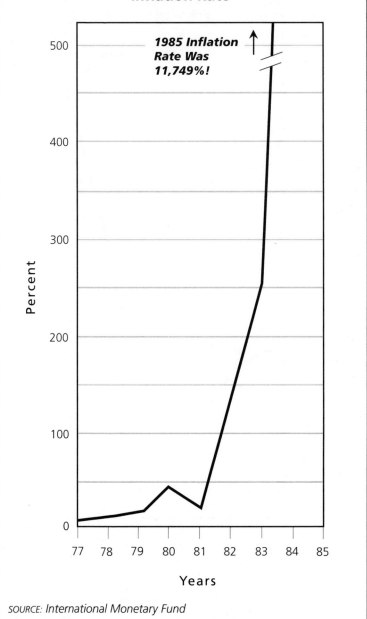

Bolivia
Inflation Rate

1985 Inflation Rate Was 11,749%!

Percent

500

400

300

200

100

0

77 78 79 80 81 82 83 84 85

Years

SOURCE: *International Monetary Fund*

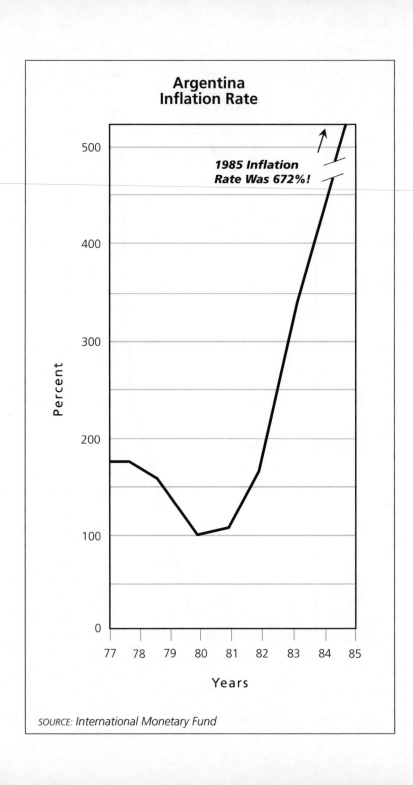

Argentina Inflation Rate

Percent

Years

1985 Inflation Rate Was 672%!

SOURCE: *International Monetary Fund*

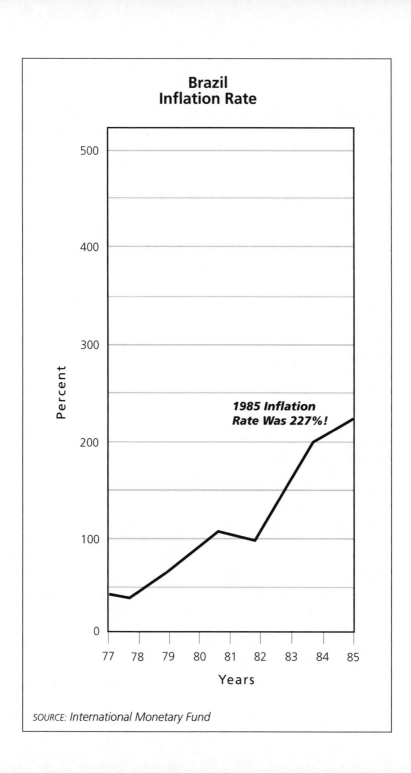

Brazil Inflation Rate

1985 Inflation Rate Was 227%!

Percent

Years

SOURCE: *International Monetary Fund*

deflation. What the charts don't disclose is that the deflation in each of these countries began with plunging real estate values and then spread to other areas, a scenario similar to the one that we in the United States are experiencing today.

Many people don't know that Argentina was a major global economic power during the first half of the twentieth century. At one point, it could boast that it was the fifth most productive nation in the world. By 1990, however, it had fallen to about seventieth, and the government had failed to take any effective action to cut its spending. Its bureaucracy was still bloated, its taxes so high they were uncollectable, and its corruption widespread and endemic. Argentina's foreign debt of $55.2 billion was the third largest in the developing world (following Mexico and Brazil), and its repayment record was so poor that investors could collect only 19 cents for every dollar they held in Argentinean debt.

In the seven years between 1983 and 1990, Argentina's per capita GDP shrank by 20 percent. Inflation in 1989 ran some 4,900 percent. In 1990, inflation ran at 1,340 percent, but that figure tells only part of the story. At one point, the annualized rate of inflation reached 20,000 percent. Argentina's per capita GDP was a paltry $2,250 and $2,560 respectively for 1989 and 1990. The country lopped six zeros off its currency in three years. The same, incidentally, is true in Brazil and Bolivia. (If the United States had a million-dollar note, scratching six zeros would reduce it to a dollar.) By 1990, then, Argentina's economy had just about bottomed out, and the people were begging for change.

In the spring of 1991, President Carlos Menem gave it to them. He introduced a new currency, cracked down on tax evaders, downsized the public sector, cut subsidies, proposed a balanced budget, and prohibited the government from printing money to finance its deficits. The results of his initiative have been astounding.

The budget deficit fell from 5 percent of GDP in 1990 to 1.8 percent of GDP in 1991; for the first quarter of 1992, the government actually ran a surplus. What's more, the economy had real growth (that is, after adjusting for inflation) of 5 percent in 1991 and had real growth of about 6 percent in 1992. Argentina hasn't solved all its problems, to be sure, but the vastly improved performance of its economy since President Menem took charge dramatically illustrates what can happen when a country finally tackles its deficit problems seriously. The policies are causing some pain, but most of the voters back them, since they realize that there will be long-term gains. Nonetheless, it has taken years of suffering to reach this point. The United States can expect to go through the same travail.

Argentina's South American neighbor Brazil, with the world's eighth-largest economy and sixth-greatest population, is a leading arms and small aircraft manufacturer and ranks second only to the United States in food exports. Yet galloping inflation and fiscal instability keep Brazil stuck in a minor role on the world stage. How galloping? A price index that was set at 100 in March 1986 reached 3,041,400 by February 1991 before it was discontinued.

Brazil's foreign debt, at $122.6 billion, is the largest in the developing world and nobody wants to own its notes. The country has often delayed repayment of its notes in the past, and it completely suspended all debt repayments in 1989. You can buy Brazilian treasury securities for about 25 percent of their face value. Like Argentina, Brazil has dropped six zeros from its currency in the last three years.

Most people don't realize just how much economic strength Brazil *could* have, if it could just rein in its runaway spending. In the early 1970s, its economy grew as fast as any in the world, expanding more than 7 percent annually from 1965 to 1980. Its GDP comes to about twice that of all of Eastern Europe, and in 1989, it had the third-largest trade surplus in the world — smaller only than Japan's and Germany's. Brazil is larger than the contiguous United States and has a population of more than 150 million. In some respects, its economic potential is greater than our own, but the political courage of its government is the same — that is, zero.

President Fernando Collor de Mello tried shock therapy when he took office in 1990. He slapped an eighteen-month freeze on 80 percent of Brazilian savings in order to halt inflationary spending. The radical measure worked, after a fashion. The inflation rate dropped from 6 percent *per day* to zero, but a deep recession followed, and the economics minister released the freeze on savings. Since the legislature kept right on spending and financing its deficits with the printing press (sound familiar?), inflation is raging once again. Prices rose by about 2,740 percent in 1990, and since then inflation has averaged approximately 20 percent *monthly* through 1992.

Brazil will continue to have severe economic problems as long as the government fails to bring its spending under control and fails to convince the public that the proposed reforms are genuine and not just business as usual.

As the nations of Eastern Europe — particularly Hungary and Poland — struggle to enter the global economy, their deficit-ridden histories and mountainous debt slow down their progress. They need to invest in infrastructure, industry, efficient federal administration, and modern financial systems, but huge portions of government resources are tied up in debt service, entitlement programs, and subsidies — not unlike our own situation in the United States.

Hungary probably has the most immediate promise of all the former Eastern Bloc countries, because it has had certain free-market liberties and substantial contact with the West. The Budapest stock exchange, for example, opened in 1964, and Hungary permitted some free-market activity as early as 1968. But the country's foreign debt of $2,000 per capita was Europe's highest in 1992. (Ours stood at $1,783 in 1992.) Foreign debt, in fact, comes to 100 percent of Hungary's GDP, and Hungarian executives and officials repeatedly cite the debt as being at the root of the nation's current problems. "It slows down the capacity of the country to acquire the capital and technology needed to improve economic performance," one embassy official noted. American industry should say the same.

Poland, the first of the Soviet Bloc countries to throw off Communist rule, introduced a "Big Bang" of economic reforms on January 1, 1990, but Poland, too, can't climb out from under its debt, which totaled about $48 billion, or close to 80 percent of the Polish GDP in 1991. Despite spending cuts, the government experienced its worst deficit ever that year, and, because its tax system collapsed, Polish officials once again resorted to the printing press. As a consequence, prices in 1991 more than doubled, and Poland's people and businesses are virtually bankrupt. Polish citizens, officially earning an average of $200 per month, spend practically everything they make just to buy food and pay rent.

Even Western Europe has a lesson or two for the United States about deficits, inflation, and dealing with debt. Italy in many ways is only a little ahead of the United States in stalking disaster. For some time now, Italy has had Western Europe's worst budget-deficit problem. The Italians' national debt surpassed 100 percent of their GDP at the end of 1990, up from 60 percent in 1980. (Ours rose from 34 percent of GDP in 1980 to 59 percent in 1990, was nearly 70 percent in 1992, and will top 100 percent in 1996.) Interest on the debt has for years been the largest item on Italy's budget. (In the United States, interest was the largest budget item in 1991; in 1993 this expense is exceeded only by the amount the government pays out in Social Security.) In 1990, Italy accounted for more than half of all government borrowing by European Community countries. (That year, the United States borrowed three times as much as Italy.)

In one respect, Italy's problem is not quite so large as the United States'. Italy's deficit would be roughly zero if it didn't have to pay interest on its debt. (In the United States, even if we excluded debt service, our federal government's budget in 1992 was still more than $100 billion in deficit.) But even though Italy has made efforts to cut its spending, it isn't out of the woods. Because its debt is so huge, it still must pay enormous amounts of interest, which causes its deficit — and debt — to continually climb, as will ours.

In Italy, however, deficits have made themselves felt in a high inflation rate, crushing interest rates, a shortage of capital, and massive unemployment. There is great inequity in the standard of living across the nation, and a consensus there holds that future generations will bear the burden of current spending. Heard this before?

Great Britain's economy a little more than a decade ago didn't so much crash as run aground. In 1976, the British government had to ask the International Monetary Fund for help in servicing its debt, an acute embarrassment to the once-mighty island kingdom. In 1979, with inflation near 14 percent, the British elected Margaret Thatcher to lighten ship. Her platform stressed fiscal conservatism, lower taxes, and a reduced public sector. Thatcher's unpleasant task was to remind Britons that though the public might make unlimited demands on the government for services, the government's resources were nonetheless finite. She had intestinal fortitude, a quality rare in the political arena.

In her years in office, Thatcher reconciled the difference between demand and supply. She lopped 100,000 civil servants off the payroll in 1980 alone, and she cut the tax rate by 3 percent. In 1984, she stood up to a national coal strike, refusing to meet wage demands that had accumulated like water in the economic bilge. She privatized many state-owned enterprises, including British Aerospace, British Airways, British Petroleum, and more. This privatization transferred some 800,000 government jobs to the private sector.

Prime Minister Thatcher did what was necessary to refloat Britain's economy so it could get under way again. She turned an $18.1 billion deficit into a $5.9 billion surplus. Thatcher used budget surpluses to pay back $47.7 billion of the country's debt, reducing it from 51 percent of GDP in 1979 to 27 percent by 1990, a remarkable feat that undoubtedly saved Great Britain.

Like any stern and demanding captain, Thatcher was not loved by all the officers and crew, who were reminded that they had to live within the limits of their resources. Nonetheless, she got England moving forward once again. From 1983 to 1990, its real annual GDP grew twice as fast as during 1973 to 1982, and real per capita GDP growth was almost one-quarter greater than the industrialized average. Unemployment, about 11 percent in the early 1980s, dropped to 6 percent in 1990. Between 1984 and 1990, Britain created three million jobs, by far the best record among large European nations; only Japan had higher labor productivity growth in the 1980s.

In an editorial reviewing Thatcher's performance, the *Financial Times* wrote, "In the 1980s, the U.K.'s economy ceased to be the laughing stock of the western world." Clinton's performance will determine whether a *New York Times* editorial, for example, will say the same for the U.S. economy years from now — or if that editorial will read: "In the 1990s, the U.S. economy totally collapsed under a crushing burden of debt."

If only we could clone Margaret Thatcher — or elect a chief executive with such strong deficit-cutting will — for our country.

Some economists think that if the United States is very, very lucky, it can fix its debt/deficit problems and suffer no more in the process than Great Britain did in the last dozen years. However, they will be proven wrong if our new president and Congress do not change from their behavior during the first few months of 1993. In the next chapter, you'll hear about some of the reality-avoidance tactics of the Clinton administration that show that this country *still* needs change — and fast.

PART
2

Averting Disaster

One thing is certain in these troubled times: What we do now will determine what happens to us later — both as individuals and as a nation.

Little time remains for us to act, and, even then, our actions must be decisive, bold, and radical if they are to prove effective.

Forestalling the demise of our country requires the commitment and participation of all of us — *now*.

10

Champagne Appetite on a Beer Income

AS a presidential candidate, Bill Clinton had a lot to say about what he would do for the nation's economy, the government's annual deficits, and the ballooning national debt. Now, as president, Clinton still talks about these issues, but, so far, he has failed to take any meaningful action. In fact, he sounds like Reagan.

When he first took office, President Clinton didn't make the deficit and national debt his first priority. Instead, he allowed his attention and political agenda to wander, spending — or mis-spending — valuable time on other issues, including his first major public-policy debate, the controversial gays-in-the-military question. One of his next moves, in February, was to introduce the Emergency Supplemental Appropriations Bill of 1993, a proposal that would have the government throw $16 billion it didn't have into a short-term, seasonal jobs program that would create absolutely no long-term value. Fortunately for the country, a Senate filibuster stopped this politically motivated and totally wasteful expenditure, and the bill was withdrawn on April 21. He also let himself be distracted by a revolving door of attorney general nominees — two of whom withdrew their names from consideration because of the short-lived controversy that the media dubbed "Nannygate."

Meanwhile, Congress has been far from blameless for the detours on the road to fiscal soundness. "It doesn't do any good to yell at us about our spending," Senator Daniel Moynihan stated in early 1993, "because we can't do anything about it." With the Democrats having chaired the crucial Appropriations Committee for the last forty years, the New York senator's statement seems disingenuous at best. Moynihan, though, has had more to say about our country's economic problems. "Now, it's our deficit," he quipped the day after the Democrats won the election. Moynihan chairs the Senate Finance Committee, which approves all appropriations before they go to the floor of the Senate — so whose deficit did he think it was the previous week?

Because of pressure from constituents at home, longtime Democratic legislators have asked for deeper cuts than Clinton proposed, but they still seem ruled by the NIMBY, or "Not In My Back Yard," principle, which makes their proposed cuts less fruitful than might otherwise have been the case. Some freshman members of Congress, by contrast, have been more than willing to make deep budget cuts. Many of them — such as Representatives Samuel Coppersmith (D-AZ), Richard Pombo (R-CA), and Nathan Deal (D-GA) — were elected because they understood the mortal danger of the federal budget deficit and clearly communicated their sincere concern to voters. But some of the other new representatives, in order to secure certain committee appointments, have let themselves get co-opted, while old-timers, such as Jamie Whitten (D-MS), have promised their constituents pork-barrel projects — in Whitten's case, the continued financing of plants that are involved in the Advanced Solid-Rocket Motor (ASRM) program. (See Chapter 12, "A Debt-Buster's Tool Kit for Congress," for details.)

Another huge roadblock to our country's secure fiscal future has also emerged in the form of an angry, drawn-out, and seemingly politically inspired argument over the administration's proposed health-care program. The goals of equalizing health care in this country and slashing skyrocketing medical costs are admirable and necessary. If we don't get these expenses under control, deficit reduction may never become a reality. But, as of this writing, the so-called health-care reform package looks as if it will end up as yet another entitlement program, adding as much as $50 to $150 billion a year in health-care costs with a heavy portion of added administrative costs.

But who cares about the country if the health-care payouts buy reelection votes?

No one except the taxpayers.

If the 1992 campaign did nothing else, it gave voters a disturbing reminder of the country's debt and deficit crisis. Polls since Clinton's first budget proposal have revealed that more than half of the country disapproves of the president's preference for taxes over spending cuts. Yet, neither the president nor Congress seems to be taking the crisis — or us — seriously. Why do we say that?

Consider the following:

- **Clinton said the size of the deficit surprised him.**

During the last campaign, both Bush and Clinton constantly cited gross underestimates of the federal budget deficit, and both candidates quickly reestimated their deficit projections following the election, as shown here in the table below. When the Bush administration came up with new — and larger — estimates of future deficits two weeks before Clinton took the oath of office, the president-elect called the news an "unsettling revelation." Both the president and the president-elect should have known that the published numbers they saw were based on unrealistic assumptions and would not come close to the real deficit. Furthermore, they constantly ignored the true deficit being offset by spending monies from our supposed "trust" funds.

The 1994 deficit was now projected to be larger than the $274

Underestimating the Budget Deficit

Year	Candidate Clinton	Post-election Clinton
1993	$295.7 billion	$332.0 billion
1994	$243.0	$264.1
1995	$174.0	$246.7
1996	$141.0	$211.7
1997	—	$214.0
1998	—	$250.5

SOURCES: "Candidate" figures from Putting People First, July 1992. Campaign plan assuming moderate economic growth. "Post-election" figures from Budget of U.S. Government, Fiscal Year 1994.

Year	Candidate Bush	Post-election Bush
1993	$341.0 billion	$327.3 billion
1994	$274.2	$292.4
1995	$218.4	$272.4
1996	$217.7	$266.4
1997	$236.7	$305.0
1998	$273.4	$319.8

SOURCES: "Candidate" figures from The President's Budget and Economic Growth Agenda, July 1992, OMB. "Post-election" figures from Budget Baselines, Historical Data & Alternatives for the Future, January 1993, OMB.

billion the Bush people had already conceded and then corrected. Back in August 1992, the Congressional Budget Office's *Economic and Budget Outlook* had upped the bad news, increasing the projected deficits for 1994 to 1997 by $161 billion. Even at that, all the projections ignored the amount that the Treasury borrows, and will borrow, from Social Security and other "trust" funds — leaving, as we've seen, IOUs in exchange. The bad numbers of the national deficit are the dirty secret that Washington officialdom, like a flock of head-down ostriches, tries to ignore.

- **The first specific economic proposal that Clinton made called for increasing the deficit.**

Clinton's theory appears to be that if he can create enough jobs and provide medical coverage for those who don't have it, regardless of the ultimate cost, he can keep his lease on the White House until the year 2000. That seemed to be the object of the so-called stimulus package that Clinton tried to push through Congress, which would have increased the size of the 1993 deficit by about $16 billion. Stan Cooper, a Democratic representative from Arizona, looked at Clinton's economic stimulus package and asked the obvious question. "Does it makes sense," he inquired, "to have one last piece of chocolate fudge pie before you go on a diet?"

This proposal to create temporary jobs with government money was, in fact, a hoax. What happened to the economics Clinton learned as a Rhodes Scholar? He should have known that real jobs are the result of economic growth in the private sector. Clinton's kind of "economic stimulus" — make-work jobs at taxpayer expense — wouldn't have stimulated real job creation at all. On the contrary, by taking investment capital out of the economy, it would have slowed it. In the end, those temporary jobs would have disappeared, or worse, become an addition to our bloated entitlement programs. Without any economic justification, it all seems to add up to an embarrassing attempt to buy future votes.

- **Next, Clinton proposed the largest tax increase in the history of the United States.**

The government already takes in 400 percent more in taxes than it did in 1983, largely because of the two record tax boosts under Reagan and Bush — but Clinton's proposed hike would be the biggest tax increase in U.S. history. There is no question that the chief executive has the same propensity to overspend as his predecessors, while the country continues its march toward financial disaster. The difference is that this time he advocates a hike in taxes on almost everything, including income taxes, corporate taxes, energy taxes, excise taxes, inheritance taxes, and taxes on foreign corporations. Some Washington insiders even expect proposals for a new payroll tax to pay for the projected national health program. Of course, the new taxes will fall most heavily on the 6 percent of the people who already pay more than 45 percent of personal income taxes. And, in contrast to Clinton's campaign platform of tax breaks for the middle class, Clinton's first economic proposal included an energy tax that would have come out of middle-class taxpayers' pockets.

In addition, the dramatic reduction in inheritance taxes under Reagan is about to be canceled out by the Clinton administration's suggested boost in these taxes. Clinton's budget, as first presented, even raised the possibility of national sales and energy taxes — until that proposal ran into a congressional stone wall. I predict that, in spite of massive new tax levies, the yearly budget deficit will continue to rise in the long term, with possibly a short-term hiatus. The same thing occurred with Reagan in 1987 and 1988. Moreover, taxes that should be used to reduce the debt will be wasted.

On top of the $67.4 billion in additional taxes that Washington would have collected just from projected economic growth between 1993 and 1994, Clinton proposed $36 billion in new taxes. Altogether, that's $103.4 billion in additional tax revenues for Congress to spend. A total of $168.9 billion in new fees and charges have also been proposed. Instead of using the extra $270 billion revenue to offset the deficit, spending was budgeted to outpace revenues by about $381 billion, as revealed by the gross deficit figures in the 1994 budget proposal.

Alan Greenspan, the chairman of the Federal Reserve, has said repeatedly, "The best way by far to cut the budget deficit is by spending cuts rather than tax increases." But in Clinton's original plan, tax increases outnumbered spending cuts by two to one.

- **Clinton's plan calls for higher taxes first, spending cuts later.**

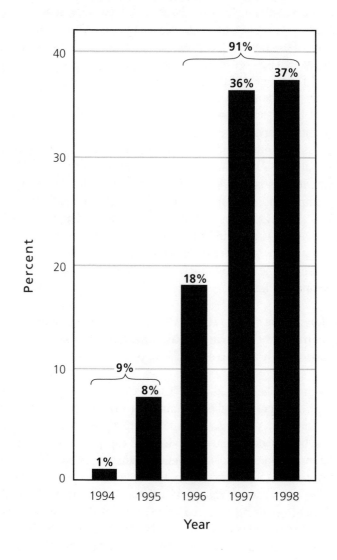

Back-end Cuts
Clinton's Proposed Spending Cuts (Excluding Social Security) as a Percentage of Total Cuts

SOURCE: OMB

Ninety-one percent of the so-called spending cuts outlined in Clinton's first budget proposal were slated to occur in 1996, 1997, and 1998, the bulk of them in his planned second term. Even if they do come about, they will have been long since submerged by ever-growing deficit expenses. In Washington, later means never. We know how quickly Congress and Clinton are blowing through the spending caps set by Bush and Congress in 1990, just as Reagan and Bush ignored the Gramm-Rudman guidelines.

If our president and members of this Congress don't have the courage to do what has to be done by trimming back reckless governmental spending, what on earth makes them think that any Congress and any president will act more honorably? Do they believe that the American people are fools, constantly willing to put up with this lack of fiscal responsibility? Clinton postponed the most important and urgent spending reforms until 1996 and 1997 — "savings" from nondefense areas amounting to about $30 billion over 1994 and 1995 and $108 billion later on. The question is: Why not now? When the deficit and debt are our worst national sicknesses, why wait two more years before we get even a minuscule and insulting dose of medicine?

- **On January 21, 1993, Clinton had the power to reinstate the Gramm-Rudman-Hollings spending caps with the stroke of a pen. He didn't.**

This means he missed a big chance to get spending under control and a chance to take advantage of one of President Bush's major blunders at the same time. In 1990, Bush and Congress made a budget deal that eliminated the cap put on the deficit by the Gramm-Rudman-Hollings Deficit Reduction Act of 1985. They agreed to let the limitation on the deficit float ever higher as spending grew every year. Did Clinton bother to find out that entitlement spending went up an average of $23.5 billion a year under Gramm-Rudman, and after that, an average of $67.5 billion yearly? Clinton didn't mention that many of the spending cuts he proposed along with tax increases were already mandated by that same 1990 deficit-reduction agreement between Bush and Congress. In fact, his proposals for spending in 1994 violated the 1990 Budget Enforcement Act by more than $5 billion in 1994 and by almost $14 billion in 1995. The president, even with a law degree from Yale, still has to figure out how to live within the law.

- **Clinton has practically ignored the nation's biggest and fastest-growing budget drain — the so-called entitlement (mandatory) portions of the budget.**

The Congressional Budget Office (CBO) projections for 1993 show discretionary spending, also called the cost of running the government, at $547 billion. For 1998, they show it at $584 billion, or virtually no increase in real terms. Entitlement spending (discussed on pages 27–28), meanwhile, will soar from $770 billion in 1993 to $1.1 trillion in 1998, or 43 percent, as the graph on page 170 shows.

Clinton has failed to realize that running a deficit to ensure the viability of entitlement programs will eventually destroy these very programs, one way or another. Allowing the deficits to continue to grow will inevitably cause more inflation. As inflation increases, the value of the benefits paid to entitlement-program beneficiaries will decrease, because the value of the dollars they are paid will fall. Ultimately, the poor will be hurt rather than helped. Inflation is a cruel tax on everyone, especially the poor. Its only specious benefit would be that it permits the government to repay its borrowing with inflated dollars.

The proposed national health-care plan is likely to be nothing more than another huge entitlement program, adding to our already skyrocketing entitlement costs. Robert D. Reischauer, director of the Congressional Budget Office, has repeatedly stated that any new plan to extend health-care coverage to millions of uninsured Americans and otherwise improve the nation's health-care system would cost more money, not less. "In the short run,

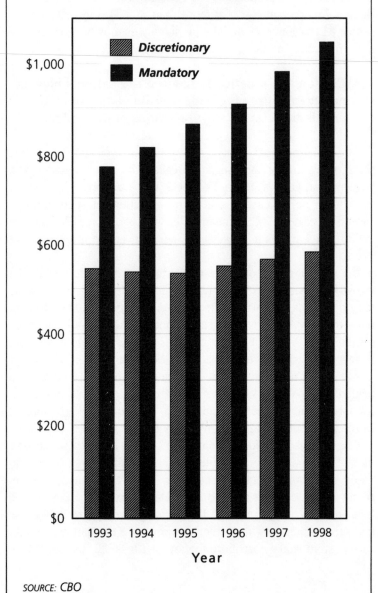

Projected Growth of Mandatory and Discretionary Spending
(In Billions of Dollars)

over the next ten years," he says, "it will be exceedingly difficult to realize any significant budgetary savings."

- **The president must stop playing word games with the budget.**

Many of the "spending cuts" included in the 1994 budget are really spending increases. Instead of making real cuts in spending, "user fees" are proposed to be collected from the public to enable spending increases in various programs. These revenues are then recorded in a subaccount to offset additional spending and are ultimately reported in the budget as spending cuts. For example, the budget proposes to triple fees on meat and poultry packers, bringing in additional revenues of $170 million. The federal meat-inspection service would then be permitted to spend $74 million more than it spent last year. The $96 million that is left after the additional spending that is proposed is then reported as a spending cut. This trick is simply masking increased spending, and is basically a lie — spending in these areas is not being cut at all. And speaking of word games, the new administration is not fooling anyone by calling taxes "contributions" and spending increases "investments." All that does is insult people's intelligence.

- **To make the national debt consist primarily of short-term bonds is to court long-term disaster.**

No financial consultant would ever advise a company to carry all its debt in short-term loans, even if short-term interest rates were far cheaper. The reason is no secret. The interest savings could be short-lived, and any increase in the short-term rates might drive the company right out of business. Only a fool or a desperate person would take such a risk. At a time when industry is taking advantage of low interest rates by extending its debt instruments, the government is doing the opposite just to claim that it benefited from a temporary reduction in the interest on our national debt. The program of shifting much of the country's debt into the short-term can only be called a blueprint for future disaster. For now, it will lower the borrowing cost. But what happens when rates go up? — and they certainly will. Already Alan Greenspan is being jawboned to hold down interest rates at a time when inflation appears just over the horizon. Even our Fed may be a political pawn. Up goes the budget deficit and, of course, the debt, too, as soon as the short-term notes have to be rolled over and financed at higher interest rates. Just recall that early in the 1980s, short-term Treasury bonds paid up to 14 percent interest.

- **Clinton has failed to put in place a strong program to reduce inefficiency and waste in government.**

Where is all the action he promised on reducing inefficiency and waste? Comptroller General Charles Bowsher prepared a report about this horrendous situation at the president's request. The report detailed billions of dollars that the government has lost through widespread fiscal mismanagement. Parts of the government, Bowsher's report said, can't even keep a decent set of financial books, and they can't collect the money they're owed. For instance, more than one-third of the $20.5 billion in loans made by the Farmers Home Administration (FmHA) are delinquent. "These widespread financial weaknesses are crippling the ability of our leaders to effectively run our federal government," the report concluded. Early on Clinton made a big show of saving money by cutting the size of the White House staff, but this "savings" was largely illusory. Nothing has been done about reducing excess workers in other parts of the government. And Congress has as many staff aides as before.

So where do we stand? As of now, the president and his administration are shirking their primary responsibility to the nation. They have not attacked the deficit by attempting to control spending, nor have they even tried to lead the government onto the path of fiscal responsibility. Congress continues to shell out cash in a manner that is totally out of proportion with national economic growth. (In 1965, congressional spending came to just 17.6 percent of GDP; by 1993 it was nearly 24 percent.) And raising taxes does nothing to rein in our senators and representatives; their appetite for spending can only be curbed with tough discipline on the part of both parties.

If the president were really serious about deficit reduction, he would propose a clear and decisive strategy, and he would enlist the support of the American people to impose that strategy on Congress. In the end, it is only political considerations that stand between us and a balanced budget. With a strong leader and a strong plan, and with the voters holding the feet of their elected representatives to the fire, we could break the back of the national debt.

We offer two such bold deficit-reduction plans in the next chapter of this book. Implementing either would definitely be a step in the right direction. Of course, the process won't be easy. And it would require all of us to finally admit that we can't keep indulging our champagne tastes on a beer income. But when you consider the alternative — total economic disaster on a scale few of us can even imagine — it doesn't sound that difficult after all.

11

What We Must Do *Now!*

A man in the prime of his life is lying on an operating table, bleeding from open wounds. A team of surgeons is busily clipping his toenails.

The United States desperately needs fiscal surgery to staunch the dollars bleeding from its deficit wounds. Congress and the president busily argue over which of the country's toenails to clip.

The operation needed to save this country already is almost too late. The patient's middle class is about to go under. Its money is about to inflate. Its economic pulse is weak, and its industrial heart is under stress. In just two years, without surgery to close its wounds, the patient — that's us — will fall into an economic coma. Then someone will have to feed us, as we're today feeding Somalia, for instance, and many of the now-independent states of what was once the Eastern Bloc. Like them, we'll be vulnerable to exploitation, dependent on the kindness of foreign strangers, and, in a word, pathetic — the hulk of a once-great nation.

I hope it doesn't happen. I hope Americans don't have to stand in line for bread; that we don't have to kowtow to foreign bankers and governments; that this great country doesn't have to yield its independence and abandon its self-respect. I hope we don't have to suffer the pain of self-inflicted shame. But the odds of American survival as a proud, independent nation have already grown terribly slim.

We will die if we don't — to switch metaphors quickly — declare war soon. Not a military war. The threat is not external. We need a fiscal war to defend us against ourselves, and we need it fast because the battle is almost lost before the fighting has even begun.

This war must have two phases. First we need an attack on the deficit. We absolutely must reduce it to zero to avert the looming crisis, and need to do so very quickly. In phase two, we must attack our debt, which almost everyone still tries to ignore.

In a war, the president takes the leadership, the Congress closes partisan ranks, and we the people work and sacrifice in whatever measure is required to support our military forces, the professionals who fight in our name.

In this war against years of continuous overspending and debt, we need to organize ourselves in much the same way, because the threat facing us is more serious and more potentially devastating than any we have ever confronted before. To fight this war, we need leadership, political unity of purpose, the work and the sacrifice of the people, and an army of experts to do battle.

President Bill Clinton, as our leader and commander-in-chief, must persuade the people that, of all the problems the country currently faces, the deficit and debt issues have to take first priority. But first he must convince himself. If these two related problems aren't fixed, he'll have to say, none of the others will matter in the long run. He must make his case with the voters, fire their enthusiasm for the battle, and then act with confidence and authority to move the country into a wartime stance. The president must demand and get the assurance of leaders in both houses of Congress and in both political parties that they will set aside partisan and personal differences and pledge their enthusiastic support to winning this war. We voters have to let both branches of government — the executive and the legislative — know that we won't stand for more delay and infighting. We have to get the word to politicians that we'll reelect those who support this war of financial independence, and that we'll oust those who don't. We must demand their commitment to victory.

This commitment to victory by politicians and citizens is essential, because no one — citizen or corporation — wants to sacrifice today for a policy that will change or fizzle tomorrow. No one in Brazil, for instance, believes what the government says about mending its deficit-spending ways. Why should they? In the past decade, Brazilian authorities have introduced eight monetary stabilization plans, five different currencies, five wage and price freezes, fifty-four sets of price control guidelines, nineteen government decrees of fiscal austerity, and eighteen changes in the official exchange rate. Brazilians call Brasilia, their capital city, "Fantasy Island." Inflation, for all the government's flailing at it, is still wildly out of control in Brazil.

Hungary, in contrast, made good on its promise to start paying the interest on its foreign debt, which has helped that nation attract more foreign investment capital than all the other former Eastern Bloc countries combined, with the exception of East Germany. Likewise, England's Margaret Thatcher acquired great credibility during her tenure as prime minster. "She was clear about what she planned to do, and she showed the resolve to stay the course," explained a British economist, "and as a result, she won the support of 99 percent of the business community and most of the public." I can only hope that President Clinton will refocus his scattered energies and do the same.

If the nation is going to win the war against its own debt and deficit, here's what the government must do:

Establish Its Credibility with the Public

The credibility of the U.S. government, or rather its current absence, is a serious handicap for a country that has to unite in its own defense. The slick gimmickry and shameful deceit now practiced by the executive and the legislative branches have to end. Our leaders must, for one, stop masking the size and the seriousness of the deficit situation. They have to start telling the truth. If we don't know what we're up against, we can't fight it, but more and more of the American people are beginning to sense how terribly serious our fiscal problem is and are angry about it.

Put a General in Charge of the War

With the people and the Congress united behind him, President Clinton must find a field general — someone such as Peter Grace or Ross Perot — whose past experience and unique qualities can recruit and lead an army of highly trained and time-tested cost-cutters who can attack and defeat the deficit. For his senior commanders, the general whom the president chooses will need to draft men and women with experience in turning failing companies around. The army's colonels would come from the country's top management consulting and accounting firms — all personnel who have spent their careers in cost reduction. Additionally, he'll need to recruit people for crisis-management task forces — specialists who are normally brought into bankrupt or near-bankrupt companies to manage cash flow for survival. The foot soldiers in this antideficit army that the field general would recruit shouldn't be administrators and operating managers from the corporate world. They should be tough cost-cutters, people who know how to spot red tape and sniff out fat and then what to do with it.

This army, numbering perhaps 1,000 to 1,500 souls in all, would work pro bono, their wages and salaries paid by their civilian employers for the duration of the war. As the Grace Commission was divided into teams, this army would be divided into battalions, each assigned to tackle overspending in a particular sector of the government. If, for instance, the commanding general divided his forces into fifty battalions, each battalion would be assigned a savings objective — say, $10 billion — to meet within one year. With luck, the front-line action in this war will require no more than three years, after which the army can disband — except for a small force of observers that would monitor government spending and warn of any new deficit outbreaks.

Create a Deficit-War Cabinet

Just as the president has a military-war cabinet, he should have a deficit-war cabinet. The president would chair this body, which would consist of top congressional leaders of both houses and of both parties and the comptroller general of the United States. The president and deficit-war cabinet would set overall strategy, support the commanding general's battle plans, and see that appropriate legislation is enacted, just as Governor Hugh Carey did when New York City nearly went bankrupt in 1975.

Part of the war cabinet's job would be to take the political heat when resistance appears from one group or another whose benefits or desires may be affected by the war. The deficit-war cabinet must keep driving home the message that there is a larger battle to be won, and that cutting costs doesn't necessarily result in fewer services or a reduction of their quality. We can reduce costs simply by doing the same jobs more efficiently. The doubters and naysayers must also be reminded that each of the programs subject to cutting will go through a cost-benefit analysis. Those programs whose benefits justify their costs should be retained, those that don't must be restructured or eliminated.

Most of us already have been forced to do more with less. Faced with declining revenues, corporations are restructuring and becoming more efficient. Similarly, individuals, pinched by recession, are reexamining their finances and streamlining their spending. Today, for example, Figgie International enjoys 65 percent higher sales while still operating on its 1985 level of spending, and has 40 percent fewer employees. If individuals and corporations can learn how to allocate resources more efficiently, so, too, can government — with a lot of help.

Make Bold Budget Changes

How should the deficit-cutting army proceed? As its first priority, it should institute sweeping, overall change; its second priority should be to slash or eliminate specific programs. In the following chapter, we give examples of specific cuts that our deficit fighters could make. For now, let's look at two possible methods for imposing overall reductions.

Our national fiscal woes aren't a result of our paying too little in taxes. Our problem is that government spending continues to grow significantly faster than our national income — a situation that has persisted since 1970. When Ronald Reagan took office in 1981, one of his main campaign promises was to balance the federal budget. At that time, spending came to 113 percent of income — that is, for every $100 that the government collected in revenue, it spent $113. Reagan, however, failed to deliver on his promise. By the end of his two terms spending had climbed to 117 percent of income.

When former president George Bush ran for office, he made the same campaign pledge as Reagan. But instead of becoming smaller during Bush's four years, the spending bite only continued to increase, rising by the end of his first term to 127 percent of income. During Bush's tenure, spending as a percentage of gross domestic product (GDP) also went up, from 22 percent to 23.5 percent.

The Congressional Budget Office (CBO) expects this ominous trend to continue under President Bill Clinton. That means for the past thirteen years — and probably continuing for three more — spending has been taking a bigger and bigger chunk out of the country's total income. More corporate and personal taxes don't help; they only allow the bite to get bigger. Unless the congressional and presidential appetites are curbed, they will soon swallow the whole nation.

Here are two bold budget changes we could take to reduce the government's craving. If the president and Congress had the courage to implement them now, they could together balance the budget in five years — and keep it balanced.

Limit Spending Growth

First, we must cap government spending growth at no higher than 4 percent a year. This strategy, called the "4 percent solution," was first devised by Scott Hodge of the Heritage Foundation. Enacting it would save about $306.6 billion in five years. Just think: 4 percent growth would give the government approximately $40 billion more to spend each year, while reducing projected spending by $306 billion in five years. Today, even a dedicated budget-cutter can't touch our mandatory programs. They grow according to whatever amounts are necessary to pay benefits to eligible beneficiaries. Since 1988, the programs have been growing an average of 10 percent a year, and are three to four times higher than our GDP.

In 1962, mandatory programs came to 5 percent of our national income and discretionary programs were 13.5 percent. Today, discretionary spending has declined to 9.2 percent, and mandatory spending has increased from 5 percent to 12.8 percent. In order to achieve the 4 percent cap in spending growth, we need to change the system by which Congress appropriates money. Congress needs to be forced to find ways to cut spending in one part of the budget before it spends money in another, so that its overall level of spending does not increase. Currently, if Congress cuts spending in one area of the budget, it does not have the power to spend that "saved" money in another area. That means lawmakers can't use savings from, say, a cut in a discretionary program to help with a pressing need in a mandatory program, and vice versa. Ironically, this system provides Congress with no incentive to cut spending in any category.

We must knock down the barriers, often called "firewalls," that exist between spending categories. The 4 percent plan would enable Congress to "borrow" (that is, cut) money from wasteful or inefficient programs, then spend that money elsewhere. With tongue firmly implanted in cheek, Scott Hodge suggests that few people would miss the $100,000 study of the century-old Hatfield-McCoy feud or the $121 million annually allotted to maintain the National Helium Reserve — which is presumably there in case we suddenly wanted to build a lot of dirigibles. Talk about inflated costs!

Eliminate COLAs

Second, we must take a break from handing out annual cost-of-living adjustments (COLAs) for federal retirement and other non-means-tested programs. Instead, adjustments can be made every five years. COLAs are unsound and can't be properly funded. There is no fundamental reason for automatic COLAs and they can't be actuarially determined. Periodic adjustments every five years can be.

For every five years the government skips increasing these benefits, federal outlays would be reduced by $125.9 billion. Furthermore, by bringing the deficit under control, we can greatly reduce the risk of inflation, which reduces the need for these adjustments in the first place. Moreover, the sacrifices people would have to make wouldn't be too hard.

We must remember that with only moderate economic growth, the government does receive between $60 to $65 billion in additional tax revenues each year. With the two programs I have suggested, we would save enough to balance the budget by fiscal 1998, providing the 4 percent limitation was observed, that entitlement programs were purged of unnecessary eligibility, and no new programs were added in the entitlement area.

The task *is* daunting — as you can see by looking at the chart on page 183. Imagine: one-fifth of our government's outlays go toward the interest on the massive national debt! This change amounts to half our government's income from personal and corporate income taxes. To call that an unproductive use of our money may be the understatement of the century.

Balanced budgets could have been achieved in Carter's era as they could be in Clinton's, with no new taxes and no drift toward socialism and class warfare. While these solutions are theoretical, they *will* work. In addition, there is still tremendous opportunity to use outsiders to cut costs in all other areas of government. We could use the surplus to pay down debt and restore fiscal sanity and responsibility to this country before it is too late.

We need to develop cost-conscious statesmen to run this country, not more politicians.

Establish Postwar Reforms

The deficit-fighting army will have another task to confront: There's no point in chopping expenditures from the government budget while leaving the government process untouched. If we do that, the same crisis we have today will develop again sooner or later, and probably sooner. Just as corporations are becoming more efficient by reducing the layers of management between workers and top executives and streamlining systems — so too must the government.

Accordingly, the cost-reduction general's troops would look for ways to reduce the number of empty suits with titles that scurry through the White House halls. They should also find ways to cut the large number of congressional committees and subcommittees that get in the way of congressional action. But theirs will not be only a search-and-destroy mission. They must help, as well, create a process through which government leaders can communicate more quickly and effectively with each other and with the American people.

The second phase of our war must be debt reduction. It's not enough just to eliminate deficit spending. We also have to reduce our outstanding national debt.

Why?

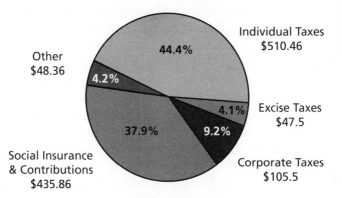

Where We Get Our Tax Revenues:
1993 Federal Receipts
(Billions of Dollars)

Individual Taxes
$510.46

44.4%

Other
$48.36

4.2%

4.1%

Excise Taxes
$47.5

37.9%

9.2%

Social Insurance
& Contributions
$435.86

Corporate Taxes
$105.5

Total: $1,148 Billion

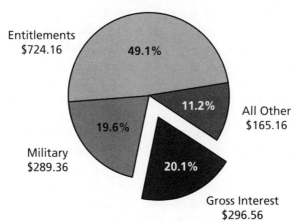

Where We Spend Them:
1993 Federal Outlays
(Billions of Dollars)

Entitlements
$724.16

49.1%

11.2%

All Other
$165.16

19.6%

20.1%

Military
$289.36

Gross Interest
$296.56

Total: $1,475 Billion

SOURCE: *OMB*

Because if we don't reduce the debt substantially and soon, we will remain vulnerable to attack by rising interest rates. The United States can't operate under the threat that this debt level poses any more than England could. As we noted in Chapter 9, Margaret Thatcher reduced England's outstanding debt from 51 percent of GDP in 1979 to 27 percent by 1990.

Even if we launch all-out war against the deficit now, the national debt will continue to climb. If interest rates remain at their currently low level — and they almost certainly will not — the interest charges will soon become the largest single expenditure the government makes. If interest rates double, which they easily could, our ability to service our debt and keep government spending within the limits of government revenues would be tested severely. The more and sooner we can cut the debt, the less vulnerable to interest rate shock we become. While interest rates are relatively low today, remember that just ten years ago short-term rates reached 14 percent and the prime rate hit 21 percent.

We *can* cut the debt — by limiting government spending growth to 4 percent a year, by putting COLAs on a five-year rather than an annual cycle, and by launching a serious effort to eliminate government waste.

Two additional steps could help, albeit in small ways, to reduce our debt. First, we should examine the possibilities of privatizing those areas of the government which could and should stand on their own in the private business arena. Second, the government might contract out on a competitive basis many of the services it now provides for citizens and for itself. At the Grace Commission, when we tested this we found potential savings of up to 50 percent. Such a move would also accomplish the government's long-range goal of improving, expanding, and creating more minority businesses.

Privatization just means selling certain government assets or operations to the private sector. Not only would we remove the operating losses from these areas from the government books, we would also collect funds from the sale of those operations, just as Great Britain under Margaret Thatcher did with the sale of British Aerospace, British Steel, and other state-owned businesses. The hardest part of privatization won't be doing it, but cutting through the plethora of federal laws that block it in one way or another. Identifying the operations to privatize would be one of the tasks of the cost-cutting general and his experts from the private sector.

Even without selling off assets, the government might find that many of its services would be performed more efficiently by a private operator. Likewise, a private company might better administer the Social Security system — the processing of claims, payment of checks, and so forth. Furthermore, if Social Security and other government trust funds were managed by private money managers, as former Delaware Governor Pete DuPont suggested during the 1988 presidential primaries, the money in these trust funds would be invested in productive ways instead of in government securities. Any professional investment manager could do better than the latter.

As important as the actions the government must take in this war to eliminate its deficits and pay down its debt, there are some expedient moves it must not make:

Don't Raise Taxes under Any Conditions

Frequently, governments opt for tax hikes over spending cuts, thereby failing to attack the root cause of their deficits. Not only do higher taxes retard economic growth, but as tax receipts grew during the 1980s, our government contrived to find ways to spend those increases and more. Politicians always will. Raising taxes does not eliminate deficit spending. It never has. We saw that demonstrated when Congress gave us our largest tax increase package in history in 1990, and then in 1991 and 1992 set all-time records for budget deficits.

Don't Raid Savings to Pay for Current Expenditures

Social Security and other federal trust funds must revert to the status of true trust accounts for the dollars that remain after expenses are deducted. The government must stop tapping these funds — including those for railroad retirement, highways, and so on — to cover up its deficits.

When it comes to Social Security, we have only two choices if we are to meet the retirement needs of our citizens in twenty-first-century America. One is to increase taxes now to pay for our Social Security benefits; the other is to increase taxes on the next generation, so the government can redeem the bonds in the Social Security account in order to pay our Social Security benefits. Either way, we will have to increase taxes. The simple fact is, with the current way fund revenues are being spent, Social Security benefits in the year 2010 will have to be paid directly out of the taxes withheld from the paychecks of people who are still working — and the ratio of workers to recipients will then be 3 to 1, down from 50 to 1 in 1939.

We need to face reality and tell some people that the generous Social Security benefits they are planning on when they retire won't be there. We need to cut the current Social Security tax and give people a tax incentive to save their own money for their own retirement. But attempts to do this will likely be derailed by politicians who can't wait to get their hands on any "excess" in order to use it for additional programs and to hide the true amount of the deficit they're creating.

Don't Allow Government Agencies to Create Debt

The danger in letting federal agencies assume or guarantee the debt of nongovernment borrowers is that taxpayers inevitably will have to make good on at least a portion of those obligations. The collapse of the thrift industry, for instance, has saddled taxpayers with as much as $500 billion in added obligations — that is the amount that the government will spend to reimburse depositors at failed savings and loans.

Loans and loan guarantees held by the Federal Home Loan Mortgage Corporation, Federal National Mortgage Association, Federal Housing Administration, Veterans Administration, and Farmers Home Administration (FmHA) — to name only a few such agencies — are part of the federal government's existing $6.6 trillion loan portfolio. Government loans and loan guarantees are ticking time bombs that have to be defused. The present liability from all these programs amounts to $224 billion.

Don't Monetize the Debt

Thus far, the United States has resisted the strategy used by so many other governments faced with overwhelming deficits: It has not tried to cover its debts by simply printing more money. We must continue that resolve; otherwise, all will be lost.

Don't Count on a Balanced-Budget Amendment to Solve Our Problems — It Will Be a Delusion

Adopting a constitutional amendment that would make it mandatory for Congress to balance the federal budget might provide a safety net for the future, but it won't prevent the crisis we're now facing. First, we must have thirty-four state legislatures approve resolutions calling for a constitutional convention. Once this occurs it will take at least three years to get the required number of thirty-eight states to ratify the amendment. We can't wait that long. With three more years of huge deficits, we'll have missed any chance of getting out from under our debt and our increased interest liability.

Moreover, any balanced-budget amendment could easily be

evaded. Congress would simply play the same tricks it has played in the past — placing expenditures off budget, classifying proposed spending increases as either emergencies or mandatory and therefore allowable, and making unrealistic spending and revenue projections. A proper balanced-budget amendment would have to eliminate or restrict these tricks legally or it would be useless.

A balanced-budget amendment won't solve the Social Security trust fund problem either. Congress could still use the Social Security trust fund surpluses to fund current expenditures, leaving only IOUs for future recipients.

A balanced-budget amendment, I fear, will only take Congress off the hook and give our legislators a smoke screen behind which to hide. It will also provide them with a ready-made excuse for increasing taxes instead of cutting wasteful government spending.

The Gramm-Rudman-Hollings Act failed because it required only a simple majority to pass amendments that eviscerated it. And according to Senator Rudman, the Democratic-controlled Congress would not let the entitlement programs, which amount to nearly 70 percent of our tax revenues, be covered by the law. If Congress does pass a balanced-budget amendment, it must change its voting rules. Currently, a simple majority can change spending and tax legislation. We need to make sure that this law is changed only under dire circumstances. Congress must also require that a so-called super-majority of two-thirds or three-fourths is necessary to override its restrictions or to increase taxes to fuel growing expenditures.

The time to launch an all-out war on deficits was yesterday, but today will have to do. However, all we have to do is make the decision to fight, and Americans and America will see some benefits flow just from that resolve. The first benefit would be the recognition worldwide that this country is determined to remain fiscally responsible and economically sound. Once we show the world that we have the will and discipline to face our toughest problem, the value of our debt instruments and our credit rating would rise immediately.

The second benefit would be a resurgence in confidence by American industry, which would spur capital investment and expansion and persuade more companies to keep their operations in this country. The technology exists that would allow more companies to continue to produce their products here in the United States. All these companies need to buy and use this technology is confidence that the government of this country is managing its affairs in a sound financial manner.

It has become popular, especially among political conservatives, to say that government is part of the problem, not part of the solution. But that's simplistic and misleading.

Government is not the answer to every problem a country faces. In many cases, probably more than we realize, the private sector would be a far better provider of the goods and services that government now tries to furnish. I've mentioned some of these in discussing privatization earlier.

But government is very much a part of the solution to the problems that threaten to overwhelm us within the next three years: our murderous deficit and crippling debt. Only the government can wage the war against its own spendthrift habits. Government leaders can — and should — draft expert civilians into the deficit-fighting army to fight the war, but the ultimate leadership and responsibility lies with the president and Congress. Our job as citizens is to demand that they accept that responsibility and get on with their job now.

If we are to keep the patient from dying on the operating room table, the surgery has to begin now.

12

A Debt-Buster's Tool Kit for Congress

SUPPOSE that in October 1993 — the beginning of the federal government's 1994 fiscal year — your congressperson sent you a list detailing exactly where your tax money will go in the next twelve months. You already know that almost every member of Congress has come out for severe budget cuts and that President Clinton has claimed that the reduction of the federal deficit and debt is a top priority for his administration. So you are optimistic that the spending list you hold in your hands will represent a greatly slimmed-down budget.

As you study the list, however, you soon come across some strange-looking items that make you rub your eyes, then look again. They must be making some wacky typographical errors at the Government Printing Office, you think at first. Are we really still shelling out for radio stations set up to broadcast anti-Communist propaganda behind an Iron Curtain that no longer exists? Are we still paying more than a whopping $100 billion a year for our military participation in NATO, so we can protect "weak" nations, such as Germany, France, and England, from attack by the former Soviet Union and what used to be its satellite countries in Eastern Europe?

Could we still be doling out cash to keep the prices of mohair and honey high? Still paying to teach civilians how to shoot rifles? And paying to advertise and market abroad Pillsbury flour, Gallo wine, and Sunsweet fruit? Are we, in fact, still paying and paying for so many seemingly foolish items that thinking about all of them makes your head spin? Well, despite all the rhetoric and hand-wringing, it seems that that is precisely what we're doing in a myriad of areas.

The question is why, and what can we do about it?

If we can enlist a deficit-cutting army and give it authority to attack our budget problems (as we outlined in the previous chapter), how might the troops proceed when it comes to looking at specific program cuts?

There is no shortage of ideas around on how to pare questionable programs such as those we just described and restore fiscal sanity to our government. This chapter offers a representative sampling of cuts that have been proposed by various debt-busting individuals and organizations, including Senators Hank Brown (R-CO) and David Boren (D-OK); former California Democrat, and one-time chairman of the House Budget Committee, Leon Panetta, now Budget Director in the Clinton administration; the Congressional Budget Office; the Heritage Foundation; and Citizens Against Government Waste.

Taken alone, these suggested cuts are not a cure-all, but must be part of a larger deficit-cutting strategy. In order to achieve a balanced budget, the cost-reduction coalition, in cooperation with Congress, must take a good hard look at each government program and decide whether it should be kept or cut. The options presented here are realistic and offer achievable spending reductions. Most important, they can be implemented if the deficit army is given the authority it will require to do the job right.

Many legislators, government watchdog organizations, and large numbers of the American people recognize the disparity between the Clinton administration's stated deficit-reduction goals and the likely end results of his budget. And many individuals also see the reluctance of most legislators to give up pet pork-barrel projects that benefit only their own regions (and help them get reelected), all at enormous expense to taxpayers around the country. It was this proclivity among legislators that let Clinton swing thirty congresspeople to vote for his budget in the House this spring. It is not surprising, then, that as we go to press, people across the nation are encouraging the president and their representatives in Congress to face the problem squarely — to focus first not on new spending programs or new tax initiatives, but rather on the battle to rein in, once and for all, our out-of-control deficits and debt. However, they are not listening; they are buying votes by a continual giveaway.

We have divided the following list of proposed spending cuts into two categories — "mandatory spending" and "discretionary spending." Mandatory spending, as its name suggests, includes programs that don't depend on annual appropriation bills, but rather are mandated by law to provide funds to every individual and organization that meets a specified set of criteria. These budget items, including entitlements such as Social Security and Medicare, now account for nearly 70 percent of federal spending and 86 percent of tax receipts and are projected to increase by at least 36 percent over the next five years. By 1998, entitlement spending alone will amount to more than 13 percent of our GDP. Discretionary spending includes programs, such as most education, science, housing, and law enforcement programs, that must be voted on by Congress and accepted by the president each year.

It is possible that many of these issues are currently being or will soon be debated. And while some of these cuts, especially in the mandatory spending category, may seem harsh at first, keep in mind that spending in this area is now close to uncontrollable; unless we make some cuts there, "deficit reduction" will remain nothing more than an empty phrase.

(We have used the fiscal year 1993 budget authorization numbers — that is, the current level of approved spending — as a reference point from which future reductions could be made. While some authorizations extend over many years, most cover the costs of a program for a single year. In addition, the one- and five-year projected savings figures are affected by such variables as severance costs and population growth. Thus, one-year savings will not always be equal to the amount of the budget authorization, and five-year savings will not always be equal to five times the one-year savings.)

Here, then, is our list:

Entitlement Cuts

1. Adjust federal retirement benefits

Fiscal Year 1993 budget authorization: $65 billion
1-year projected savings: $990 million
5-year projected savings: $14 billion

Military and civilian retirees from the federal government pocket substantially greater benefits than their counterparts from the private sector, a disparity that proponents say is meant to compensate federal employees for receiving salaries that are generally lower than those in the private sector. Yet some studies have found that federal workers are actually paid *more* than private-sector employees with similar training and experience. (Other studies, though, claim the opposite is true.) Even with the following small reductions, however, federal workers would still be better off than employees doing comparable work in private companies. Suggested cuts: Eliminate cost-of-living adjustments (COLAs) altogether. Failing that, defer COLAs until retirees reach the age of sixty-two; lower those COLA additions to 1 percent below the rate of inflation; and make other modifications to the existing regulations, such as calculating initial benefits based on the so-called straight-line average from beginning to ending salaries — rather than the last several years — of a worker's salary. Remember that in private industry, retirement before age sixty-five results in reduced benefits because of the longer period of time the pension will be paid. Also, industry in general does not favor indexing with COLAs because pensions cannot be actuarially determined for proper funding.

2. Eliminate the Market Promotion Program (MPP)

Fiscal Year 1993 budget authorization: $200 million
1-year projected savings: $200 million
5-year projected savings: $1 billion

The Dole Food Company, Inc., is the world's largest supplier of fruits and vegetables. Yet, while it made a handsome operating income of more than $200 million in 1991, the government handed it another $2.4 million to advertise overseas. Sunsweet Growers collected $3.7 million for the same purpose; Gallo Wines received $5.1 million in government largesse; and Blue Diamond Nuts collected $6.2 million.

These, mind you, are only a handful of the country's largest and most successful companies that benefit each year from the Market Promotion Program, a welfare-for-the-rich scheme that handed out $200 million of taxpayer funds in 1991 alone to promote the products of private companies abroad. The program, originally called the Targeted Export Assistance (TEA) Program and passed as part of the 1985 farm bill, became law in 1986 and was renamed the Market Promotion Program in 1990.

The people in charge of this generous program have tripped up once or twice — for one, when Gunze, Japan's largest underwear maker, received $1 million in Japanese advertising (produced and purchased by the Cotton Council International), in exchange for mentioning in its ads that its underwear was made from American cotton. Another memorable moment came in 1991 when the major share of the MPP's handouts were allotted to Brown-Forman distilleries — coincidentally, one of the top contributors to President Bush's reelection campaign.

This is one program that should get the ax immediately. It's a safe bet that the fruit and vegetable growers will get along just fine without it.

3. Eliminate Social Security benefits for children of retirees who are between ages sixty-two and sixty-four

Fiscal Year 1993 budget authorization: $1.5 billion
1-year projected savings: $75 million
5-year projected savings: $1.8 billion

Unmarried children of retired workers are eligible to receive a monthly payment equal to one-half of their parents' basic Social Security benefit, as long as the children are under eighteen, unmarried, or become disabled before they reach age twenty-two. That means that workers under age sixty-five actually have an incentive to retire while their children still qualify for this aid. Eliminating this benefit would encourage early retirees to stay in the work force longer and save the government close to $2 billion over five years.

4. Eliminate price supports for honey, mohair, and wool

Fiscal Year 1993 budget authorization: $30 million
1-year projected savings: $30 million
5-year projected savings: $820 million

Can the United States survive without subsidizing domestic beekeepers, angora goat breeders, and sheep ranchers? The members of Congress who initiated these governmental handouts for what can only be called marginal industries apparently didn't think so, but we respectfully disagree. Aren't we taxpayers tired of getting stung and shorn?

5. Reduce Medicare payments to teaching hospitals

Fiscal Year 1993 budget authorization: $3.1 billion
1-year projected savings: $1.65 billion
5-year projected savings: $10.95 billion

Every patient in each of the United States' approximately 1,100 teaching hospitals (one-sixth of the country's 6,000 facilities) gets charged more for services than would be the case in an ordinary hospital. Why the discrepancy? So-called indirect educational costs for the medical training the hospitals provide their interns and residents are automatically added to each patient's tab.

All insurers, including Medicare, pay some portion of these costs. However, each year, the bill to Medicare automatically climbs by 7.7 percent when a hospital's intern-to-patient ratio increases a mere 0.1 percent. This hike in Medicare payments, according to CBO data, comes to more than the actual cost increases that result from adding more interns. A 3 percent increase, says the CBO, would be sufficient.

6. Reduce farm deficiency payments by lowering target prices

Fiscal Year 1993 budget authorization: $13.3 billion
1-year projected savings: $400 million
5-year projected savings: $11.2 billion

The government sets high artificial "target prices" for corn, wheat, rice, and cotton, then pays the growers the difference between the target and the actual market price of the crop. So if a bushel of corn sells for $5 on the open market but the government says it should sell for $8, the farmer gets to pocket an extra $3.

Cut those phony target prices by just 3 percent, and we will begin to bring farmers back into the free-market world, please our foreign trading partners, and save billions without causing undue damage to the agriculture industry.

7. Phase out Medicare's disproportionate share adjustment

Fiscal Year 1993 budget authorization: $2.5 billion
1-year projected savings: $470 million
5-year projected savings: $9.5 billion

Hospitals that treat large numbers of indigent patients are supposed to get higher reimbursements from Medicare. Fifteen hundred hospitals collect this extra cash, yet only 150 of them have truly disproportionately higher costs. Gradually eliminating all but the hospitals with legitimate claims would be a move for savings and fair play at the same time.

8. Limit the growth of Medicare, Medicaid, and other mandatory spending programs

Fiscal Year 1993 budget authorization: $407 billion
1-year savings: $15 billion
5-year savings: $257 billion

The rapid expansion of such mandatory spending programs as Medicare and Medicaid threatens to overwhelm our ability to fulfill these obligations. If the government would contain the use and cost of the services that these programs underwrite (both currently growing at double-digit rates), new beneficiaries could still be added when they became eligible, and cost-of-living adjustments could still be granted without affecting the programs' fundamental soundness.

Discretionary Spending Cuts

1. Cut in half spending allowances for federal office furniture and decoration

Fiscal Year 1993 budget authorization: $2 billion
1-year projected savings: $1 billion
5-year projected savings: $5 billion

Each year, the government buys enough hardwood desks, re-
clining chairs, mahogany tables, sofas, and oriental rugs to furnish
a small country — all for the offices of bureaucrats. A huge warehouse in Washington is packed with slightly used furnishings re-
jected by choosy new tenants when they take office. Could the
bureaucratic shoppers be asked to make an oriental rug and a
walnut desk last at least a year? Or even five?

2. Slash federal agency overhead expenses

Fiscal Year 1993 budget authorization: $110 billion
1-year projected savings: $11.6 billion
5-year projected savings: $65 billion

For the last quarter-century, every U.S. president has promised to cut government overhead. Unfortunately, all too predictably, few of these politicians have kept their word, and every year
expenses grow by about 6 percent.

Granted, Jimmy Carter did turn out most of the lights in the
White House, and Bill Clinton claims to have reduced the White
House staff (at least in the Travel Office), but the net gains, if
they existed at all, have been hard to discern.

Of course, the bulk of the overhead is found in federal agencies,
with such expenses as telephones, rents, utilities, printing, ship-
ping, janitorial services, and so forth.

Federal agencies should be forced to pursue such simple expedients as, for example, aggressively searching for cheaper phone systems and services in the very competitive telecommunications industry. Also, many cities have ample office space available at competitively priced rents. Why not lock in long-term leases at the current low rates? Leaving the base expense alone and cutting only the rate of growth by 10 percent — a move that would still allow these costs to increase by some 18 percent over five years — would save billions.

3. Lower federal travel costs by 15 percent

Fiscal Year 1993 budget authorization: $2.3 billion
1-year projected savings: $380 million
5-year projected savings: $2 billion

Even if we left military and postal-service travel out of the picture, government travel costs are climbing at double-digit rates. With computer modems, fax machines, and telephones handy, the need to meet face-to-face should decrease, not increase. Where are all these people going at our expense?

4. Sell most government-owned aircraft and nonpostal vehicles

Fiscal Year 1993 budget authorization: $3 billion
1-year projected savings: $2.5 billion
5-year projected savings: $12.5 billion

The federal government owns and operates a huge fleet of 1,200 civilian aircraft and about 340,000 automobiles at excessive cost to the taxpayer. More than enough privately owned taxis, rental cars, and aircraft are available for charter — at considerable savings overall. Consider that a 25-hour, round-trip flight from Washington, D.C., to Tokyo on *Air Force One* and its companion jet costs taxpayers about $700,000 — more, if you include a stop in L.A. for a haircut. Even a private charter from Washington to Tokyo costs less — about $600,000 less, to be precise. Of course, the same trip could be made on a scheduled commercial airline flight for just $1,500. But the in-flight movie might not be good enough to please our federal employees.

5. Reduce congressional and White House staffs

Fiscal Year 1993 budget authorization: $3.1 billion
1-year projected savings: $780 million
5-year projected savings: $3.9 billion

Private-sector companies know that when the red ink starts flowing, owners look at ways to cut overhead.

Government should be no different. Downsizing must become a fact of life in the federal government. Yet the size of congressional staffs have ballooned right along with the deficit. Even with significant work force cuts of 25 percent, the United States legislative staff will still be six times larger than the legislative staff of any other country worldwide. And we brag about American productivity!

6. Cut salaries of federal civilian employees by 2 percent

Fiscal Year 1993 budget authorization: $80 billion
1-year projected savings: $1.4 billion
5-year projected savings: $8.8 billion

When private-sector companies get in profit trouble or a recession, they have to trim salaries, benefits, and personnel. Our country isn't just in trouble; it's in a financial crisis and has called on retired people, the well-to-do, and the middle class to sacrifice. So why isn't the bureaucracy subject to a little austerity as well?

7. Change vacation leave compensation and overtime pay practices for some managers and supervisors

Fiscal Year 1993 budget authorization: $90 million
1-year projected savings: $90 million
5-year projected savings: $540 million

Most federal employees may accumulate up to a generous thirty days of unused vacation leave time. Top managers, however, can (and most do) accumulate unused leave without limit. Why should average taxpayers dole out millions each year for a special perk that supplements the six-figure incomes of senior executives, who can earn performance bonuses up to 20 percent of their annual salary?

The federal government also pays special, unapproved overtime to managers and supervisors involved in law enforcement. The problem is, these managers are usually engaged in the normal administrative functions that other managers perform without extra pay.

If we put an end to these special perks, the savings in outlays over five years would be enormous.

8. Reduce civilian work force in the military by assigning additional peacetime duties to military personnel

Fiscal Year 1993 budget authorization: $20 billion
1-year projected savings: $260 million
5-year projected savings: $1.8 billion

The Department of Defense employs 250,000 civilian personnel to provide support for operations at military bases. Civilians perform functions ranging from fire and police protection to maintenance and property repair. Why can't many of these duties be assigned to military personnel in existing deployable combat units located at military installations? Military doctors, for example, already provide medical services for civilian employees and dependents, and Air Force engineers currently perform all types of civil engineering and maintenance work. The civilian work force could easily be reduced by 10,000 (or 4 percent) without hurting services. And by fulfilling these functions at bases, military personnel would receive training in some of the very skills they would need in a combat situation. The Department of Defense could actually improve the quality of its installations through this initiative.

9. Privatize military commissaries

Fiscal Year 1993 budget authorization: $400 million
1-year projected savings: $290 million
5-year projected savings: $4.2 billion

One hundred and fifty years ago, the U.S. government established military commissaries at army posts far from civilization, such as the outposts established in Kearney, Nebraska, and Minot, North Dakota. There, soldiers and their families could purchase food and sundries at very low cost — thanks to federal subsidies. The military commissary is still with us today — in such rugged inaccessible places as San Diego (four), San Francisco (five), and Washington, D.C. (six). We're convinced that our military personnel wouldn't suffer unduly, if at all, if they, like the rest of us, had to do their shopping at a local supermarket or drugstore — or even at one of the proliferating low-price chains. In fact, they might even end up saving money.

10. Eliminate inefficient or underused veterans' medical facilities

Fiscal Year 1993 budget authorization: $13.3 billion
1-year projected savings: $65 million
5-year projected savings: $1.1 billion

The Department of Veterans Affairs (VA) operates more than 170 hospitals, some 130 nursing homes, and more than 350 outpatient clinics nationwide. Some small VA hospitals are close to better-equipped private facilities. Many VA hospitals have empty beds, and a substantial number operate under substandard conditions. The government could close some of these facilities and transfer their patients to nearby private facilities with the VA picking up the tab for patient care; others could be converted to high-demand nursing-care units.

11. Cancel NASA's Advanced Solid-Rocket Motor Program (ASRM)

Fiscal Year 1993 budget authorization: $350 million
1-year projected savings: $170 million
5-year projected savings: $1.65 billion

NASA originally chose solid rocket fuel for the space shuttle because it was less expensive in the short run, even though liquid fuel had always been used for human space flight. The ASRM program was intended to open the way to a bigger shuttle payload capability, which would be necessary to carry astronauts and materials back and forth to a permanent space station. But with the space station itself cut back and its future in doubt, further research seems pointless. Although first-year severance costs would limit savings in the short term, the long-term results would prove impressive.

12. Eliminate Rural Development Administration (RDA) grants, loans, and grant guarantees

Fiscal Year 1993 budget authorization: $560 million
1-year projected savings: $20 million
5-year projected savings: $1.38 billion

These funding initiatives were always intended to spur economic development in low-income and distressed rural communities. Research by the nonprofit Center for Community Change has found, however, that, far from providing help to poverty-level regions, two of the RDA's largest programs — water and waste disposal and business and industry development — are more likely to benefit higher-income communities, which receive larger amounts of assistance in any case. Besides, shouldn't states or localities be supporting local projects, not a federal agency such as the RDA?

13. Eliminate the National Board for the Promotion of Rifle Practice

Fiscal Year 1993 budget authorization: $3 million
1-year projected savings: $2.4 million
5-year projected savings: $14 million

"What's that?" you say. Believe it or not, the Department of Defense spends millions each year to operate rifle ranges, teach civilians marksmanship, and send rifle teams to competitions, all in the name of "encouraging the use of long guns." While shutting down the program would eat up $1 million over five years in closing and severance costs, taxpayers would still greatly benefit from the projected $14 million savings over five years. This is a small-ticket item, but it represents the many small items out there that can be eliminated or cut. Cumulatively, they would add up to a large number of dollars saved.

14. Cut the amount given to law-enforcement agencies attempting to reduce the supply of illegal drugs

Fiscal Year 1993 budget authorization: $7 billion
1-year projected savings: $470 million
5-year projected savings: $9.4 billion

Funds for this effort have more than doubled since 1988, yet indications abound that we are losing the war on drug runners and suppliers. Many experts believe that the customers are at the root of the problem, and our money would be better spent attempting to eliminate demand, not supply. Even a phased-in one-third cutback would leave the program with more money than it received in 1988.

15. Eliminate special-purpose Housing and Urban Development (HUD) grants

Fiscal Year 1993 budget authorization: $26 million
1-year projected savings: $25 million
5-year projected savings: $990 million

This pork barrel is small, but our legislators love it. Restoring a "historic" building in Idaho or immortalizing Lawrence Welk's birthplace is popular in the home district. The only problem is that it takes away money that could be used for some real housing needs.

16. Eliminate highway demonstration projects

Fiscal Year 1993 budget authorization: $325 million
1-year projected savings: $185 million
5-year projected savings: $3.9 billion

A favorite of legislators who are eager to curry favor at home, this program is intended to fund the development of so-called experimental roads and highways that in some way "demonstrate" methods of enhancing or improving highway construction. Recent studies have found, however, that more than 10 percent of these projects could never qualify for funding under regular highway grant programs, because the roadways that result don't serve any practical purpose. The Baltimore/Washington Parkway, for example, cost $15 million, yet it runs parallel to an existing interstate. About half of the projects don't even appear in state transportation plans, a good indicator that many of the projects are paved with pork.

17. Eliminate Community Development Block Grants (CDBG)

Fiscal Year 1993 budget authorization: $4 billion
1-year projected savings: $160 million
5-year projected savings: $14.2 billion

Intended for urban renewal and for spurring economic development in poor areas of cities, these funds have been misused by local politicians. Cities, for example, have frequently used the grants to lure businesses from other localities — an action that simply transfers the need for renewal to the city that lost its business. Other examples of misuse or downright fraud: Chester, Pennsylvania, used $1.8 million in CDBG funds for loans and grants to enable municipal employees and their relatives to buy cars and to purchase airline tickets to conventions, which were never attended. In another instance, the city of Troy, New York, used $1.65 million of these grants to make two loans to its professional hockey team.

True economic development — expanding upon or upgrading existing facilities, or building brand-new ones — is a function of the private sector, not the federal government. As Tom Lantos, a Democratic congressman from California, remarked in 1991 hearings that looked into the abuse of these grants: "Some of the projects being funded by federal tax dollars belong in 'Ripley's Believe It or Not.'"

18. Eliminate Impact Aid

Fiscal Year 1993 budget authorization: $750 million
1-year projected savings: $600 million
5-year projected savings: $3.85 billion

Children whose parents live on military bases or other federal property go to local schools, but the parents pay no school taxes. The so-called Impact Aid program compensates the localities for the loss of those tax revenues. This fee to communities doesn't take into account the fact that people living on bases or other federal installations inject a large flow of money into local economies — more than enough to compensate for the services they receive.

19. Cut federal subsidies for urban mass-transit systems

Fiscal Year 1993 budget authorization: $3.6 billion
1-year projected savings: $530 million
5-year projected savings: $6.25 billion

The federal government pays up to 80 percent of the cost of new rail lines or other capital improvements to mass-transit systems. It also covers up to 50 percent of their operating deficits. The original idea behind subsidizing mass transit was to cut gasoline consumption and air pollution. But it hasn't worked. Rightly or wrongly, Americans prefer their cars, and only 6.5 percent of home-workplace round trips are on mass transit. Cut investment costs to 50 percent, and let the passengers make up deficits through higher fares.

20. Phase out American military involvement in NATO

Fiscal Year 1993 budget authorization: $100 billion
1-year projected savings: $20 billion
5-year projected savings: $100 billion

According to scholars at such think tanks as the Cato Institute and the Hoover Institution, the price tag for American military support of NATO runs somewhere between $100 billion and $200 billion annually. Yet maintaining a military presence overseas to "defend" Western Europe from the menace of Communist aggression — the original intent of NATO — has lost much of its urgency with the collapse of the former Soviet Union and the fall of the Iron Curtain. It's time to get out of Europe and — using even the most conservative estimates — save billions from a phased withdrawal of troops and material.

21. End funding for the Legal Services Corporation

Fiscal Year 1993 budget authorization: $370 million
1-year projected savings: $370 million
5-year projected savings: $1.9 billion

The Legal Services Commission is an independent not-for-profit organization that was initially intended to provide free legal aid to low-income people. However, the program seems to have abandoned its original mission of helping the poor with routine legal problems. Responsibility for funding and control of legal aid programs may be more appropriately placed on states and localities who can closely monitor programs and insure they respond to the specific local needs of the poor.

The simple reductions we've outlined here in both discretionary and mandatory spending add up to a total of $60 billion in projected first-year savings and $555 billion in projected five-year savings. The total projected five-year amount is enough to achieve an average of $111 billion in deficit reduction annually. While that amount alone doesn't solve the deficit problem, these are only examples of how spending could be reduced without the burden of new taxes. What's more, they are only a small part of the spending cuts that could be made. As we said, they are merely a representative sampling of some of the hundreds of deficit-reduction proposals that have been put forth by various savings-minded individuals and entities, including the present budget director.

Ideally, the president and Congress should implement overall spending-reduction policies, such as the 4 percent cap and the COLA cutbacks mentioned in Chapter 11. With the momentum from such an effort we can keep pushing forward to cut spending on a program-by-program basis. If the job is done with wisdom and fairness, the average citizen does not have to suffer undue hardship in the process, and the country could have an unprecedented resurgence.

Someone has to recognize the gravity of the situation that this country faces and take both positive and aggressive action. It's too bad that there is not a leader in place who could recognize that such a strong performance would assure him or her an exalted place in American history.

13

A Debt-Buster's Tool Kit for You

WHAT can we private citizens — workers, managers, investors, and voters — do to get our debt and deficit under control? Are we merely hapless, helpless victims of shortsighted, self-serving, and demagoguing politicians? Can we only follow them into chaos even if we can see it coming?

No and no. On the contrary, I'm convinced that we ordinary citizens are the key to halting America's slide into economic oblivion. We're victims only if we let ourselves be victimized.

Since the 1992 presidential election, the federal deficit has become a front-burner issue for the American people, and, consequently, politicians have had to sit up and take notice.

We *must* keep up the pressure and strike while the issue is still red-hot. There may never be a better time to make a difference. National polls show that deficit reduction is the number-one issue on voters' minds, and politicians are finally beginning to pay attention to their constituents' demands.

Politicians from both parties were critical of President Clinton's first economic proposal for being too short on spending cuts and long on taxes. That's a good sign. Our lawmakers, however, won't go far enough unless voters continue to demand that they act responsibly.

Obviously, the average American has no direct control over decisions affecting the debt and deficit, but elected officials and lawmakers don't pull the levers of public policy in a vacuum. They make the decisions they think are necessary to remain in office. As writer H. L. Mencken once put it, "The politicians know what the public wants and plan to give it to us good and hard."

That means it is our responsibility to continue to send our elected representatives an unambiguous signal: We *demand* fiscal stability, and we will do what we must to get it.

You now understand the threat that the federal debt and continued deficits pose to you, your family, your community, and your country. You understand that we're enjoying a "free" lunch today but passing the tab along to our children and grandchildren.

This book won't convince lawmakers that the American public wants action. Only you can do that. You *have* to, to assure your own, your parents', and your children's economic survival. And you *can* play a role in rescuing the country.

What you have to do is to get your message across to your fellow citizens and to Washington. The debt and deficit are not the country's only problems. But they're the most pressing. Until we get them under control, we can do little to nothing about any of the others.

Getting the country's debt and deficit under control involves our voting, to be sure, but as important as our vote is, it's only a first step. There's much more that we citizens can — and must — do if we are to solve America's first-priority problem.

The special-interest lobbyists won't do it. Economists won't do it. Staff professionals and bureaucrats won't do it. Left alone, the president and members of Congress won't do it, either. Washington insiders, these are the people who created America's debt and deficit problem and have allowed it to reach the crisis stage. We know that they won't fix it until fixing it is clearly in their own best political interests, and that is something that voters like you and me determine.

I know how to solve America's debt and deficit crises; so do you. Now we must get our message across in ways that government officials cannot fail to hear and understand. We currently have the largest freshman class in Congress in nearly two decades. That means new opportunities for change exist, because so many of these fresh faces were elected with a mandate from voters to change the system — to reform radically the way the government has managed itself and our tax dollars. They are, however, under great pressure from their parties to get in line. Committee appointments and pork-barrel projects are powerful inducements.

They will cave in one by one and as a class unless you don't let them.

What's more, these newly elected members are easier targets at election time — so they *will* pay attention. First-termers are aware they are vulnerable and are eager to please on issues they perceive voters care about.

That said, here's what you can do:

1. Vote

We know. People are turned off by the political process — to the point where voter turnout has fallen to nearly 50 percent in many elections. But dropping out isn't the answer. A single vote still has potency. If you doubt it, consider that in 1964, Senator Howard Cannon of Nevada won reelection to his Senate seat by only forty-eight votes. Get to know your legislators' records on budget proposals. Grill them on their stands and tell them you will vote for them the next time they run *only* if their records are satisfactory. Then, follow through.

2. Write or Call Your Representatives in Washington

No, it's not hopeless, and they do listen. People accuse their congresspeople of many sins, but they are rarely accused of ignoring the direct demands of their constituents. That's because most of our legislators have only one thing on their minds — getting re-elected — and the way they do that is to pay attention to what voters back home in their district say.

Members of Congress frequently base their decisions on how to vote on an issue directly on the number of positive or negative letters they receive from constituents. Some legislators use their mail count on a pending bill as the *sole* determinant for how they vote. So voicing your opinion can be crucial in getting responsible legislation passed on the fiscal crisis we now face.

When calling or writing, be assertive but courteous. Convey your concern clearly and forcefully, and demand politely that your elected official be accountable to you. The actions of our elected "leaders" can make it tempting to let loose with a verbal or written fusillade, but that approach almost never works.

Above all, be timely. A call or letter that comes months before an important vote or weeks after the legislation has passed won't do much good. The most critical times for sending a letter or making a call come during the initial drafting of a bill, right after a bill has been passed, during the drafting of new regulations to implement a law, or during the reconsideration of existing regulations.

It helps to write on your own letterhead. In any case, you should always sign your name and give your address. That way, your legislators know you're willing to stand up and be counted.

Keep letters brief and to the point. One page is ample to provide key facts, state your convictions, and ask for action. If you're writing about a specific piece of legislation, identify it by its popular name or bill number. (See "Learn How the Congressional Budget Process Works — and Influence It" for more information.)

For the most part, you should send letters to your own representatives. They're the ones who need to hear your views, and what you say can help that legislator make decisions that will affect the people and businesses in his or her state.

If appropriate, praise your legislator's performance. He or she, like most of us, will respond favorably to a pat on the back. Here's a suggested structure for your letter:

The salutation should read "Dear Representative/Senator (name):"

Begin by stating your reason for writing. For example:

- If the government doesn't act now to control its runaway debt and deficit, this country will experience a catastrophic breakdown by 1995. As a concerned citizen and voter, I demand that you be fiscally responsible for this country and take action to reduce the federal debt.
- During the 1992 campaign season, we heard a lot of lip service paid to debt reduction. Now, only a short time into this term, we voters recognize that much of what you and your colleagues promised, you lack the will or skill to accomplish.
- Witness the economic plan put forward by President Clinton. His plan is imbalanced, loaded down with tax increases, and far too light on spending cuts, all of which are put off until the years he expects to be in his *second* term of office. That is arrogance and deceit.

Next outline your concerns and make your arguments. Consider including some of these elements:

- I and an increasing number of my fellow Americans believe that our federal debt burden is the single most important problem facing the country today; indeed, solving it is tantamount to fighting a war.
- Our current course will lead us to economic devastation by the mid-1990s. No country since the time of the Romans has ever gotten away with running a huge deficit year after year without paying a ruinous price.
- I find it intolerable that interest on the debt is nearly the

largest expense in the federal budget and eats up 61 cents of every dollar we pay in personal income taxes.

- I am concerned for my children and grandchildren. Money is being diverted from uses that could increase wealth and productivity for future generations and it is being spent in nonproductive, short-term areas that will not benefit us or our country.
- I am fed up that no one is doing anything to solve the problem. I am concerned that my elected officials seem long on words, but short on action. I am all too aware that our leaders in Washington concentrate not on solutions that would reduce the debt but on ways to mask the size of the "official" deficit.
- President Clinton's economic plan is just another case of a politician's sleight of hand that poses as deficit reduction but in reality amounts to nothing more than an elaborate accounting shell game. How dumb does he think the American people are?
- I am becoming actively and personally involved in the campaign to reduce our debt. Besides writing to you and other elected officials, I am encouraging the media to cover the issue and speaking out in my own community. I am forming an organization which will fight for this country's well-being.
- I find your performance on the debt and deficit issue unsatisfactory. [Or, I applaud your performance on the debt and deficit so far. Keep up the good work.]

Your conclusion should call for specific action. Some elements that might be included:

- The problem is still reversible, but we need to take action immediately.
- I expect you to become fully committed and actively involved in debt reduction and to push for fiscally

responsible legislation. I will hold you and all elected officials responsible for your actions on this issue. Your performance on matters relating to this all-important matter will be the absolute litmus test for my vote.

Here's an example of an effective letter:

Dear Representative (name):

As a concerned citizen, I am deeply troubled by your inaction and silence on the issue of the national deficit and debt.

Your constituents recognize fiscal hocus-pocus when they see it. We elected you to represent us responsibly, and you are accountable to the public you serve.

Twice each month, I sit down to pay the household bills. I know exactly who must be paid and how much. As do most responsible American citizens, I never write a check that exceeds my budget. I follow the same rule when I purchase clothing, items for the household, or anything else. I keep within my budget.

Every household, every business, every institution, every person in America operates this way as a matter of routine — with the exception of the federal government. How did our government get into the habit of not living within its means like the rest of us? Perhaps you could explain to me how and why our government has chosen not to abide by this most fundamental of economic principles.

Any individual — or any business or institution — would be bankrupt long ago if we acted in this irresponsible manner — every institution, that is, but the federal government.

How can you justify this method of bookkeeping? What happens when we have no credit left?

I demand that you and the other members of Congress

begin treating America's checkbook the same way the rest of us treat ours. The government must learn to live within its means and adhere to the discipline of a balanced budget. No longer can I tolerate this government irresponsibility.

Since you serve as my representative, I hold you personally accountable for remedying this untenable situation.

I also know exactly how to enforce my demands — at the ballot box — and so does every other U.S. citizen of voting age. I look forward to your response.

Sincerely,
(full name and address)

Where to Write

Write your U.S. representative at the following address:

The Hon. (name)
House Office Building
Washington, DC 20515

Write your U.S. senators at the following address:

The Hon. (name)
Senate Office Building
Washington, DC 20510

or call the main switchboard at the Capitol: 202/224-3121.

Write to the president at the following address:

The President
The White House
Washington, DC 20500

or call the main switchboard at the White House: 202/456-1414.

3. Organize a Letter-Writing Campaign

With just a little extra effort, you can multiply the effectiveness of your letter by making it the foundation of a letter-writing campaign. If you are part of a citizens' group (see the next section), ask each member of your organization to write, and encourage those outside of the group to write as well. Begin by recruiting your family and friends. That should be an easy sell, because the government's fiscal irresponsibility and our runaway national debt are unacceptable to everyone. Get children involved as well and have them write their own letters. They're the ones who will be the big losers as we sell ourselves down the fiscal river, and their words will have an impact. Whether the letter writer is a child or an adult, ask each participant in the campaign to write his or her own original letters, perhaps using yours as a springboard. Postcards and form letters don't pack as great a punch, though any correspondence is better than nothing.

4. Become Involved in a Citizens' Action Group

Citizens' action groups, otherwise known as grass-roots organizations, bring people together who share a common grievance, then help them turn their emotions into effective, targeted action. Several grass-roots organizations dedicated to making government more efficient already exist. If your area doesn't have a local chapter, consider forming one. If none of the organizations we list below appeal to you, consider creating your own.

The following organizations share an interest in effective and efficient government. Many of these groups publish newsletters that keep readers posted on timely developments on appropriations bills, the budget, tax bills, and so forth. These can be a great resource for identifying whom to contact and how but, more important, *when,* so your letter or call counts the most. You can find out more about their specific orientation by calling or writing.

Citizens Against Government Waste
1301 Connecticut Avenue, N.W.
Suite 400
Washington, DC 20036
Telephone: 1-800/BE-ANGRY or 202/467-5300

National Taxpayers Union
325 Pennsylvania Avenue, S.E.
Washington, DC 20003
Telephone: 202/543-1300

Lead or Leave
1100 Connecticut Avenue N.W.
Suite 1300
Washington, DC 20036
202/857-0808

United We Stand America, Inc.
7616 LBJ Freeway, Suite 727
Dallas, Texas 75251
214/450-8874 (Media Hotline)
214/960-9100

Committee for a Responsible Federal Budget
220 1/2 E Street, N.E.
Washington, DC 20002
202/547-4484

Citizens for a Sound Economy
470 L'Enfant Plaza, S.W.
Suite 7112
Washington, DC 20024
Telephone: 202/488-8200

Americans for Tax Reform
1301 Connecticut Avenue, N.W.
Suite 444
Washington, DC 20036
Telephone: 202/785-0266

As a member of one or more citizens' action groups, you may want to influence your group to endorse members of Congress, all of whom will be candidates again at some point in the future. Political candidates covet endorsements, and endorsements from governmental watchdog groups are particularly sought after.

Action groups should make endorsements carefully, based on criteria related to the official's position and track record on reducing the debt and deficit.

If you would like to start your own citizens' group, begin by establishing a core group of people who share your concern about our nation's crisis. Start by talking to those around you — friends, neighbors, co-workers, and members of your professional or civic organizations — about the dangers posed by the runaway federal debt. Once you have built a base of concerned citizens, decide on a name for your group and a regular meeting time and place. To help enlist additional members, publicize your meetings with postings on community bulletin boards — at your workplace or at local libraries, for example — and through advertisements in local newspapers or in company or professional organization newsletters.

As a group, become informed about the legislative process and formulate and agree on a mission statement aimed at influencing legislators to take action on the debt crisis. Working together, your group can convince others that this issue is critical to our nation's survival.

The group should designate a leader to take primary responsibility for legislative advocacy. The leader should be reliable and credible; articulate, persuasive, and outgoing; and able to advocate both offensively to get legislation passed and defensively to prevent legislation *from* passing.

He or she should:

- Keep track of pertinent legislation by following it through the legislative process and advocating for or against it. (See "Learn How the Congressional Budget Process Works — and Influence It," following.)
- Assist the group in organizing and training its members to follow and influence the legislative process.
- Network the group with other legislative advocates and professional lobbyists to develop common goals.

Here are some tips to help your group become more visible and effective:

- Publicize to the local media the group's formation and the appointment of the leader. (See "Use the News Media to Promote Your Cause," page 232.)
- Find out the names of similar citizens' groups.
- Become familiar with the legislative officials who have an impact on federal budget decision-making and ask to be put on their mailing lists. (See "Learn How the Congressional Budget Process Works — and Influence It," page 222.)
- Encourage members to compile lists of people they can call on to join in advocacy efforts.

Your group can establish special ad hoc committees to carry out specific objectives, such as coordinating a letter-writing campaign or planning an event. For example, you might ask a prominent business leader in your community to become part of an ad hoc committee that will sponsor a community forum on the federal debt crisis. Once you've contacted the people you want to become involved in the committee, call a meeting to carry out its mission, and appoint ad hoc committee coleaders to follow through. Again, use announcements in local media or notices on community bulletin boards to attract participants.

Any citizens' group, especially a new one, can benefit from contacting other groups, organizations, and opinion leaders to form a coalition. That is nothing more than an arrangement among a combination of groups, organizations, and/or individuals to work toward a common legislative objective by coordinating the advocacy effort and, thereby, dramatically increasing its effectiveness.

Here are a few guidelines to make it easier to manage a coalition:

- Form a committee with members from the two or more groups to coordinate the coalition's activities.
- Establish and maintain a regular means of communication among the coalition members, through regular meetings, a telephone directory, a monthly newsletter, and so forth.
- Make sure that all members of the coalition understand that no one will speak for the coalition on any issue other than the debt or deficit.
- Do not let the coalition stray from its primary purpose. Keep it focused.

5. Learn How the Congressional Budget Process Works — and Influence It

Ordinary citizens need to understand the twists and turns the annual budget takes on its way to passage if they are to influence it. Getting up to speed isn't all that difficult, although our legislators might prefer to have us think otherwise.

The congressional budget process begins when the president submits his budget to Congress in early February, about eight months before the start of the fiscal year on October 1. The House and Senate budget committees, along with the appropriate subcommittees, must then formulate a budget resolution by April 15.

The resolution contains revenue and spending levels for the next five fiscal years, but does not give specific dollar amounts for individual programs.

During the summer and early fall, Congress hammers out the details of spending, revenues, and the level of the public debt for the upcoming fiscal year. At the same time, federal agencies submit budgets to Congress and appeal to the president and Congress for funds.

The first step in influencing the budget process is to find out who serves on the Senate and House budget committees and sub-committees. *The Congressional Directory* ($16) lists committee and subcommittee members and chairpersons. Published annually, it is an invaluable source of information about members of Congress and their staffs and is available from libraries or the Government Printing Office (GPO). To order documents from the GPO, write or call:

Superintendent of Documents
U.S. Government Printing Office
Washington, DC 20402
Telephone: 202/783-3238

Once you identify key legislators on the budget committees, write or call them. You'll find the main addresses and telephone numbers on page 217.

If you have facts you think the congressional committee holding hearings on a bill should know, write to the committee chairperson. You can also request copies of hearings and reports from relevant committees. Contact the budget committee directly to request a list of committee hearing dates so you can time your correspondence to coincide with specific bills. Call the Senate Budget Committee at 202/224-0642, or the House Budget Committee at 202/226-7200.

You can also work with your local representative to influence the budget process. Arrange a meeting with the representative or his or her staff to discuss key issues. (See "Visit Your Representatives," on page 225.)

You should know that a piece of legislation can go through as many as twenty-five steps before it becomes law. Legislation begins in a congressional subcommittee or a full committee. You should contact committee members when pertinent legislation is about to come before that committee. Another key time to get in touch with your legislators is when a bill is about to come before the full Senate or House. You should contact both your senators if the bill originates in the Senate and your representative if it originates in the House. To obtain a copy of a bill, write or call your representative's or senators' district office.

These sources will help you track the progress of legislation:

- The *Congressional Record* ($225 annually) is a daily account of all floor activity in Congress. It includes descriptions of bills introduced, bills reported out of committees, and hearing schedules. You can find the *Congressional Record* in libraries or obtain it from the GPO.
- The *Congressional Quarterly* ($1,299 annually) is a weekly news report and analysis of activity in Congress. It includes analyses of bills and proposals before Congress, as well as news stories on the people and issues behind these proposals. The *Congressional Quarterly* is available for reference at most libraries.
- The *Federal Register* ($375 annually) contains notices of executive branch and regulatory agency meetings and rule-making, proposed regulations, information on hearings, comment periods, contacts for additional information, final regulations, and effective dates. It is published daily and available from libraries or the GPO.
- Legislative Status Office — You can call 202/225-1772 to check the status of legislation in both the House and Senate and to get dates of committee hearings.
- U.S. Capitol — You can reach the office of any member of

Congress and all committees and subcommittees by calling
202/224-3121.

- Federal government switchboard — If you do not know the
direct number of a government department or agency, call
202/245-6000 and the operator will connect you.

6. Visit Your Representatives

One effective — yet often overlooked — way of communicating
with your legislators is simply to visit them in person, either at
their district offices or in Washington. Face-to-face contact pre-
sents an opportunity for a more meaningful exchange on an issue
and can set the groundwork for an ongoing relationship. A personal
visit will, at the least, get their attention.

It's not hard to arrange a visit. After all, your representative
and senators are supposed to serve as *your* proxy in government.
Just call the district office of your legislator and ask a staff member
to make an appointment for you. All representatives and senators
operate at least one office in their district, and most plan well in
advance the dates they will be there. Some set aside every weekend. If you're in Washington, stop in at your legislator's office,
even if you haven't made an appointment. Chances are, you won't
be turned away.

If your representative is unavailable at times that are convenient to you, ask to meet with a legislative assistant. The visit
won't be wasted. These staff aides are frequently better informed
on specific subjects than their boss, since they're the people
charged with briefing officials, writing floor statements, and drafting amendments, among other tasks.

A single visit may not accomplish your objective. But it can have
an impact on your representatives and can establish a basis for an
ongoing communication that could prove effective in the long run.

To get the most out of a legislative visit, prepare yourself with
facts and figures in advance. You may find that you are more
knowledgeable about the debt and deficit than either your legis-

lators or their aides, especially if they are not involved with the committee or subcommittees handling the issue.

Take the opportunity to state that you believe the debt crisis is the most critical issue facing our country, and you feel it is your responsibility — and theirs — to stay informed and involved.

Share the valuable insights and information you have learned that have led you to your strong convictions. Your legislators may just learn something from you and will certainly be reminded that there are concerned and active citizens on this topic in their district. Let them know how you assess their performance on the deficit issue, and make clear to them that you will continue to monitor their performance in pressing for fiscal stability for this country.

7. Ask the Tough Questions

Whether you telephone or write your elected officials and representatives — or meet with them in person — be tough. They've nearly destroyed our country with their big-spending ways (from the following chart you can see that almost half of our congress-people are big spenders, while only 12.2 percent are debt-busters), and now's no time to tippy-toe around the issues.

Here are some questions you can ask your elected officials — and candidates for office — to find out the importance they attach to the federal deficit and debt:

- Where would you rank the debt and the deficit on the nation's list of priorities?
- What specific actions do you plan to take to reduce the debt and the deficit?
- Will you promise not to run for office again if you make no progress in addressing the problem of the debt and the deficit?
- How do you explain a $400 billion deficit in 1992, the year we were promised a balanced budget?

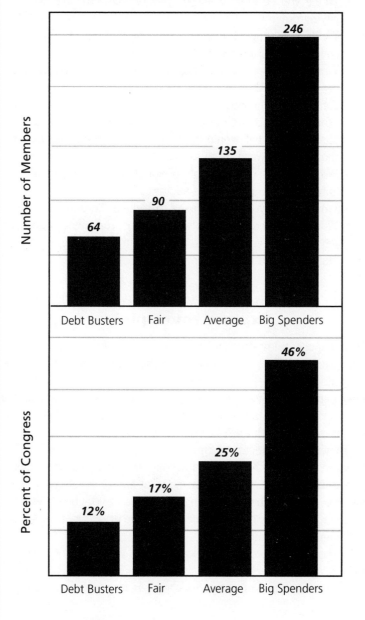

Spending Scorecard of the 102nd Congress

Number of Members

64	90	135	246
Debt Busters	Fair	Average	Big Spenders

Percent of Congress

12%	17%	25%	46%
Debt Busters	Fair	Average	Big Spenders

SOURCE: *National Taxpayers Union*

- Would you be in favor of not only reducing the deficit, but paying down the debt?
- Would you support a reduction in the number of congressional committees and subcommittees?
- Would you support reducing expenditures in all government programs, both those that are discretionary and those considered mandatory?
- Would you support the formation of a private-sector debt-buster team that would make recommendations similar to those put forward by the Grace Commission?
- Would you support the sale of some of our government enterprises to the private sector?
- Would you favor raising taxes to reduce the debt?
- Would you please tell me where the government is going to get the money to pay our Social Security benefits in the year 2010 and thereafter?

8. Use the News Media to Express Your Opinion

Newspapers, television, and radio are all effective vehicles for getting your views on the debt and deficit crises known and discussed. A simple letter to the editor in your daily or weekly newspaper can have a wide-ranging effect. Daily newspapers in the top 100 U.S. markets reach anywhere from 50,000 to 1.2 million readers with each issue.

To write an effective letter to the editor, keep it brief. The average letter to the editor is around 150 to 250 words. That's one double-spaced typewritten page at most. Keep your letter simple, as well. The average person reads at a high-school level.

Try to grab your readers' attention in the first sentence, so they will want to continue to read.

Make a clear, accurate, logical case for your point of view, and back it up with facts.

In the introduction, summarize your main point. For example:

- This country will experience a complete financial breakdown or be irreparably damaged by the mid-1990s unless we force the government to act now to substantially rein in the federal debt.

The body of the letter should include your opinions and facts to support them. For example:

- The federal debt is the biggest threat facing the country today; solving it is tantamount to fighting a war.
- Inaction will kill this country. Politicians have been long on talk but short on action when it comes to this pressing problem.
- It took this country more than two hundred years to run up its first $1 trillion in debt. It took only ten more years to add another $3 trillion; by 1996, our debt will total more than the entire industrial output of the United States.
- What does that mean in everyday terms? It means that the equivalent of 61 cents of every dollar each of us pays in personal income taxes goes to pay off interest on the debt. Interest on the debt is larger than the combined budgets for the departments of Agriculture, Education, Energy, Housing and Urban Development, Interior, Justice, Labor, State, Transportation, and Veterans Affairs.
- We all know that no person can consistently spend more than he or she takes in; nor can any business. Well, neither can government.

Conclude your letter with a call to action. For example:

- During the 1992 campaign, lawmakers promised us that they would be agents of change. They swore they would be advocates for changing the way the federal government operated. They said they would cut waste. Reduce the deficit. Put an end to congressional perks and privileges.

Break the gridlock. From the looks of things, since the election it's still business as usual in Washington.

- We're being hurt, and it's up to us, as citizens, to sound the alarm. Everyone should call or write his or her elected officials and demand action and accountability. Our elected officials, left to themselves, do not have the political will to introduce meaningful change. That's why we must pull together now and make them do so.
- We must also speak out in our community about this crisis. All of us should try to talk to neighbors, friends, and colleagues about the magnitude of the problem.
- The time to act is now, before our debt becomes totally unmanageable, and this great country is left broke and in ruins.

Be certain to sign your name and address and include your daytime phone number. Most newspapers will not print anonymous letters, although some will withhold your name from print if you request.

Here's an example of an effective letter to the editor:

To the Editor:
Bankruptcy.
We all know that's what happens when we continually live beyond our means. And, that's exactly where the federal government is heading. But the size of that bounced check doesn't seem to bother the politicians in Washington. In fact, President Clinton's illusory plan to reduce the deficit actually adds to our debt.

Last year our government spent the equivalent of 61 cents of every tax dollar it collects from individuals just in paying interest on the national debt. The government took in $1.1 trillion and paid out $1.5 trillion. That amounted to an overdraft of $400 billion in 1992, including monies meant for the long-term viability of Social Security.

You and I could never live that way — paying out more

than the amount of our paycheck on a regular basis. What makes our government any different?

Most of us buy what we can afford. That seems a pretty simple rule to me. Maybe it's too simple for the folks in Washington.

Sincerely,
(your full name)

You can also try your hand at an op-ed article, so called because it appears opposite the editorial page. Local newspapers usually are receptive to thoughtful, well-written editorials or personal commentaries on subjects of concern to the community, particularly if you can show you're an expert on the subject or head of an organization. Check with the editor or editorial director for the newspaper's guidelines on length or any other specific requirements.

In writing the article, follow the guidelines for a letter to the editor — clearly state your views on the subject of our nation's debt, support your opinion with evidence from this book or other sources, and suggest what should be done to solve the problem. Since the hardcover version of this book came out, many citizens have heeded this call. We know of hundreds of newspapers nationwide that have published strong letters to the editor drawing attention to the severity of the national debt and quoting or mentioning our book as support.

Local radio and television stations provide another powerful forum for expressing your views on the national debt. Most stations provide time for news and public service programming. Take advantage of these opportunities to get the issue before a wider audience.

Contact the editorial directors of all the radio and television stations in your area. Many stations take formal positions on issues in on-air editorials. Urge each station to run an editorial about the seriousness of the national debt and the importance of doing something now to get the problem under control. Then ask if you can give a guest editorial. Many stations offer an "in my opinion" segment, which provides an opportunity for the public to address important issues. Or see if you can set up an on-air interview.

If you do get an interview opportunity, make your message concise and try to articulate it in a polished manner. Make sure to practice your delivery until you feel comfortable. Understand the arguments on both sides of the issue, so you can answer questions with authority. A good performance will add to your credibility as a valuable media source on the debt and deficit.

You should also contact the public affairs director at each radio and television station in your area. Most stations air weekly public affairs programs, which, with a little prodding, could focus considerable time on the national debt.

Contact the news directors and program directors at all local outlets as well and suggest that they consider a debate, telethon, or other special program on the issue of the debt and deficit. Broadcasters regularly plan such special programming, especially during the ratings periods. We as authors are practicing what we preach. We have been very active during the past year in trying to reach the American public through the media. We have written several "op-ed" commentaries for national publications, including the *Washington Times*. Gerry Swanson and I have appeared on dozens of national radio and television programs, including the "Today Show" on NBC, "Larry King Live" and "Moneyline" on CNN, and "Smart Money" on CNBC, as well as numerous local and regional broadcast programs. In addition, editorials, book reviews, and articles featuring or mentioning the book have appeared in over 350 newspapers and magazines across the United States and Canada.

9. Use the News Media to Promote Your Cause

Coverage of the debt and deficit crises by newspapers and television and radio stations in your community can go a long way toward creating greater concern about the issue. You can solicit coverage ranging from the announcement of a rally at City Hall to the launching of a city-wide letter-writing campaign about the impact of the debt and deficit crises on your own community. Although you can act as an individual, you will probably have more credibility with the media — and get better results — if you represent a grass-roots organization. Use these tools to get your message across:

News Release

A news release is nothing more than a short article, written in basic, factual style ("who, what, where, when, why, and how"), announcing a specific activity or event — perhaps a rally or letter-writing campaign or the election of officers of an organization. Keep the release short and to the point and include the telephone number of someone who can answer any questions or provide more information. If you want an event covered, make sure the release gets to the appropriate editors, news directors, and reporters well in advance (at least two or three days), so they can arrange for coverage. Call each news organization to find out where and to whom you should send your release. Don't forget the suburban weekly as well as dailies in your area.

Pitch Letter

A pitch letter is a brief, persuasive, personalized letter that "pitches" or suggests a story idea to an editor or news director. Think, for example, how the debt crisis affects your community and its people and point to specific areas for media attention. If you belong to a formal organization, use a pitch letter to encourage members of the media to speak with an expert from your group. Send supporting documentation, such as debt figures, and follow up with a phone call.

Fact Sheet

A grass-roots organization may provide a fact sheet to reporters and editors that they can use as a convenient reference when writing their story. Usually no more than two pages, the fact sheet should include key points about the organization (its purpose, type and number of members, officers, and so forth). It should also summarize important facts about the debt, the deficit, and the impending crisis. Cite this book and other books or articles as sources.

10. Organize a Petition Drive

The best way to influence an elected official to do something about the budget crisis is to demonstrate that the majority of his or her constituents feel strongly that something must be done. Organizing a petition drive is one way of getting that message across. Dozens or hundreds of signatures send a clear signal to legislators that their constituents understand the importance of taking action on the debt and deficit — and won't reelect them if they do not.

To begin a petition drive, draft a statement that states your objective and the action that you would like the elected official to take. For example:

> We recognize the federal debt and the deficit as the two most serious problems facing our country today. Lack of action on these problems will destroy our country. Accordingly, we demand that our political leaders act now to reduce the debt and deficit. We urge you and other elected officials to take action today.

Below the statement, provide lines for signatures and addresses. Make a number of copies of the petition and distribute them to people to solicit signatures.

You can solicit signatures in public places, such as street corners or parks, and, subject to company policies, in many privately owned places as well, such as factories or shopping malls.

Once you have collected a respectable number of signatures,

compile the copies of the petition and either mail them to your representative or deliver them in person.

11. Arrange Public Speaking Engagements

Group functions and community and neighborhood meetings can provide valuable forums for getting the debt and deficit issues before local opinion leaders and the public. By speaking to business groups, professional associations, or community organizations, you can help increase awareness and understanding of the debt and deficit crises and of the need for citizen action.

To find appropriate forums, start with your local chamber of commerce and public library reference desk. They can provide the names of civic, professional, religious, and other community organizations such as the Kiwanis, Rotary, and Lions clubs. Or simply ask your friends, neighbors, and associates the names of groups to which they belong.

Once you've identified potential forums, write a letter to each group's program chairperson. The letter should state what you want to talk about and why the group's members should want to listen to you.

Specify that you want to discuss the impact of the debt and deficit problems on everyday citizens and will suggest concrete steps people can take to bring about positive change. Suggest a title for your talk that clearly identifies its topic — for example, "Government's Destruction of the American Economy and How to Stop It." You may also want to include a brief profile of yourself to show that you are, indeed, well versed on the topic. Keep the letter short and to the point, preferably no more than one page.

After a few weeks, follow up your letter with a telephone call. Remind the program chairman why you feel the topic is critically important. Remember, many set their programs well in advance, so get there "fastest with the mostest."

If you do obtain a speaking engagement, do your homework — not only on your topic, but also on the host organization, its members, and any speaking guidelines, such as the length of time you may speak.

Know your audience. Ask the group's chairperson or membership director to provide you with a profile of members. Then, tailor your comments for that audience by stating specifically how the issue affects them and using illustrations, examples, and anecdotes that they can relate to their own experience or area of expertise.

For example, Kiwanis clubs are primarily made up of small-business owners and entrepreneurs. So, if you speak before that group, consider making analogies to running a company when you discuss the gross mismanagement of this country and the critical need to reduce spending and increase efficiency if we are to survive.

Your presentation's main goals and key points, however, won't change from audience to audience. You should always present yourself as a knowledgeable source, establish the validity of your case, emphasize the need for action, and let those in attendance know what they can do to help bring about needed change. Make your presentation both dynamic and informative.

Following are some key points you might want to emphasize:

1. The federal debt and deficit are the two most serious problems facing our country today.

- Our debt has passed $4 trillion. That means that the government owes more than $16,000 for every man, woman, and child in America.
- The interest on our debt alone is nearly the largest single item in the federal budget. It is larger than Social Security or the combined budgets for the departments of Agriculture, Education, Energy, Housing and Urban Development, Interior, Justice, Labor, State, Transportation, and Veterans Affairs. For every dollar we

pay in personal income taxes, the equivalent of 61 cents
goes toward paying interest on the debt.

- If present trends continue, the debt will total more than the
  entire industrial output (GDP) of the United States by
  1996.

2. Our elected officials have failed to do anything to reverse
the trend.

- It took the federal government more than two hundred
  years to run up its first $1 trillion in debt; it has taken us
  only ten more years to reach $4 trillion. In 1992 alone,
  President Bush ran up a larger deficit than any other
  president did — with the exception of Ronald Reagan (who
  had eight years versus Bush's four).
- Elected officials focus their energies and resources on
  hiding the deficit figures, not on coming up with ways to
  reduce the debt.

3. We are already experiencing the consequences of unchecked
spending and government inaction, which will spell the breakdown
of our economy by the mid-1990s.

- The United States has gone from being the largest creditor
  nation to the largest debtor nation in the world. With this
  reversal in status, our once-powerful reputation has
  vanished. History tells us that no country has ever run a
  large deficit year after year without paying a ruinous price.
  Experience tells us that the same holds true for individuals
  and businesses.
- Money that we should be spending on programs to produce
  wealth and increase productivity for our country's future is
  instead being squandered to service the debt.
- The crisis is growing so fast, we will experience a complete
  financial catastrophe by the mid-1990s.

4. We must act immediately if we are to save our country.

- It is imperative that we as citizens force our elected officials to take fiscal responsibility. We must demand accountability. We must call or write our elected officials and insist that they take immediate action.
- There are other actions we can all take: We can speak out within our own community; write op-ed articles and letters to the editor in our local newspapers; encourage the media to cover this vital issue; and organize or participate in letter-writing campaigns, petition drives, and protests.
- The time to tackle the problem is now, before our debt becomes completely uncontrollable, and this great country of ours is left in ruins.

12. Stage Public Events and Demonstrations

Public events and demonstrations that are well organized and publicized can make a powerful statement to citizens in your community about the importance and urgency of reducing the federal debt and deficit. They can prove especially useful in generating enthusiasm for candidates, elected officials, and legislation that support aggressive debt reduction.

Any kind of mass event — whether a rally, parade, or demonstration — demands careful planning and aggressive promotion if it is to succeed.

Take special care in selecting the time for your event. The best time for staging a rally to support or oppose a candidate, for example, is in the closing weeks of the election, when a significant number of voters are still undecided. You can also time your demonstration or rally to coincide with or complement a newsworthy event, such as the government's release of deficit and debt figures for the upcoming fiscal year.

Hold the event in a central location that will draw attention and is easily accessible. If you are staging a rally or meeting, make sure necessary facilities, including a platform, microphone, chairs, and so on, are available. If you hold an event in a public place outdoors — your town square, for example — contact your city hall to see if you need a permit. You may need to complete an application for services such as security personnel and speaking facilities.

Consider using banners, literature, and handouts to drive your message home.

Organize a rally or meeting around one or more credible speakers who can deliver brief, inspiring addresses. Choose people who are well-known, animated presenters and have appropriate backgrounds or experience on the topic. It doesn't hurt to have a core of well-trained and well-placed cheerleaders lead applause and generate enthusiasm. Remember to close with a call to action that lets those in attendance know what they can do. You may want to pass out handouts with tips for suggested actions or form letters for a specific campaign.

You may also want to consider organizing a parade, so you can make use of attention-getting devices such as a band, creative costumes, or striking floats. Be careful, however, that the pageantry doesn't overwhelm the message. Remember: Your event is designed to create enthusiasm and spur action, but it won't be effective unless your message comes through loud and clear.

A key to the success of virtually any event is publicizing it thoroughly in advance through every means possible. Pursue publicity opportunities in newspapers and on radio, distribute handbills and direct mailers, and use paid advertising and sound trucks where appropriate.

Early in the planning process, make telephone calls or visits to local concerned citizens' groups and community organizations to enlist their participation and support. Doing so adds credibility to your efforts and ensures a solid turnout.

13. Make the Debt and Deficit the Subject of a Town Hall Meeting

You can also use more established forums to get the deficit issue to the front of your government and community agenda. For example, your city council may have "open meetings" on a regular basis, at which citizens can voice concerns on specific subjects. Visit your city hall or check your local newspaper for a community calendar that posts the time, place, and agenda of these open meetings. While you must follow the protocol of the meeting, there may be an opportunity for you to introduce your own topic and address the council with your concerns about the debt and federal government inaction.

You can also attempt to get a specific forum, or town meeting, held on the particular topic of the debt. Write or telephone your councilperson. (If you don't know who that is, call your city council or the board of elections and tell them where you live. They will tell you your district and your council member.) He or she can then take your concerns or suggestions for such a forum to a city council meeting where they may arrange to have your topic discussed.

To find out what other kinds of forums or options are available for a citizen to speak out in your community, try contacting your local clerk of council or chamber of commerce.

14. Tap into Political Action Committees (PACs)

You can also seek a voice in the political arena through Political Action Committees, or PACs. These are groups of people not affiliated with a party or candidate who contribute money to specific candidates for public office.

PACs give you the chance to pool your money with others and thereby have a greater impact on the election of a particular candidate with whom you agree. Since federal law forbids corporations from making direct contributions to candidates, many companies have set up their own PACs through which employees can funnel donations and choose which candidates to support. You can encourage other PAC members to support candidates who will take action on the federal debt problem.

To participate in a political action committee, ask your employer if your company has a PAC and, if so, how to get on that committee. If your business doesn't have a PAC, check into PACs representing trade unions, professions, cooperatives, and ideological groups. If you're interested in starting a PAC that is not established or administered by a company or other organization, contact the Federal Election Commission for rules and regulations (800/424-9530).

14

The Questions You Ask Most

WE wrote *Bankruptcy 1995* because we hoped our book would open people's eyes to the economic time bomb that our wastrel politicians have been courting since Lyndon Johnson occupied the Oval Office in the mid-1960s. Even so, we were totally unprepared for the incredible and immediate response that the book received from concerned Americans around the nation. The hardcover edition went through eighteen printings, totaling more than 300,000 copies, and, as of this writing, *Bankruptcy 1995* has occupied a place on the *New York Times* bestseller list for almost nine months.

Here's something else we never expected: Since the book was first published in the late summer of 1992, readers have sent me tens of thousands of letters, many of them containing questions that deserve an answer. Unfortunately, as much as I would have liked, it was impossible for me to respond individually to everyone — not, that is, if I wanted to sleep occasionally and try to run two businesses that, unlike the federal government, must meet their expenses with real income from sales — recession or not. You can rest assured, though, that I've tried to read each of those letters, and I can tell you that the people who wrote them are just as frightened and as angry as they should be at what our elected politicians have done to our country. Because I couldn't answer all the letters personally, I have taken the liberty — forgivable, I hope — of summarizing the most frequently asked questions and responding to them in this chapter, written especially for this new softcover edition of the book. (Though this chapter contains much new information, it also serves as a partial summary of some of *Bankruptcy 1995's* most salient points.)

I'll begin, then, with the most frequently asked question. In most of the letters it goes something like this:

QUESTION: *Do our elected officials in Washington really understand the seriousness of our deficit problem?*

As unbelievable as it may seem, the president and most members of Congress still don't get it or won't admit they don't get it. Some of them may be mouthing the right words about the cataclysmic dangers that the deficit poses to our economic security, but their cowardly actions — or inactions — don't match their brave statements. I worry that some people may be lulled by the talk into believing that this Congress and the Clinton administration are actually taking action that will lead to the elimination of the problem. They aren't. In fact, they haven't even come close. In the long run they are certain to exacerbate the problem.

In May 1993, when the Senate approved the president's budget plan, Senate Majority Leader George Mitchell said what we all wanted to hear: "We can't keep piling up this impossibly high debt and telling the American people that there is not a problem." But so far, that's precisely what they are doing. The deficit continues to grow, the government's debt piles up at record rates, the Treasury is still borrowing from Social Security and other trust funds to finance the government's current spending, the president and most legislators continue to play a numbers game in order to mislead voters and keep them from knowing the true magnitude of the problem, and they still think that increased taxes — especially on the so-called rich — are a panacea. They are not and have never been, nor will they ever be.

QUESTION: *How bad is the deficit right now?*

Unbelievably bad. In 1992, the amount spent on entitlement programs alone actually exceeded the total of personal and corporate income taxes that the government collected, as you can see on the graph on page 245. That's right. Nearly every dollar of income tax the government collects is already consumed by just this one spending category. Entitlements, you recall, are programs, such as Aid to Families with Dependent Children (AFDC) and Medicaid, that pay benefits to anyone who qualifies. So no spending caps exist for these programs. Whatever they cost each year is the amount that the federal government must pay out. That means the government must depend on the rest of the revenue it collects — Social Security and excise taxes, for example — to cover all other functions of government, including interest on the debt; and what those revenues don't cover, we are forced to borrow at an increasing rate.

If that's not frightening enough for you, consider this appalling fact: By 1995, entitlement programs and interest on our debt will eat up every penny of government revenues, as the graph also shows. That means within two years, every function of the federal government — from national defense to environmental protection to drug research to meat inspection — will all be paid for with borrowed funds. Let me say that again: By 1995, after the government finishes paying the cost of entitlement programs and debt interest, it won't have a nickel left. Every other government service, from submarine repair to park rangers' salaries, will be paid for with borrowed funds.

That's how bad the deficit is, and long term it will get much worse.

Receipts versus Spending

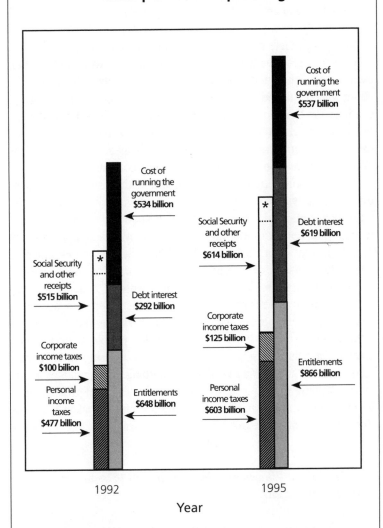

1992

1995

Year

* Receipts borrowed from trust fund surpluses amounted to $96 billion in 1992, and are projected to be $107 billion in 1995. The balances collected are paid out to satisfy current recipients' needs.

SOURCES: *OMB; CBO; DRI/Grace Commission.*

QUESTION: *Do you think the president and Congress can solve this problem alone?*

No. But in fact, no one else can. So we have to force them to solve it, because, as history has shown us, they won't act on their own. Large and incredibly complex corporations all across the country have turned themselves inside-out to reengineer their operations for the radically different conditions that exist in today's business environment. It wasn't easy for them, and it won't be easy for the government, but that doesn't mean our "leaders" in Washington can continue on their present course.

The companies that haven't reinvented themselves, for whatever reason, will probably fail. It's as simple as that. Just as surely, if the government doesn't get its deficit spending under control, it will collapse and bring the country's economy crashing down with it. I hope that every voter in the United States will continue to keep the pressure on the president and on his or her representatives in Congress. As we've said in Chapter 13, politicians pay close attention to letters and telephone calls when they appear in large enough numbers to indicate that voters are taking an active interest in an issue. It's not too much for people to write their elected officials every couple of months — praising them on the rare occasion when they've done something courageous but otherwise holding their feet to the proverbial fire. The letters needn't be long. They need only be direct and forceful and clearly convey this simple, but unmistakable, message: Bring the budget deficit down now and tackle the debt issue.

QUESTION: *Why do you object so strongly to using tax increases to reduce our deficit?*

That's an easy one. Every time we have increased taxes, presumably to reduce the deficit, Congress has used the added revenues to boost government spending well beyond the additional monies flowing in. Reagan and Bush passed what were the first and second largest tax increase packages in our history, and still did not bring down our deficit — instead, the deficit increased at a record pace. Some studies estimate, for example, that for every $1 in new revenues that Congress raised when it passed the Budget Enforcement Act of 1990 — the so-called deficit-control act — it has increased spending by $1.80. In other words, Congress spent almost twice as much as the new taxes it had approved brought in. This kind of behavior is outrageous, and we have absolutely no reason to believe that this Congress and this president would behave any differently. Do we want to take the risk? I don't think so.

Moreover, if the president and Congress would just make a serious effort to eliminate waste in government, we would not need new taxes to cut the deficit. Furthermore, increased taxes do not stimulate the economy. Every time we increase taxes, industry retreats, frequently dragging down the growth of the economy.

QUESTION: *Congress reported a deficit of $290 billion for 1992. Yet, you say the deficit was more than $400 billion that year. Which number is correct?*

One of my biggest complaints is that Washington not only refuses to take action on the deficit problem, it continually tries to mask its true size. Actual deficit spending for 1992, for example, reached $403.7 billion, as the Treasury Department's own numbers show. That's the gross deficit, or the real difference between the revenue the government took in that year and the money it paid out. But the Treasury Department reports a 1992 net deficit of just $290 billion. Why the disparity?

The difference between the two numbers comes from the fact that the Treasury Department subtracts from the deficit the amount that the government "borrows" from Social Security and other trust funds and government accounts. The graph on page

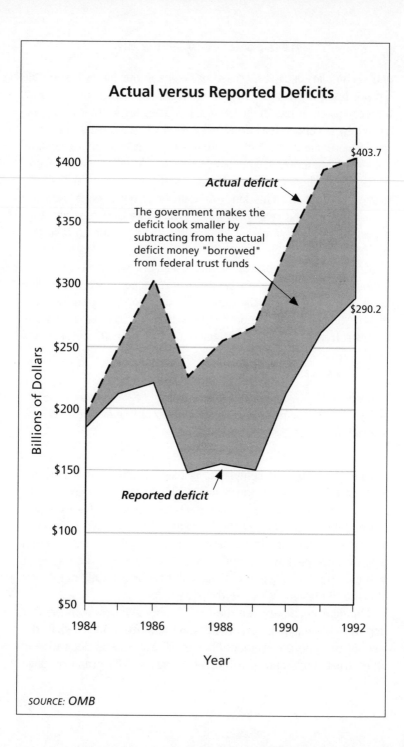

Actual versus Reported Deficits

Billions of Dollars

$403.7

Actual deficit

The government makes the deficit look smaller by subtracting from the actual deficit money "borrowed" from federal trust funds

$290.2

Reported deficit

$400

$350

$300

$250

$200

$150

$100

$50

1984   1986   1988   1990   1992

Year

SOURCE: *OMB*

248 shows the difference between the amount the government reports as the deficit and the real deficit.

In 1992, that difference came to more than $100 billion. How does the government justify that kind of financial finagling? It simply ignores the fact that the money pouring into the Social Security account is supposed to accumulate there in order to pay benefits to today's workers after they retire. That money was not intended to pay government's day-to-day expenses. It was collected for a specific purpose — to be deposited in a trust — and to count it as part of the government's general revenue is to abuse the trust of all those people depending on Social Security to help finance their retirements, especially younger workers. More to the point, it's just a cheap trick the government can use to make its own profligacy appear less serious than it actually is. The real deficit in 1992, as you can see in the chart on page 248, came to more than $400 billion, nearly 40 percent more than the government would like to fess up to. But no amount of finagling can change that fact.

QUESTION: *What would happen to the deficit if the federal government kept their accounts the way corporations must keep theirs?*

If the U.S. government were a corporation or an individual and continued to grossly mismanage its finances year after year, it would be forced to declare bankruptcy. A company's creditors and shareholders would refuse to support an organization that continued to set records for outspending its receipts. If the government were required to conform to the same accounting standards that it imposes on private corporations, it would have reported not a $290 billion deficit last year, but a deficit of more than $850 billion — three times larger.

Why the huge difference? It's simply another example of how the government writes the rules, so that it can continue to mislead taxpayers and voters about the extent of its excessive spending. Specifically, the government doesn't require its own bookkeepers to take into account its future obligation to make pension payments to current and former civilian and military government workers. These so-called unfunded pension liabilities mount up every year. Corporations, on the other hand, must annually put aside money to cover future pension obligations, and they must count these pension liabilities as expenses against income in the year the obligation is incurred. And beginning this year, the Securities and Exchange Commission also requires corporations to estimate and report as an expense the total future cost of such nonpension benefits as life insurance and health and dental care.

Government, by contrast, has no requirement to put aside money for future pension payments. It just pays these obligations out of current revenues when they come due. Consequently, the government allows itself to wait until pension payments actually get paid before showing them as costs on its books. If the government had counted as expenses all of the future pension obligations it incurred last year, the federal budget deficit would have climbed, as I've just pointed out, to more than $850 billion. What is sauce for the goose, as they say, should be sauce for the gander. As with so many of the dishonest, if not downright illegal, dodges that the government permits itself, the rules that apply to you and me regarding pension liabilities should be made to apply to the people spending our tax dollars as well.

QUESTION: *Why are interest rates at a twenty-year low?*

A number of reasons exist for the low interest rates we have today. The Federal Reserve, for one, has been pumping large amounts of reserves into the banking system, which gives us a large supply of money available for borrowing. Second, our economy is experiencing a very slow recovery from the 1991 recession; therefore, there isn't a large demand for money. And the other leading industrialized nations of the world are not borrowing in the international financial markets. Because the money supply, then, is so large, the United States is able to sell its bonds at interest rates that are the lowest we've had in twenty years. This drop in interest rates could give the president and Congress temporary breathing room to develop a long-term solution to the debt and deficit problem. We must not forget, however, that in 1983 short-term rates soared to 14 percent, and the prime rate stood at 21 percent. If interest rates return to the high levels of the early 1980s — which is not at all implausible — our current federal budget deficit would explode, with interest on the debt absorbing nearly half the government's total revenues.

QUESTION: *Do you agree with Ross Perot's objectives?*

The short answer is "yes." Ross Perot and I share many concerns about the way lobbyists and our elected officials conduct business in Washington. My primary concern — and his — is the size of the current debt and deficit and the wasteful government spending that continues to take place as well as the constant pressure from lobbyists who have no basic interest in this country's well-being. We are both worried about our elected officials' lack of accountability, and we want those officials to take action now to preserve the future of our children and grandchildren. "A Debt-Buster's Tool Kit for You" urges people to take part in the political process. Ross Perot's organization, United We Stand America, has the same objectives. We want people to think that their voices can be heard, that they can make a difference in the political process. We want them to take action and replace the people in Washington who refuse to make an honest and serious effort to develop long-term solutions to our debt and deficit problems. Like Mr. Perot, I believe Americans are willing and able to bear the cost and make the sacrifices, as long as they know their efforts will be rewarded with sound fiscal policy.

Also, I'd like to see the creation of a strong third party to give Americans an alternate choice.

QUESTION: *Are there similarities between the economic chaos in Russia today and the debt and deficit crisis facing the United States?*

Though our economic systems are quite different, the end result of the former Soviet Union's deficit spending provides us with a good example of the pain created by fiscal irresponsibility. The speed with which the Russian system disintegrated shows just how fast a world power can become a third-rate player in the global economic market. The political will in Russia has so far been insufficient to allow that country to make the necessary cuts in government spending and to restrict the undesirable growth of the money supply. The Russian government has continued to finance wasteful government projects by printing rubles at an outrageous rate. The predictable result of this rapid growth in the Russian money supply has been hyperinflation.

It is hyperinflation that has spurred capital to flee the country and to turn economic growth negative. Predictably, it has also caused extreme hardship for the people of Russia, with the poor, as usual, hit the hardest. Much of the savings in Russia that individuals and families accumulated over many years has disappeared. Hyperinflation and the resulting devaluation of the ruble have resulted in those citizens' hard-earned savings becoming worthless, thereby forcing Russians to rely on barter to survive.

The International Monetary Fund (IMF) and industrialized nations of the West are now dictating how this former world power conducts its internal economic affairs. Both are threatening to cut off aid, because if inflation continues, the money given Russia will not stay in the country. These are precisely the same conditions that could occur in the United States if we don't get our deficit and debt under control — and soon.

Some critics say that the Russian government thinks that the country's sheer size makes it exempt from the IMF rules and that it does not have to bite the bullet and make sacrifices. If Russia appears to be on the verge of collapse, these same people say, the West will come along and bail them out. The truth is the lack of confidence in the ruble and the daily power struggles within the Russian government mean that Russia must take strong action to cut its government deficit, because a Western bailout is by no means a sure bet. If we follow Russia's example, we're only a short time away from suffering the same fate.

QUESTION: *I thought there was a ceiling on our national debt. Am I wrong?*

You're not wrong — well, not exactly. A ceiling does exist, but it has never acted as a ceiling. The Budget Enforcement Act of 1990, which we have mentioned previously, set a debt ceiling of $4.145 trillion. In April of 1993, however, Congress and the president quickly adopted a temporary new ceiling of $4.370 trillion, a limit that expires in September 1993. In the past, the task of raising the debt ceiling has been linked to budget reform. The original Balanced Budget and Emergency Control Act of 1985 — better known as Gramm-Rudman-Hollings — and its amendments in 1987 and 1990 all coincided with increases in the existing debt ceilings. Not only did the budget reforms not work, but the statutory limits on the debt were totally useless in controlling government spending. Instead, they served only as an insult to the intelligence of the American voting public. We raise the debt ceiling to suit the whims of Congress. There have been thirty-two increases in thirteen years.

Those, then, are the questions that most bothered the people who wrote or faxed me during the months following *Bankruptcy 1995*'s hardcover release in September 1992. Naturally, I am gratified that so many ordinary citizens and voters cared enough about the issues the book raised to take the time to write, to comment, and, often, to ask for more information. I am also encouraged to note how well most of those who wrote me seemed to understand the dramatic seriousness of the issues that I had raised — better, I would judge, than the politicians who spend so much time talking about the deficit and so little time working to shrink it.

Now that nearly a year has passed since our book's publication, a new question has begun to appear in my daily mail. Writers want to know if I still think that bankruptcy will come to the United States in 1995, which is now just slightly more than a year in the future. In other words, were the predictions I made correct? The answer is: Just about. It should be small comfort to anyone, however, to observe that lower-than-expected interest rates on the national debt have given us perhaps a year or two grace period. As Reagan experienced in 1987 and 1988, there was a short sideways movement (see graph on page 42). But long term, the upward trend will increase dramatically.

Our problem as Americans is that we're entirely too trusting. We have been spoiled by being lucky enough to have had a few great presidents, some competent ones, and only two whose administrations let corruption run wild. We find it hard to believe that a president would lie to us or that the honorable men and women we elect to Congress would cheat us out of our savings. We look around and see only the bustling marketplace of the largest economy on earth. As we currently travel in Europe to collect data for another book, at least one economist tells us, "You are only ten years behind Brazil."

Our other problem is that we Americans are all republicans — with a small "r" — at heart. The Founding Fathers told us that if we elected wise men to govern us and make our laws, we could go about our daily business of commerce, or farming, or learning, or homemaking, or protecting society, with no misgivings. We believed them and, for most of the time in our history, our republican system has worked.

But what I'm saying to you now is that our system is broken; it no longer works. We trusted those astute men and women with our money and our bookkeeping, and they have failed miserably to keep us solvent. Then, they lied to us about what the account books show. Next, they tried to stave off the inevitable disaster by stopgap measures — borrowing from the pension fund and offering flimsy Band-Aid remedies, such as President Clinton's "deficit-reduction" budget. Just like other stopgap measures, this one won't work. What I have said to America in this book is not gloom-and-doom prophecy but the cold, inescapable truth that our past tells us about our future.

What will work? We must stop being trusting republicans and become militant democrats — with a small "d." The original meaning of democracy was that all power flows from the people. We must show our muscle and exert that power in every legitimate way we can in a great national movement to bring back financial sanity. At the same time, we must, as a people, understand and accept that we cannot make unreasonable demands for services that our government cannot afford. We cannot indulge our champagne appetite on a beer income. Not only must we start electing men and women who mean what they say when they talk about honesty and thrift, we must start recall movements for elected officials whose actions don't match their promises. We must use every ounce of pressure we can bring to bear on Congress and other elected officials to start learning some of the lessons I have outlined in this book.

And we must never let up until we finish the job, or as a great nation we will be finished.

Epilogue

They are killing our country, and by now you know who I mean. You understand how serious our plight is and that we have very little time — a few months, a year at the most — to mobilize the citizens and the leaders of our country to take up the fight against deficit spending and the mounting debt that otherwise will destroy the United States as we know it.

Get it out of your mind that economic and political collapse can't happen in this country, or that we can deal with it once it happens. It can and — as the chart on page 258 shows — will happen here unless we move to stop it now. You can't beat cancer once you've died, and by the mid-1990s, the United States as we know it will most likely be dead.

The one point I have tried to stress more than any other in this book is that the responsibility for raising the alarm and goading public officials into action is ours — yours and mine. I suggested ways in Chapter 13 in which each of us can act individually. I also showed how we can work collectively through one or another of the watchdog citizen groups in Washington. What price are you willing to pay to save your country? Middle-class Americans have

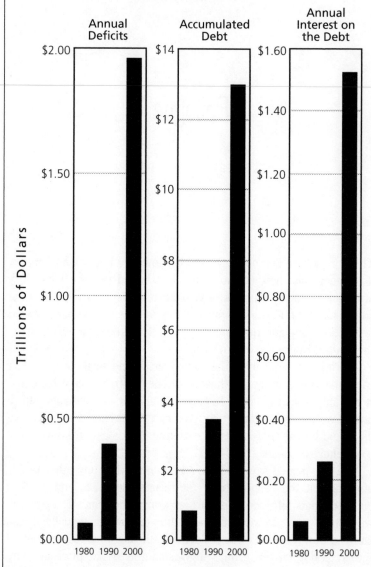

Budget Deficits, Debt and Interest Payments

Annual Deficits

Accumulated Debt

Annual Interest on the Debt

Trillions of Dollars

YEARS

SOURCES: OMB; DRI/Grace Commission

a choice. They can pay a modest price now, or they can wait a few more years and lose everything they've ever had.

In rereading the manuscript of this book, I find myself still startled by the statistics it contains. These are numbers that I have been working with and developing for the last nine years, but they still have the power to shock and upset me. When I look at the graph, which I put in our 1985 annual report, of our country's public debt stretching back more than 200 years (the graph is reproduced on page 260), and I see the dramatic change — the hockey stick — that began to take place so few years ago, I see clearly that in squandering its birthright, one generation of Americans — our generation — has betrayed the courage, faith, sacrifices, and hard work of many generations of Americans, who sweated to build a free and rich nation and then handed it over to us.

We should be ashamed.

Properly speaking, debt isn't even our problem. Our deficits and debt are simply tools that our ever-eager-to-please politicians use to provide their constituents with what we say we want. By piling borrowing upon borrowing, we've been able to spend money that we don't have on nonproductive projects and programs that most of us wouldn't condone if we had to pay for them with real tax dollars.

The good news and the bad is that neither we nor any other nation can continue the sin of deficit spending indefinitely. The laws of economics eventually exact their punishment, and we are dangerously close to getting ours. Just as interest compounds in a savings account, it compounds on our debt. The $4 trillion we owed in 1992 becomes $6.56 trillion in 1995 and $13 trillion by the year 2000 just from the accumulation of deficits and interest alone. Only a fool would contend that this insanity doesn't have to end.

Take a look at the charts. They make the point that whether we look at debt, deficit, or interest, the country is about to be blown away. They also show why former Senator Rudman can say that our money will be worthless by 1997.

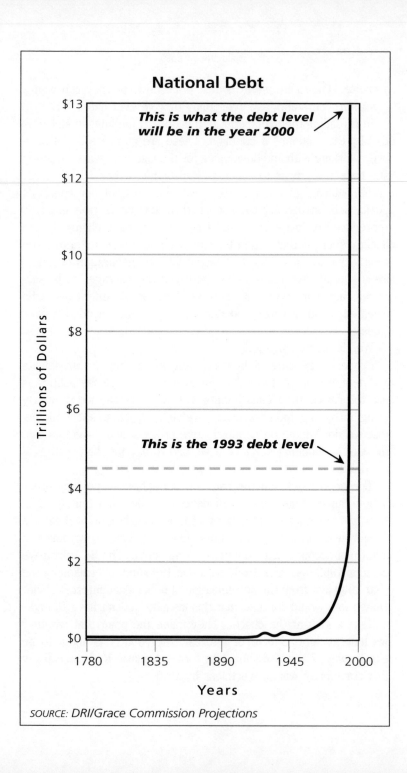

I am also saddened when I see what has happened to politics in the United States. Many people — nearly half of us, to judge by recent voter turnouts — have opted out of the process. In the face of both foreign and domestic interest groups and corporate lobbying, too many people think the single citizen has no voice. But a citizen does have a voice. Senators and congresspeople tell me that as few as two hundred calls or letters from constituents for or against a particular bill will often influence their votes.

By failing to use our voices, we've conceded the creation of a political caste system in America and given elected officials leave to assign to themselves the prerogatives of a collective monarchy. Politicians chide the wealthy but vote themselves salaries that place them in the top 5 percent of incomes in America. The perks they allow themselves ought to be an embarrassment. They pass laws that restrict our rights and freedoms while they exempt themselves from, for instance, the civil rights, antidiscrimination, and sexual harassment laws.

By living in splendid isolation, this elected monarchy has lost touch with the concerns of its constituents and has even come to believe that it is exempt from the laws it doesn't pass — the laws of economics. If you just balance your checkbook every month, you're living closer to economic reality than most members of Congress, the president, and his budget director.

We have allowed ourselves to draw so close to the point at which our debt will compound out of control that I'm not confident that we have the guts and the will to save ourselves. In Congress, there is almost universal use of the NIMBY factor — "Not In My Back Yard." There's so little time to waste, and the spending cuts we have to make are going to prove so painful to so many of us. We cannot, for instance, continue to index entitlement programs — including Social Security, Medicaid, and AFDC — to the inflation rate, but just freezing those payments alone won't end the deficit. Being fair — do we cut food stamps or farm supports or both? — is going to be so hard that I wonder if we can bring ourselves to make those choices. Certainly Congress and the president won't.

But I do know what will be worse.

With the outline of the action we need to take so clear in front of us, the tragedy greater than failure would be for us not to act at all, for us not to try to save our country. America's decline would go on, accelerating so quickly that within a generation, younger Americans will not even know what they have lost. But we will know, and we will have to live with the knowledge of that loss for the rest of our days.

If you don't think it's your responsibility to get involved in putting pressure on people in government or those running for office, remember that it's your future that's at stake here — yours and mine. The fact of the matter is, if you don't watch out for yourself, your family, and your country, who will? If you think my example of Weimar Germany's collapse is too far in the past to matter, consider Russia today. It's only the latest reminder of how fast a country can come apart when control is lost.

The United States will unravel just as quickly, and if we don't want that to happen, we've got to start acting to stop it now. The image of a crippled and dying America is just too horrible to contemplate.

Remember, democracy never lasts long. It soon wastes, exhausts, murders itself. There never was a democracy yet that did not commit suicide. It is in vain to say that democracy is less vain, less proud, less selfish, less ambitious, or less avaricious than aristocracy or monarchy. It is not true, in fact, and nowhere appears in history. Those passions are the same in all men, under all forms of simple government, and, when unchecked, produce the same effects of fraud, violence, and cruelty. . . .
— John Quincy Adams

I place economy among the first and most important virtues, and public debt as the greatest danger to be feared.
— Thomas Jefferson

Glossary

BANKRUPTCY: The condition of being declared insolvent by a court of law. Following this declaration, the control of the assets of the bankrupt entity are transferred to a court-appointed official, who then liquidates the assets and sees that creditors are treated fairly. Bankruptcy can be voluntary or involuntary.

BUDGET AUTHORIZATION: The amount of money appropriated by Congress for a specific program. While some budget authorities extend over multiple years, most cover the costs of a program for a single year.

CAPITAL: The durable items necessary for production, such as plants and equipment. The value of capital is determined by the income it generates in the future.

COMPOUNDING OF INTEREST: The process by which interest is earned on the principal (the original amount) and on the sums of all interest already earned. For example, if $100 is deposited into an account earning 10 percent compounded annually, at the end of year one, $10 is earned; at the end of year two, $11 in interest is earned — $10 on the principal, plus $1 on the interest accumulated.

CREDITOR: An entity (a person, corporation, or country, for example) that lends money to another on the promise of future payment and to which money is due. A creditor nation is a nation whose public and private sectors owe less money to other nations' public and private sectors than vice versa.

CURRENCY SPECULATION: The buying and selling of foreign currencies in the hopes that their value will increase relative to the value of your own country's currency.

DEBT (government debt or federal debt): The total amount of accumulated borrowings over the years by the government; in other words, the total amount of money the government has spent, including interest on borrowings, in excess of the revenue it has brought in. Internal debt is the amount borrowed by the government and owed to itself or its own citizens. Foreign or external debt is the amount of the federal debt that is owed to foreigners.

DEBTOR: An entity that borrows money from another and owes future payment. A debtor nation is a country whose public and private sectors owe more money to other countries' public and private sectors than vice versa.

DEFAULT: Failure to pay money that is owed to creditors.

DEFICIT: Also called budget deficit, this is the amount of government expenditures that exceed taxes and other revenues over a specified period.

DEVALUATION: A decrease in the official price, or worth, of a nation's currency when expressed in terms of other nations' currencies or in terms of gold.

DI: Disability Insurance (see SOCIAL SECURITY).

ENTITLEMENTS: Programs of government aid that automatically entitle anyone who meets certain criteria to government assistance either in the form of money or in something that costs money, like food stamps or health care. Examples of entitlement programs include Social Security, Medicare and Medicaid, and Aid to Families with Dependent Children.

EXPENDITURES: All money spent by the government.

FEDERAL RESERVE BANKS: The operating arms of the central banking system. The banks of America's banks, they hold the cash reserves of depositing institutions and make loans to them. They also provide checking accounts for the U.S. Treasury, and issue and redeem government securities.

FICA: Federal Insurance Contributions Act, the taxing authority for the Social Security system.

FISCAL CONSERVATISM: Cautious fiscal policy; attempting to keep government spending in line with revenues.

FISCAL POLICY: The manipulation of federal taxation and expenditures with the intent of achieving specific objectives. Usually these objectives are to smooth out the swings in the business cycle and to maintain a growing, high-employment economy free from high or volatile inflation.

GDP (Gross Domestic Product): The value of all final goods and services produced by a nation, excluding any goods and services produced and consumed abroad with ties to local residents, for a particular period, such as a year or a quarter. GDP is the universal, accepted measurement of the value of a country's output. It is considered a more accurate measure than GNP (Gross National Product), a similar measure which includes goods produced and consumed in other countries.

GRACE COMMISSION, THE: Formally referred to as the President's Private Sector Survey on Cost Control, this was a task force established by President Ronald Reagan in 1982 to find ways to eliminate government waste. The commission, made up of 160 business leaders and two thousand corporate employees, was headed by J. Peter Grace, chairman of W. R. Grace & Company.

GRAMM-RUDMAN-HOLLINGS ACT: Also called the Balanced Budget and Emergency Deficit Control Act of 1985, this legislation required the federal budget deficit to be lowered in increments for the following five fiscal years, and to reach zero by 1991. Failure to meet targets was to result in automatic spending cuts. The act was revised in 1987 and 1990, and no longer has a balanced-budget target date.

HI: Hospital Insurance (see MEDICARE).

HYPERINFLATION: A condition of inflation that is so severe — ranging from 1,000 percent to even 1 billion percent — that people try to get rid of their currency before prices render the money worthless. Technically, it is defined as a monthly inflation rate exceeding 50 percent.

INDIVIDUAL RETIREMENT ACCOUNT (IRA): A self-directed pension plan which provides a tax deduction for annual contributions of up to $2,000 and allows earnings on the contributions to accumulate tax-free until retirement. IRAs were introduced in 1977.

INFLATION: The percentage annual increase in a general price level. It is commonly measured by the Consumer Price Index (CPI), which places a value on the cost of living by pricing a fixed basket of consumer goods. The percentage increase in the CPI for any given year is equivalent to that year's inflation rate.

INSOLVENT: Unable to meet debts or discharge liabilities, often leading to bankruptcy.

INTEREST: The return paid to those who lend money by those who borrow it. Interest rates determine the price paid for borrowing money for a period of time. For example, if the interest rate on a loan is 10 percent annually, then interest on a $1,000 loan would be $100 the first year.

MANDATORY SPENDING: Those items in the government budget that are automatically financed without annual congressional approval, particularly entitlement programs.

MARSHALL PLAN: The foreign-aid plan adopted by the United States following World War II under which the United States gave billions in grants and loans to rebuild Western Europe.

MEDICAID: A federal-state matching entitlement program providing medical assistance for low-income persons who are aged, blind, disabled, members of families with dependent children, and certain other pregnant women and children. Programs vary from state to state in terms of persons covered, types of benefits offered, and amounts of payments.

MEDICARE: The federally administered health-insurance program for all persons over age sixty-five. "Part A" Medicare consists of Hospital Insurance (HI). "Part B" is Supplementary Medical Insurance (SMI), for which enrollees pay a monthly premium.

MONETARY POLICY: The actions taken by a nation's central bank, such as the U.S. Federal Reserve Bank (FRB), in determining the availability of money, interest rates, and credit conditions.

MONETIZING (monetizing the debt): The process of increasing currency in circulation by selling public debt to — in the case of the United States — the Federal Reserve Bank. The FRB pays for Treasury bonds with a check, and the check is deposited in a bank, becoming part of our money supply, with no real money to back it up.

NOMINAL INTEREST RATE: The rate of interest expressed in dollars of current value, not adjusted for inflation.

OASDI: Old-Age, Survivors and Disability Insurance (see SOCIAL SECURITY).

OASDHI: Old-Age, Survivors, Disability and Hospital Insurance (see SOCIAL SECURITY).

OASI: Old-Age and Survivors Insurance (see SOCIAL SECURITY).

PAY-AS-YOU-GO: A system in which current outlays are funded by current receipts. Social Security became a pay-as-you-go system, rather than a trust fund, in 1939.

PORK-BARRELING: Passing legislation for a project that is not necessarily needed, but is used as a means of demonstrating service to voters and gaining reelection. Much "pork-barrel legislation" is passed through a system of "logrolling," or vote trading, under which legislators pass another legislator's pet project regardless of merit, in order to ensure that their own proposals are passed.

PRIVATIZING: Transferring a government-provided service or asset to a private entity.

REAL INTEREST RATE: The interest rate adjusted to account for inflation. It is equal to the nominal interest rate less the rate of inflation.

RECESSION: A period in which a downturn in GDP — or negative economic growth — is experienced for two or more consecutive quarters. A severe prolonged recession is a depression.

REVENUES: Money brought into an operation, such as the money taken in by the federal government through individual and corporate income tax, Social Security tax, excise taxes, and various fees.

SECURITIES: Also called government securities, these are legal forms of indebtedness, or IOUs, issued by a government in exchange for cash, with the promise to pay specified or variable interest rates.

SOCIAL SECURITY: Implemented in 1935 solely as an old-age insurance pension plan, with tax contributions from covered workers going into a trust fund and being repaid with interest to those same workers upon their retirement. In 1939, changed by Congress to a "pay-as-you-go" plan, whereby tax contributions of the current work force finance the benefits of those already retired. At the same time, the scope of Social Security was expanded to include benefit payments to spouses and dependent children of retired workers, as well as survivors of deceased covered workers and retirees (OASI, or Old Age and Survivors Insurance). Later expanded again as OASDI (Old-Age, Survivors and Dependents Insurance), which eventually became OASDHI, administering OASI, DI (Disability Insurance), HI (Hospital Insurance, or Medicare "Part A"), and other benefit programs.

SUPPLY-SIDE ECONOMICS: An economic theory promoted by President Ronald Reagan in the 1980s, which held that the incentive effects of across-the-board cuts in personal and business taxes would stimulate individuals' work efforts and business investment, leading to increased tax revenues and economic growth.

SURPLUS: The amount of taxes and other government revenues that exceeds government expenditures in an annual budget.

SURTAX: An extra or additional tax levied on taxes owed or items already taxed.

TAX REBATE: A partial return to the payer on the amount taxed.

TRUST FUND: A legal arrangement by which property, usually money, is held by one party for the benefit of another. Until 1939 (in the original Social Security trust fund), taxes paid by a worker were held by the federal government until the worker's retirement, at which time the contributions, plus interest, were returned to the worker in the form of a monthly pension.

VALUE ADDED TAX (VAT): A tax levied at each stage of the production process that taxes a business on the value it has added. VAT is levied on a company as a percentage of its "value added," the difference between the value of goods produced and the cost of materials and supplies that are used in producing goods.

Chapter Notes

Most current and historical numbers were drawn from the OMB's *Budget of the United States Government* for Fiscal Year 1993 or 1994, or from the OMB's *Budget Baselines, Historical Data, and Alternatives for the Future,* issued in January 1993.

The deficit figures cited reflect the net deficit through 1984. Beginning with 1985, the deficit figures cited reflect the gross deficit, or the total amount of government borrowing before monies were "borrowed" from federal trust funds to artificially "reduce" the deficit figures reported to the public. (Beginning with 1985, trust fund surpluses began increasing substantially thanks to an earlier Social Security tax increase, and therefore, after that time, a significant amount of trust fund surpluses have been used to lower the net deficit.)

Data that did not come from the above sources is discussed in the notes that follow.

Chapter 2

Page 24: The 1995 debt and interest figures are based on projections made by the economic forecasting firm of Data Resources Inc. (DRI), as reported by the President's Private Sector Survey on Cost Control — better known as the Grace Commission — in its 1984 report to President Reagan. These figures have proved to be far more accurate than the government's own projections. The DRI/Grace Commission projections pegged the 1990 debt at $3.2 trillion and 1990 interest payments at $252.3 billion. The debt figure proved to be right on target, and the interest figure was less than 5 percent under the actual number. DRI supplied projections for 1990 and 2000, and we have arrived at figures for interim years by calculating the rate of change necessary to achieve the DRI/Grace Commission projections. The 1991 revenue figure used to calculate the interest/tax receipt ratio came from the OMB.

Page 27: Though "entitlements" are generally considered to be those programs that provide assistance to anyone who meets preordained criteria, neither the Senate, the House of Representatives, nor the OMB were able to supply a list of entitlement programs. According to the OMB, its figures for "mandatory programs" are equivalent to entitlements, so they are used interchangeably.

Page 29: The percentage comparing entitlement programs with spending, not including spending on debt interest, is based on the CBO's projection for 1993 entitlement spending, from the CBO's *Economic and Budget Outlook: Fiscal Years 1994–1998.*

Page 34: The gray portions of the bars on the deficit chart show the difference between the net deficit and the gross deficit. The black portion of the bar shows the amount of the net deficit; the gray portion shows the amount of borrowing from trust funds and other government accounts; the entire bar shows the gross deficit.

Page 37: The Cost of Living Adjustment for Social Security in 1991 amounted to $13.4 billion, over the base amount of approximately $250 billion, according to the Bureau of Economic Analysis.

Page 38: Refer to note for page 34.

Page 40: The figures for future deficit growth are calculated according to the annual increase in the 1982 DRI/Grace Commission debt projections, which have proven to be accurate thus far. If the deficit merely continues to rise at the same rate it has throughout the Bush administration, it will climb even higher: $761.2 billion in 1994, and $1,050.5 billion in 1995. The future interest figures are also based on DRI/Grace Commission projections.

Page 44: Refer to note for page 34.

Chapter 3

Page 45: Information on the Grace Commission comes from my personal experience as cochairman, and from *War on Waste,* the report issued by the President's Private Sector Survey on Cost Control and published by Macmillan Publishing Company in 1984.

Page 46: Figures on federal dollars spent on defense purchases are cited in *Burning Money: The Waste of Your Tax Dollars,* by Peter Grace.

Page 47: Information and figures relating to the Rural Electrification Administration came from The Heritage Foundation.

Page 47: The figure cited for U.S. Forest Service outlays, $487 million, includes road maintenance and construction costs directly or indirectly affiliated with road building, and came from *Citizens' Guide to the Forest Service Budget,* issued by Cascade Holistic Economic Consultants of Portland, Oregon.

Page 48: According to the OMB, 1,607 Grace Commission recommendations have been acted on, saving $152.4 billion through 1989. Citizens Against Government Waste, the nonprofit advocacy group formed to carry on the work of the Grace Commission, reports that its efforts added $45 billion in savings in 1990.

Page 48: Information relating to the Gramm-Rudman-Hollings Act came from the office of Senator Ernest F. Hollings.

Page 51: According to The Heritage Foundation's 1992 *A Prosperity Plan for America,* the government claimed that the 1990 budget deal cut spending by $290 billion over five years, though its "own projections have spending being 'cut' from $1.290 trillion in fiscal 1991 to $1.521 trillion in fiscal 1995 . . . a $231 billion spending increase."

Page 51: The increase in the amount Congress budgeted was calculated using the January 1991 estimates for 1991 and 1992 outlays, from the January 1991 *Economic and Budget Outlook* issued by the Congressional Budget Office (CBO).

Page 51: The percentages that Congress reported its 1990 budget package would save were calculated by comparing the estimated savings on deficit reductions, for 1991 and 1992, with the 1991 and 1992 outlay projections existing at the time of the budget summit; figures come from the House Budget Committee.

Page 52: Off-budget federal entities are federally owned and controlled, but their transactions are specifically excluded from the budget totals by law. When the U.S. Postal Service became "off-budget," the $1.8 billion projected spending became "savings," since it was not included in the total projected outlays, and therefore, not calculated into the projected deficit. Historical spending projections and deficit figures for the U.S. Postal Service came from the CBO.

Page 53: Financial information on the Pension Benefit Guarantee Corporation came from OMB's *Budget of the United States Government for Fiscal Year 1993*.

Page 54: *The Economic and Budget Outlook: Fiscal Years 1993–1997*, issued by the CBO, reports that "the economy's failure to live up to expectations," as well as other "policy" and "technical" factors, caused an average annual shortfall of $44.7 billion between congressional estimates and actual deficits from 1980 to 1991. If, for example, economic growth is 1 percent lower than estimated and unemployment 1 percent higher, the 1993 deficit would be $76 billion higher than projected and the 1995 deficit $132 billion higher.

Page 57: As of 1992, Social Security and other trust funds held $1.004 trillion in bonds used to finance government debt, according to the CBO's *Economic and Budget Outlook: Fiscal Years 1993–1997*.

Page 58: Information on the Gramm-Rudman-Hollings Act came from the office of Senator Ernest F. Hollings.

Page 60: The idea that the Budget Reconciliation Act of 1990 was intended to cut $2 in spending for every $1 in taxes came from The Heritage Foundation's 1992 *A Prosperity Plan for America*.

Chapter 4

Information on the history and present financial status of the Social Security system comes from a variety of sources, including documents issued by the General Accounting Office, the Social Security Administration, The Brookings Institution, and the CATO Institute. The majority of the data comes from the *1993 Annual Report of the Federal Old-Age & Survivors Insurance and Disability Insurance Trust Fund*, issued in April 1993 by the Social Security Board of Trustees, and the *1992 Green Book*, issued in May 1992 by the Committee on Ways and Means of the U.S. House of Representatives.

Information that did not come from these sources is described below:

Page 67: The graph reflects average-to-high wage earners with annual salaries of $50,000 to $75,000. Data for twenty-five- to sixty-three-year-olds' contribution and return from the Social Security system comes from a study conducted by The Wyatt Company consultants and actuaries. We've assumed that cost-of-living adjustments (COLAs) remain at 4 percent per year. The present value of future Social Security benefits is based on a 6 percent annual interest rate — that is, a 2 percent real rate of return. According to Wyatt, the current average retirement age is sixty-three. While this graph shows that today's average-to-high wage earners are entitled to receive much less back from the Social Security system than they have contributed, similar studies show that low-wage earners ($15,000 annual salaries) are entitled to receive much more than they have contributed upon retirement.

Page 72: The relatively high increase in the "cumulative debt" column from 1982 to 1983, and the relatively small increase from 1985 to 1986, reflect that $17.5 billion was borrowed by Social Security from the Disability Insurance (DI) and Hospital Insurance (HI) accounts beginning in 1982, and was paid back by 1986.

Page 78: Martin Feldsteins' study, "Social Security, Induced Retirement, and Aggregate Capital Accumulation" (*Journal of Political Economy,* 1974), estimated the net impact of Social Security on private savings by analyzing savings behavior in the United States since 1929. The results of his study suggested that Social Security reduces personal savings by about 40 percent.

Chapter 5

Page 83: The U.S. debt projections referred to here are the same DRI/Grace Commission projections mentioned earlier.

Page 88: According to the OMB, the federal government ran a very small surplus — about $3 billion — in 1969 but had an "on-budget" deficit of about $500 million that year. The last "on-budget" surplus was in 1960 — the final year of the Eisenhower administration.

Page 88: In 1995, according to DRI/Grace Commission interest projections and OMB revenue projections, interest will top $619 billion while personal income tax will reach $603 billion. 1995 debt and interest figures are based on the DRI/Grace Commission projections, while projected tax revenue comes from the OMB. OMB debt and interest projections for 1995 are $5.32 trillion and $354.2 billion, respectively.

Page 90: As mentioned earlier, at the suggestion of the OMB, the figure used for 1992 "entitlements" came from the OMB's data for "mandatory programs."

Page 90: Mandatory spending programs include Social Security, Medicare and Medicaid, veterans benefits, unemployment compensation, food and nutrition assistance, and many energy, agriculture, and international-affairs programs.

Chapter 6

Much of this chapter is conjectural, based on observations Gerry Swanson and his team made in countries around the world. However, certain figures are based on existing projections, as noted below.

Page 98: According to the Senate Foreign Relations Committee, President Bush requested $12 billion in humanitarian and technical assistance funds for the former Soviet nations. The $12 billion figure was corroborated by the *Washington Post* on May 5, 1992.

Page 98: The 1991 Treasury bond rates on this page came from the Treasury Department's Bureau of Public Debt.

Page 106: In addition to having to finance the annual deficit, each year the federal government also must refinance one-third of its existing debt. According to the OMB, 34 percent of the debt outstanding will mature in less than one year, and 70 percent will mature within five years. Therefore, higher interest rates will quickly translate into increased interest payments.

Page 108: Interest as a percentage of revenues, excluding Social Security, rises to 96 percent in 1997, according to DRI/Grace Commission interest projections and OMB revenue projections. Social Security receipts were backed out of total revenues because they are in effect savings intended to finance future Social Security benefits.

Chapter 7

Page 112: The 1996 debt/GDP ratio was calculated using the DRI/Grace Commission debt projection and OMB GDP projection.

Page 115: Figures on foreign ownership of U.S. debt came from the OMB's *Budget of the United States Government for Fiscal Year 1993*.

Page 117: Foreign ownership of U.S.-based assets came from the CBO's Fiscal Analysis Division.

Page 123: Information on private domestic investment in nonresidential plant and equipment came from the Bureau of Economic Analysis at the U.S. Department of Commerce.

Page 123: Figures on Italian inflation and bond rates were supplied by the Italian embassy in Washington, D.C. According to the International Monetary Fund's *World Economic Outlook* of May 1991, Canada and the United States were the only major industrialized nations that had negative economic growth in 1991.

Page 125: The study mentioned from the Federal Reserve Bank of Cleveland was done by Michael Bryan in August 1990, and was called "Inflation and Growth: Working More vs. Working Better."

Page 127: As noted earlier, in 1969 we had a negligible surplus of $3 billion, and an "on-budget" deficit of $500 million.

Page 128: According to the Conference Board's Consumer Confidence Index (1985 = 100), the level of confidence in May 1993 was 61.5 percent, which is lower than the October 1992 level.

Chapter 8

Much of the material in chapters 8 and 9 came from interviews conducted by Gerry Swanson and his research team. In order to gain high access and ensure candor, the team promised interview subjects anonymity, so no specific sources will be identified. However, the interviews were held with highly placed authorities, and facts were not used in this book unless corroborated by multiple sources.

Page 131: Poland's 1991 inflation rate was provided by the CIA's *World Fact Book* research division.

Page 134: Fuel tax and tax evasion estimates were supplied by a consular official in the U.S. embassy in Italy.

Page 135: The 1992 estimated range of tax dollars lost due to unreported income came from the Internal Revenue Service (IRS). The term "unreported income" is synonomous with "underground economy," according to the IRS.

Page 137: One of the individuals who described credit circles to us was a European consultant who had recently transferred to Hungary, where he bought a $300,000 house for which he was forced to pay cash.

Page 141: According to the *World Economic Outlook* issued by the International Monetary Fund, the United States and Canada both suffered per capita GNP losses in 1990, and U.S. economic growth lagged behind the average of the other Group of Seven nations (including the United Kingdom, Canada, Japan, Germany, France, and Italy).

Page 144: The figure of $450 million in U.S. aid to Eastern Europe came from the U.S. Agency for International Development, while the West German figure came from Chancellor Helmut Kohl, as reported in the *Wall Street Journal*'s international edition on February 10, 1992.

Chapter 9

(See introductory note to Chapter 8 regarding information from interviews conducted by Gerry Swanson and his research team.)

Page 145: Our sources for historical information on inflation include *Dying of Money* by Jens Parsson, *Inflation Through the Ages: Economic, Social, Psychological and Historical Aspects* by Nathan Schmukler and Edward Marcus, *The Penniless Billionaires* by Max Shapiro, and *The Hyperinflation Collection* by Gerald Stone and Ralph Byrns.

Page 148: Figures used to calculate the deficit totals for 1994 and 1995 were drawn from the DRI/Grace Commission debt projections, while the 1995 GDP came from the OMB.

Pages 152: *The Economist* of April 18, 1992, in an article called "Argentina's Economy," reported that Argentina's economy had fallen to "around 70th" in the world. The same article discussed the value of Argentine debt, inflation, budget deficits and economic growth. Argentina's per capita GDP was provided by the CIA's *World Fact Book* research division.

Page 153: Information on Brazil's debt came from a survey on Brazil published in the December 7, 1991, issue of *The Economist*.

Page 153: Brazilian inflation information came from the 1992 International Reports of IBC USA Publications Inc. Brazil Service, published April 15, 1992.

Page 155: Poland was given an opportunity by its creditors to reduce its debt from $48 billion to $28 billion if it met certain conditions.

Page 155: Figures for the U.S. debt-to-GDP ratio for 1980 and 1992 are from *Budget of the United States Government for Fiscal Year 1993* issued by the OMB. The 1996 debt figure is based on the DRI/Grace Commission projections.

Page 155: Italy's 1990 deficit — or the amount it borrowed in 1990 — was about $73 billion, according to the March 1, 1991, Country Report on Italy published by IBC USA Licensing Inc.

Page 156: Information on changes in the British economy during Margaret Thatcher's reign came from *Business Week*, "She Didn't Spare the Rod — or Finish the Job," December 10, 1990; British Information Services of New York; and England's Office of Treasury.

Chapter 10

Page 161: President Clinton's proposed $16.3 billion economic stimulus package was first outlined in his report *A Vision of Change for America*, issued in February 1993. No spending cuts were proposed to offset the additional spending this stimulus package would have entailed.

Page 166: The Internal Revenue Service Statistics of Income, September 1992, reported that 6 percent of taxpayers earn yearly salaries of $75,000 or more, and that their tax contributions amount to 45 percent of all personal income taxes.

Page 166: The projected amount of additional taxes to be collected due to economic growth between 1993 and 1994 and the amount of President Clinton's new tax proposals for 1994 are reported in the *Budget of the United States Government for Fiscal Year 1994*.

Page 166: The entire amount of President Clinton's proposed new user fees and charges was reported in a *Washington Times* article, "When is a cut not a cut?" (May 3, 1993). According to the *Times*, many new fees are included in the president's 1994 budget, with the additional revenues being reported as "spending cuts" in the president's Fiscal Year 1994 budget proposal. The fees are hidden in columns headed "offsetting collections" and "reimbursable obligations."

Page 168: The average annual entitlement spending increase of $67.5 billion a year since 1990 is based on the OMB's figures for 1991 and

1992 "mandatory program" spending, and on CBO projections for 1993 mandatory program spending.

Page 171: The portrayal of user fees as spending cuts in President Clinton's Fiscal Year 1994 budget proposal was reported in *The Washington Times* article, "When is a cut not a cut?," May 3, 1993. (See note about page 166 for more information.)

Chapter 11

Page 180: Information about "The 4 Percent Solution" was drawn from an article by Scott A. Hodge in the Heritage Foundation's report "A Prosperity Plan for America, Fiscal 1993." The estimate of $306.6 billion savings achieved over five years is based on spending projections issued by the OMB in its July 15, 1991 *Mid-Session Review of the Budget.*

Page 181: Estimates of savings achieved by freezing cost-of-living adjustments to people on federal retirement programs were drawn from the CBO's February 1993 report *Reducing the Deficit: Spending and Revenue Options.*

Page 186: Figures on Social Security benefits are from the Social Security Administrations' 1992 *Trustees' Report.*

Page 186: The 1992 face value of federal credit and insurance programs totals $6.6 trillion, according to the OMB's *Budget of the United States Government for Fiscal Year 1993.* Included in this total are $157 billion in direct loans, $587 billion in guaranteed loans, $4.7 trillion in federal insurance and $1.1 trillion in government-sponsored enterprise loans. The "present value of future costs," or the estimate of projected losses in each program's portfolio, is $224 billion, according to the OMB.

Chapter 12

Information about the suggested spending cuts listed in this chapter was drawn from a variety of sources including: "Balanced Budget Amendment Options," issued by Leon Panetta (as chairman of the House Budget Committee) in May 1992; "Cutting Spending First," issued in March 1993 by the Republican members of the House Committee on the Budget; the statement of U.S. Senator David L. Boren, "Bipartisan Deficit Reduction Plan," issued in May 1993; "The Clinton Challenge Answered," issued in March 1993 by the Heritage Foundation in response to President Clinton's "challenge" for individuals or organizations to find more spending cuts than were included in the president's first budget proposal; "The 1993 Waste Tax Summary," prepared by Citizens Against Government Waste; and *Reducing the Deficit: Spending and Revenue Options*, issued by the Congressional Budget Office in February 1993.

Chapter 14

Page 245: Because the federal government does not follow Generally Accepted Accounting Principles (GAAP), the total of government outlays on discretionary programs, gross debt interest, and entitlement programs does not match the amount the government reports as total outlays. That is because money is borrowed from various government trust funds to reduce the amount of reported total spending.

Page 247: *The Final Monthly Treasury Statement of Receipts and Outlays of the United States Government for Fiscal Year 1992*, issued by the Department of the Treasury Financial Management Service, reports that the amount of "total public securities net of premium and discount" was $403.4 billion. This figure was later revised to $403.7 billion. Various amounts are deducted, including monies from trust fund surpluses, to arrive at the net deficit of $290.2 billion.

Page 249: Information about the size of the deficit according to GAAP was drawn from "The Straight Shooter" issued by Econometric Publications, Ridgewood, N.J., which reported that the 1992 deficit was actually as high as $850 billion if calculated according to GAAP. *Barron's,* the national financial weekly newspaper, corroborated this figure in an April 12, 1993, article.

Page 253: The number of debt-ceiling increases comes from the federal government's Bureau of Public Debt.

Epilogue

Page 259: Debt figures for 1995 and 2000 came from the DRI/Grace Commission projections.

Index

283